Women in Spiritual and Communitarian
Societies in the United States

D1003134

Utopianism and Communitarianism
LYMAN TOWER SARGENT AND GREGORY CLAEYS
Series Editors

Women in Spiritual and Communitarian
Societies in the United States

Edited by
Wendy E. Chmielewski,
Louis J. Kern, *and*
Marlyn Klee-Hartzell

SYRACUSE UNIVERSITY PRESS

First Edition 1993
93 94 95 96 97 98 99   6 5 4 3 2 1

The paper used in this publication meets the minimum requirements of American National
Standard for Information Sciences – Permanence of Paper for Printed Library Materials, ANSI
Z39.48-1984. ∞™

Library of Congress Cataloging-in-Publication Data

Women in spiritual and communitarian societies in the United States/
    edited by Wendy E. Chmielewski, Louis J. Kern, and Marlyn Klee-
    Hartzell. – 1st ed.
          p.   cm. – (Utopianism and communitarianism)
    Includes bibliographical references and index.
    ISBN 0-8156-2568-5 (alk. paper). – ISBN 0-8156-2569-3 (pbk. :
alk. paper)
        1. – Collective settlements – United States – History.   2. Communal
living – United States – History.   3. Utopian socialism – United
States – History.   4. Monasticism and religious orders for women –
United States – History.   5. Women – United States – History.
        I. Chmielewski, Wendy E.   II. Kern, Louis J., 1943–
III. Klee-Hartzell, Marlyn.   IV. Series.
HX653.W57   1992
335'.973 – dc20   92-10609

Manufactured in the United States of America

We dedicate this book to our mothers:

Regina Rosenthal Chmielewski
in memory (1924–1991)

Ruth Virginia Lambertson Kern

Lillian May Klee Hartzell

"Away with your man-visions! Women propose to reject them all, and begin to dream dreams for themselves."

Grateful acknowledgment is made to the following for permission to quote from manuscript collections and to reprint previously published material:

Friends Historical Library of Swarthmore College for permission to quote from letters in the Fisher-Warner Papers in its collection, quoted in Carol A. Kolmerten's article, "Women's Experiences in the American Owenite Communities."

Vassar College, Rare Books and Manuscripts Division, for permission to quote passages from Amy L. Reed, ed., *Letters From Brook Farm, 1844–1847* (Vassar College, 1928), in Lucy M. Freibert's article, "Creative Women of Brook Farm."

Winterthur Portfolio: A Journal of American Material Culture 25, nos. 2/3 (Summer/Autumn 1990), a publication of the Henry Francis duPont Winterthur Museum, for permission to reprint portions of an article by Beverly Gordon, "Victorian Fancy Goods: Another Reappraisal of Shaker Material Culture."

The University of Chicago, © 1992 by The University of Chicago. All rights reserved. For permission to publish a condensed version of Priscilla J. Brewer's article, "'Tho' of the Weaker Sex': A Reassessment of Gender Equality among the Shakers," *Signs: Journal of Women in Culture and Society* 17, no. 3 (Spring 1992).

Archdiocese of Boston for permission to reprint portions of an article by Mary J. Oates, "'The Good Sisters': The Work and Position of Catholic Churchwomen in Boston, 1870–1940," which originally appeared in *Catholic Boston: Studies in Religion and Community, 1870–1970,* ed. R. E. Sullivan and J. M. O'Toole (Archdiocese of Boston, 1985).

Women's Studies Department, University of Michigan, for permission to reprint Kathy Marquis's article, "'Diamond Cut Diamond': Mormon Women and the Cult of Domesticity in the Nineteenth Century," which originally appeared in *University of Michigan Papers in Women's Studies* 2, no. 2 (1977).

Mel Albin and Dom Cavallo, eds., *Family Life in America, 1620–2000* (St. James, N.Y.: Revisionary Press, 1981), for permission to reprint portions of an article by Marlyn Dalsimer, "Bible Communists: Female Socialization and Family Life in the Oneida Community."

Contents

Illustrations   xiii

Preface   xv

Contributors   xvii

Introduction

     MARLYN KLEE-HARTZELL   3

PART ONE

Women's Search for Community
Religious, Secular, Feminist

1. Sojourner Truth

     Utopian Vision and Search for Community, 1797–1883

       WENDY E. CHMIELEWSKI   21

2. Women's Experiences in the American Owenite Communities

       CAROL A. KOLMERTEN   38

3. Heaven on Earth

     The Woman's Commonwealth, 1867–1983

       WENDY E. CHMIELEWSKI   52

PART TWO

Women's Creativity in Community

4. Creative Women of Brook Farm

       LUCY M. FREIBERT   75

5. Shaker Fancy Goods
   *Women's Work and Presentation of Self in the
   Community Context in the Victorian Era*
   BEVERLY GORDON   89

6. "In the Bonds of True Love and Friendship"
   *Some Meanings of "Gospel Affection"
   and "Gospel Union" in Shaker Sisters' Letters and Poems*
   ROSEMARY D. GOODEN   104

PART THREE

Women and Structures of Leadership in Community

7. Sexual Equality and Economic Authority
   The Shaker Experience, 1784–1900
   KAREN K. NICKLESS and PAMELA J. NICKLESS   119

8. "Tho' of the Weaker Sex"
   A Reassessment of Gender Equality among the Shakers
   PRISCILLA J. BREWER   133

9. Organizing for Service
   *Challenges to Community Life and Work Decisions
   in Catholic Sisterhoods, 1850–1940*
   MARY J. OATES   150

PART FOUR

Women's Status and Male Power in Community

10. "Diamond Cut Diamond"
    The Mormon Wife vs. the True Woman, 1840–1890
    KATHY MARQUIS   169

11. Family Love, True Womanliness, Motherhood, and
    the Socialization of Girls in the Oneida Community,
    1848–1880
    MARLYN KLEE-HARTZELL   182

12. Pronatalism, Midwifery, and Synergistic Marriage
*Spiritual Enlightenment and Sexual Ideology
on The Farm (Tennessee)*
LOUIS J. KERN   201

13. Female Education in the Lubavitcher Community
The Beth Rivkah and Machon Chana Schools
BONNIE MORRIS   221

PART FIVE

Women's Voices
Personal Experiences of Community

14. Colony Girl
A Hutterite Childhood
RUTH BAER LAMBACH   241

15. The Power of Feminism at Twin Oaks Community
ZENA GOLDENBERG   256

Index   267

Illustrations

1. Sojourner Truth (ca. 1797–1883) 34
2. Frances Wright (1795–1852), founder of the
   Nashoba Community 47
3. Members of the Woman's Commonwealth, ca. 1904 64
4. Georgiana Bruce Kirby (1818–1887), Abby Morton Díaz
   (1821–1904), and Marianne Dwight Orvis (1816–1901) 78
5. Detail of poplar cloth woven by Shaker sisters, ca. 1920 93
6. Two finished poplar boxes made by Shaker sisters in 1908 94
7. Design for a miniature Swiss cottage, *Godey's Lady's Book*, 1867 96
8. "Little Companions" from *Peterson's Magazine*, 1865 99
9. Shaker Sister Martha Burger in fancy goods store, ca. 1900 101
10. "A Special Visit" of four Shaker sisters, ca. 1915 105
11. Shaker Sisters Catharine and Phebe Van Houten, 1887 107
12. A Shaker schoolmistress and pupils at Canterbury
    Shaker Village 121
13. Shaker Sister Sarah Collins weaving a chair seat 122
14. Shaker sisters and girls working in the laundry 143
15. Eldress Emma Neale and Sister Sadie Neale 144
16. Three Shaker sisters making pastries 145
17. Novice Sisters of Notre Dame going roller skating, ca. 1940 155
18. Mormon silk workers 177
19. "Exit Brigham Young," 1877 cartoon of Mormon plural
    marriage 178
20. Oneida Community members at their Summer House, 1866 194
21. A bag bee at the Oneida Community, ca. 1860s 195

22. Midwives and infant at The Farm, 1970s   209

23. Hasidic women dancing at a Succos festival, 1990   233

24. The Baer family, Forest River Colony, 1954   247

25. Twin Oaks women hauling garbage, 1987   261

Preface

THIS BOOK MARKS A BEGINNING of an exploration of women's experiences in U.S. spiritual and communitarian societies. The idea for the volume took hold at the thirteenth annual meeting of the Communal Studies Association held at Canterbury, New Hampshire, Shaker Village in October 1986. Because this was the first meeting of the CSA to focus on gender issues (and by implication, on women's experiences), many scholars at the conference presented papers using the new lens of feminist scholarship and perspectives. Out of this experience, we decided that a book surveying the most recent feminist scholarship on women in spiritual and communal societies was needed.

For several years we actively solicited papers for this volume. We wrote letters to academic departments and advertised the proposal for the book at conferences and in newsletters. Many people submitted manuscripts. For this book we selected the papers that we think best represent the new scholarship on women's experiences in spiritual and communal societies. Ten of the articles have never before been published.

We have organized the volume thematically into five sections, and within each section, the articles are presented in an approximate chronological order. A short introduction, providing basic background information not included in the articles, precedes each section. We made the decision to present works cited at the end of each article, so that interested readers would have a beginning point for research on a particular topic or community. The works cited sections are not extensive bibliographies but suggestions for additional sources. The index was prepared by Twin Oaks Indexing, Louisa, Virginia.

During the five years that it has taken to bring this collection to publication, many people have encouraged us and helped us. We especially thank the authors of the individual articles for contributing their scholarship and their ideas: Priscilla J. Brewer, Lucy M. Freibert, Zena Goldenberg, Rosemary D. Gooden, Beverly Gordon, Carol A. Kolmerten, Ruth Baer Lambach, Kathy Marquis, Bonnie Morris, Karen K. Nickless, Pamela J.

Nickless, and Mary J. Oates. Obviously, we could not have produced this
book without their work, not to mention their patient attention to any
number of drafts and revisions. We also thank Lyman Tower Sargent and
Gregory Claeys, general editors of the Utopianism and Communitarian Series,
for encouraging our project. Our editor at Syracuse University Press, Cynthia Maude-Gembler, has guided the book through many stages. We thank
her for believing in the importance of the book and for answering all our
questions.

One of the delights of preparing the volume has been the selection of
illustrations and photographs to accompany the text. In that selection process we relied on collectors, librarians, archivists, and curators of many re-
positories to help us locate appropriate graphics. We thank these individuals;
they are the friendliest professionals we have met in a long time. They are:
Albert Bates (The Farm); Sister Frances Bernardine, S.N.D. (Sisters of Notre
Dame de Namur); Richard Brooker (Richard Brooker Collection); Mary
Ellen Chijioke (Friends Historical Library of Swarthmore College); Caro-
lyn A. Davis (George Arents Research Library at Syracuse University); Wayne
Furman (New York Public Library); Jerry Grant (Shaker Museum at Old
Chatham, New York); Pamela Kirschner (National Portrait Gallery); Nancy
S. MacKechnie (Vassar College Library); Richard McKinstry (Winterthur
Museum); Ronald Patkus (Archdiocese of Boston); Patricia Paladines (New-
York Historical Society); June Sprigg (Hancock Shaker Village); Maggie Stier
(Fruitlands Museum); Scott Swank and Cynthia Hunt (Canterbury Shaker
Village); and Craig Williams (New York State Museum at Albany, New York).
Several authors also contributed their personal photographs to the book;
we thank Zena Goldenberg, Beverly Gordon, Ruth Baer Lambach, and
Bonnie Morris.

Contributors

PRISCILLA J. BREWER is associate professor of American studies at the University of South Florida in Tampa. She received her Ph.D. in American civilization from Brown University in 1987. Her research interests include material culture and women's history. Her publications on the Shakers include *Shaker Communities, Shaker Lives* (1986).

WENDY E. CHMIELEWSKI is the George R. Cooley curator of the Swarthmore College Peace Collection. She received her Ph.D. in women's history from the State University of New York at Binghamton. She has written extensively on the subject of women and feminism in nineteenth-century U.S. communitarian societies. She is currently working on the role of women in the ante-bellum peace movement in the United States.

LUCY M. FREIBERT, professor of English, directs the English honors program at the University of Louisville. In 1983 she presented a paper, "The Role of the Artist in the Commune," at the First International Conference on Utopian Studies, Reggio Calabria, Italy. Her article "World Views in Utopian Novels by Women" appeared in the *Journal of Popular Culture* (1983). With Barbara A. White, she edited *Hidden Hands: An Anthology of American Women Writers, 1790–1870* (1985).

ZENA GOLDENBERG holds an M.A. in anthropology from the University of Illinois at Chicago and a B.A. in English from the University of Wisconsin at Madison. She is grateful to the members of Twin Oaks for welcoming her into their lives.

ROSEMARY D. GOODEN is assistant professor of history at De Paul University. She received a Ph.D. in American studies from the University of Michigan. Her article "A Preliminary Examination of the Shaker Attitude Toward Work" appeared in *Communal Societies* (1983). Gooden was awarded a Leverhulme Fellowship for the 1988–1989 academic year at the University of Exeter, England, where she co-organized an international symposium on the Shakers in March 1989. She is presently working on a study of devotional language entitled "The Language of Devotion in Nineteenth-Century American Religion."

BEVERLY GORDON is associate professor in the environment, textiles, and design department at the University of Wisconsin. She teaches courses and advises students in the fields of design history and material culture and serves as the director of the Helen Allen Textile Collection. Gordon worked at Hancock Shaker Village from 1973 to 1977. Her publications include *Shaker Textile Arts* (1980) and "Dress in American Communal Societies," *Communal Societies* (1985).

LOUIS J. KERN is professor of history at Hofstra University, where he teaches American cultural, social, and intellectual history, American studies, and film. He is the author of *An Ordered Love: Sex Roles and Sexuality in Victorian Utopias: The Shakers, the Mormons, and the Oneida Community* (1981).

MARLYN KLEE-HARTZELL is associate professor of political science at Adelphi University. She has previously published articles on women and family in the Oneida Community and on contemporary public policies and Chinese women in *Feminist Studies* and *Review of Radical Political Economics*. With the publication of this book, she has reclaimed her maternal and paternal surnames.

CAROL A. KOLMERTEN is professor of English and director of the honors program at Hood College. Author of *Women in Utopia: The Ideology of Gender in the American Owenite Communities* (1990) and editor of Alice Ilgenfritz Jones and Ella Merchant's *Unveiling a Parallel* (1991), she has published a variety of articles on both historical and fictional utopias. She is currently working on a cultural biography of Ernestine L. Rose and the woman's rights conventions of the 1850s.

RUTH BAER LAMBACH graduated from college in 1965 with a teaching degree in German and English and taught in the public schools of Milwaukee for several years. She has also pursued graduate studies in linguistics. Since 1981 she has worked at Truman College in Chicago as the coordinator of the Refugee Program, which offers English instruction and prepares students to live in a modern society. Lambach writes: "I became a citizen of the United States in 1988. After thirty years on the 'outside', I think I am ready to accept the awesome responsibility of freedom. At the party for this event I asked each person to bring a definition of 'freedom'. My favorite comes from Robert Frost who said, 'Freedom is being easy in your harness.'"

KATHY MARQUIS is a reference archivist at the Minnesota Historical Society. She has held previous archival positions at the Massachusetts Institute of Technology and the Schlesinger Library on the History of Women in America. She holds a master's degree in library science from Simmons College and a bachelor's degree in history from the University of Michigan.

BONNIE MORRIS received her Ph.D. in women's history from the State University of New York at Binghamton, after completing her doctoral dissertation on Hasidic women. Morris was a visiting fellow at Dartmouth College's Humanities Research Institute and has taught in the women's studies and religion program of Harvard Divinity School. She is currently assistant professor of history at St. Lawrence University. Morris also coordinates workshops for Jewish women at music festivals.

KAREN K. NICKLESS is an independent scholar and historical consultant in Columbia, S.C. She has published on the Shakers in *Communal Studies* and is currently at work, with her sister, on a book on the role of the Shaker sisters.

PAMELA J. NICKLESS is associate professor of economics and director of women's studies at the University of North Carolina at Asheville. She has published in the *Journal of Economic History* and *Communal Studies*. She is currently at work on a study of nineteenth-century North Carolina businesswomen.

MARY J. OATES, professor of economics at Regis College, has written extensively on the education and occupational choices of Catholic women. She is the editor of *Higher Education for Catholic Women: An Historical Anthology* (1987) and the author of "Catholic Laywomen in the Labor Force, 1850–1950," in *American Catholic Women*, ed. Karen Kennelly (1989). Oates is currently writing a book on the American Catholic philanthropic tradition.

Women in Spiritual and Communitarian
Societies in the United States

Introduction

MARLYN KLEE-HARTZELL

COMMUNAL AND UTOPIAN IMPULSES are as old as American history. Indeed, since 1630 when English Puritans established their city on a hill at Massachusetts Bay, many have looked to North America as a continent uniquely suited to experimentation and reformation of human society. Americans are fond of their utopian past. For more than a century, scholars and social commentators have scrutinized and evaluated communal societies, leaders, and movements.

Until recently, however, the experiences and perspectives of women participants in communal endeavors have received scant attention. Beginning about two decades ago, and paralleling a period of intense social upheaval in the United States, scholars began investigating the experiences of those Americans previously hidden from history. Buoyed and propelled by various liberation movements, "invisible" Americans—ethnic minorities, Native Americans, working people, and, of course, women—began to demand their due in the story of our collective national experience. These new subjects of history have transformed our academic curricula and, indeed, our national culture and language. Of these many transformations, none has been more dynamic and vibrant than the emerging discipline called women's studies. Women's studies is more than simply studying women. At its best, women's studies has changed the way we see, hear, speak, and think about our past, present, and future. As a transdisciplinary endeavor, women's studies offers us new theory, new vocabulary, and new questions about ourselves and our society.

We place this volume squarely within the context of feminist scholarship and discourse. The goals of this book are three: (1) to recover women's experiences in U.S. spiritual and communitarian societies; (2) to interpret those experiences, using the tools of contemporary feminist theory and

3

analysis; and (3) to encourage further studies of American communalism, with gender at the *center* rather than at the periphery of investigation.

We need to know more about women and communities not only because this information will give us a fuller understanding of our national communitarian past but also because many communal societies have deliberately attempted to change gendered behaviors and institutions that are the core of women's social experience: work, sexuality, marriage, child rearing, education, artistic expression, and political decision making. In a communal society, the first challenges to be addressed, both theoretically and practically, were pressing questions about how to make a living, how to govern, how to organize sexuality and procreation, and how to socialize the young into communal values. Further, because many communards believed that mainstream society was corrupt or, at the very least, inadequate to meet human needs, many people joined communities in the hope of transforming social relations. Communities' attempts to seek a better way to live—their philosophies and social practices, their successes and failures—give us an interpretive window on our national culture. One of the most basic questions this anthology raises, therefore, is, Have spiritual and communal societies offered women a better life?

At the same time, it is important to acknowledge that many communal societies have not been interested in progressive social change, particularly regarding gender relations, but instead were *retreats* from "the world." In other words, some (especially religious) communards felt that entirely too much change had already occurred. Some communities have tried to restore a lost earlier era, for example, by restoring patriarchal norms or preindustrial work patterns. In other words, we cannot assume that all communal societies are progressive from a feminist perspective. Nevertheless, many communities claimed that they offered some emancipatory possibilities for members, including women. We can learn from their critiques of the outside world and also from the concrete steps they took to make their societies better than the mainstream experience.

Each author in this collection raises feminist questions and uses feminist tools of analysis. Yet each article raises more questions than it can possibly address, for we are at the beginning stages of our endeavor to incorporate a feminist perspective into communitarian studies. (We were reminded of how far we have to go by a manuscript we received [and declined] for this collection that purported to discuss marriage and family in a particular community and hardly ever mentioned *women* in the text.)

Several of the articles expand our definition of community. Wendy E. Chmielewski's examination of Sojourner Truth's search for community offers us an unusual perspective on this great American heroine who is better known for her abolitionist and woman's rights activism. Yet Chmielewski reminds us that Truth's life was consistently informed by a religious sojourn toward a community of believers and doers, toward a vision of righteousness, salvation, and social justice. Her quest impelled Sojourner Truth toward many different community associations during her long and productive life.

We also include two articles about religious women who comprise communities that are generally not included in the field of communitarian studies: Lubavitcher women of Crown Heights, Brooklyn, New York, and Catholic sisters of the Boston diocese. Bonnie Morris's discussion of Lubavitcher women's education raises many fascinating questions, including how a tight-knit and conservative social group can assimilate new women converts into its society, particularly when these converts bring to it educational credentials, skills, and worldly experiences to which women raised from childhood inside the society have not been exposed. Another question implicit in Morris's article is how and whether the Lubavitchers can resist and mold the outside influences of contemporary feminism to retain the loyalty of women in their essentially patriarchal culture. A similar theme of women's needs for growth, development, and autonomy appears in Mary J. Oates's discussion of Catholic sisterhoods. She describes a process whereby Catholic sisters have attempted to increase their authority and to protect their female-directed institutions within the wider structure of a patriarchal and bureaucratic church structure. Another question posed by the Lubavitcher and Catholic sisterhoods' experiences is whether any intentional community can realistically keep the outside world at bay; that is, can a community boycott the influences of mainstream society and remain different or apart—whether for progressive or for reactionary reasons?

Kathy Marquis and Marlyn Klee-Hartzell implicity deal with the same question when they examine, respectively, Mormon and Oneida women's situations and compare them with those of their worldly counterparts and with notions of ideal womanhood outside these nineteenth-century societies. Both authors find that although the Mormons and the Oneida communists had decidedly unusual marriage and sexual arrangements and claimed to emancipate women, their idealization of "true womanliness" (Welter 1966) and their gendered marriage and work roles were remarkably similar, although not identical, to those of mainstream society. This knowledge should caution us that communal practices can seem quite daring and even liberatory but still adhere to patriarchal structures and values. Another interesting comparison offered by articles in this volume is the status of motherhood in two religious, male-led communes: the Oneida Community of the nineteenth century and The Farm (Tennessee) of the 1970s. Whereas the Oneida Community strictly limited women's opportunities to become mothers and restricted mothers' intimacy with their children, Louis J. Kern argues that The Farm raised childbirth and motherhood to sacramental status. Midwifery, an occupation monopolized by women, and a celebratory pronatalism were at the ideological center of communal practices of love and spirituality at The Farm. How did these two very different perspectives on motherhood affect the status of women in these communities?

A prominent feature of recent women's studies scholarship has been the rediscovery and interpretation of women's writings, especially private writings such as personal narratives, letters, and diaries. From this process of excavation and revelation we have learned to listen to women's voices as well as to women's silences (McConnell-Ginet, Borker, and Furman 1980; Olsen 1979; Rich 1979; Washington 1987). Carol A. Kolmerten uses unpublished women's letters in her study of women in Owenite communities to suggest that women (especially married women) were not satisfied with their communitarian experiences. Rosemary D. Gooden's discussion of the letters, poems, and acrostics Shaker sisters exchanged with each other examines similar sources but uses the perspective of women's friendship and affection as its major interpretive tool. Her emphasis on female friendship and spiritual networks is consistent with another strong theme of contemporary women's studies: "the female world of love and ritual" (Smith-Rosenberg 1975).

Lucy M. Freibert examines creative works (novels, essays, drawings, and paintings) by three Brook Farm women. Her study illustrates yet another perspective, which communitarian scholars call a developmental approach. Freibert traces the creative activities of Brook Farm women *throughout* their lives, particularly after the community dissolved, and concludes that the essentially nurturant environment of Brook Farm informed and sometimes provided direct materials for their creative activities. Freibert reminds us that the effects of communal living are not limited to one's residence in community but extend throughout the life of the communards and, indeed, throughout the lives of their descendants.

Although most of the communities treated in this book deal with mixed male and female societies, we are delighted to include one article about the Sanctified Sisters of Belton, Texas (and later, Washington, D.C.), also known as the Woman's Commonwealth. As Wendy E. Chmielewski points out, although the sisters couched their community in terms of respectable religious goals of the period, their female leadership, their rejection of oppressive marriages, and their drive to autonomy lead us to conclude that the Sanctified Sisters were self-consciously feminist. Chmielewski also raises the issue of community as a sanctuary from wife-abuse and family violence.

Of all the communitarian efforts in the United States, perhaps none is better known today than the Shakers (United Society of Believers in Christ's Second Appearing), who are widely admired for their aesthetics, artistry, and work ethic. From a feminist perspective, however, the fact that the Society of Believers was founded by a woman, Mother Ann Lee, piques our interest. Because so many American communal societies were founded and dominated by men, a feminist analysis of Shaker society gives us an opportunity to examine these communities founded on a mother ideology. We ask, for example, what effect Mother Ann Lee's spiritual beliefs and legacy had upon the self-image and self-expression of Shaker sisters. Rosemary D. Gooden's article suggests that love, affection, and "gospel union" among women were strong themes in Shaker sisters' writings. Many of these expressions drew on maternal images of comfort and tenderness and invoked Mother Ann's protective love. It appears that community was a place of refuge and safety for Shaker sisters. Because the Shaker sisters lived and worked in sex-segregated units, were they freer to be "women-identified women" (Rich 1980) than were women in the male-dominated communities of the period?

Further, because sisters have outnumbered and outlived brethren in twentieth-century Shaker societies, the latter years of Shaker history give us an opportunity to examine female styles of leadership and the decisions sisters made. Authors Karen K. Nickless, Pamela J. Nickless, and Priscilla J. Brewer examine issues of female leadership and power in Shaker society. Nickless and Nickless attribute Shaker interest in female equality to influences *outside* the Society of Believers, rather than to internal religious beliefs. Further, they remind us that symmetrical officeholding (for example, deacon/deaconess) among the Shakers did not necessarily mean symmetrical power and influence in the society. Brewer concludes that despite Ann Lee's position as "Mother" in Shaker belief and doctrine, Shakers held traditional assumptions about gender roles and preferred male leadership; women's leadership was not accepted without a struggle within the society and was facilitated, in part, by the fact that Shaker sisters began to outnumber brethren in the nineteenth century.

A classic question posed by early women's studies scholars was, "Why have there been no great women artists?" (Nochlin 1973). Exploring the relationship of artistic expression to the social experiences of most women, feminist scholars conclude that women have indeed produced artistic works, but not in the same domains or numbers as male artists. Because of their childbearing and childrearing responsibilities, as well as their lack of training, of economic resources, and of public power, many women have been unable to produce art—paintings and sculpture—as we generally think of it. Instead, we have learned to look for women's artistry in new places, and especially in the domestic sphere where most women have lived their lives and exerted their influence. As a consequence, we have come to appreciate woman-made objects like quilts, textiles, and humble household items and, further, to realize that within these objects, women often tell the stories of their lives. Beverly Gordon situates her article on Shaker fancy goods within this feminist and material culture tradition, by emphasizing the ideas of Shaker sisters' identity and purposefulness embodied in the goods they made. Gordon draws out this analysis by underscoring the pride and economic power Shaker craftswomen achieved through their sale of fancy goods to the outside world.

Finally, we conclude the anthology with two first-person accounts of twentieth-century communal life. Ruth Baer Lambach relates a compelling narrative of her life as a colony girl amidst the German pietistic community of the Hutterites—rural communards who practice rigid sex roles and keep women and girls busy with reproduction tasks. Zena Goldenberg's analysis of women's culture at Twin Oaks takes the participant-observer stance of an anthropologist, rather than that of a member of the commune. Goldenberg highlights Twin Oakers' commitment to eradicating sexism from their work and language, but at the same time, she finds that the vibrancy of women-only activities in the community has caused some male members to feel excluded and resentful. At Twin Oaks in 1987, women seemed to have had an advantage in personal and collective growth opportunities and in setting the standards for community behavior, as evidenced by their strong campaign against male "wolfing." These two first-person accounts of twentieth-century communities give us a sample of the great diversity of contemporary communal societies and the radically different places of women in each.

Although we, the editors, are satisfied with the quality and diversity of the articles in this book, we are acutely aware that one book cannot convey the breadth of the American communal experience, nor can it raise every question and issue we would like to explore. In particular, we would like to encourage feminist inquiry that would examine in greater depth the boundaries and limitations of community itself. In other words, what *is* a feminist definition of *community?* We need as well to know much more about why women have joined communal societies—what they were seeking and what they found. As we learn more about communal societies, we expect to find that, among other motivations, women joined communities seeking sanctuary from family violence and abuse, as well as economic refuge for the widowed, divorced, and abandoned. This theme certainly needs further exploration.

Another theme that warrants further investigation is the expression of women's spirituality in community. Many articles in this book reveal the importance of dreams, visions, revelations, spirit manifestations, and gifts of inspiration that have guided women in their search for spiritual meaning. Sojourner Truth, the Sanctified Sisters of Belton, Texas, and Shaker women all based their vision of community on various forms of spiritual revelation. Prayer, worship, meditation, and religious ritual have provided important touchstones for women in many communities surveyed in this volume. One of the notable results of contemporary feminism has been the growth of many small groups of women – both inside and outside established religions – who are quietly engaged in serious spiritual sojourns. Many contemporary women find spiritual empowerment in eco-feminism; in disarmament and pacifist movements (like the Greenham Common and Seneca Falls encampments); in feminist poetry, novels, and music; in covens; and in the rediscovery of symbols and rituals of female power from the ancient past (Adler 1986). These contemporary spiritual manifestations link American women to the nineteenth-century women who also sought community and spiritual meaning in their lives (Braude 1989). We need to know more about women's spirituality as it manifests itself in community, both in the past and in the present.

Not only have American women been attracted to spritual and communal life, but many have been impelled to leave (secede from) community. We wonder if women have left communal societies in equal proportions to men. In her study of eight charismatic communities of the nineteenth century, Sue Wright (1989) found that male members predominated in the formative stages of community building, but that women predominated in the consolidation and decline stages. We wonder if this has been a general pattern in communal life, and if so, why?

One famous apostate (seceder), Mary Marshall Dyer, left the Enfield, New Hampshire, Shaker community in 1816. Because mothers had no legal rights to their children in this period, Mary Dyer was unable to take her five children with her (born before she and Joseph Dyer joined in 1812) and spent the rest of her life pressing lawsuits and public campaigns to regain her children. She did not succeed, despite her anguished plea: "Give me my children. I ask no more." The Enfield Shaker community fought Mary Dyer tooth and nail and, with their superior economic and legal resources, prevented her from recovering her children. Was Mary Dyer merely a troublemaker, or insane, as the Shakers contended? Her story (and the extensive literature, including lawsuits, her case developed) begs for a feminist interpretation. Undoubtedly, many other stories of women apostates, of both the nineteenth and twentieth centuries still need to be recovered and interpreted.

Probably one of the most fruitful yet difficult subjects of feminist interpretation concerns sexuality and procreation in U.S. communal societies.
We know that sexuality is historically and socially determined, but we need
more feminist analyses of specific communal sexual practices. How do we
evaluate, for example, the great diversity of sexual practices of communal
societies: celibacy (Shakers), complex marriage (Oneida), plural marriage
(Mormons), community prohibitions against the use of birth control (Hutterites), and celebratory pronatalism (The Farm)?

What, to take one example, did or does celibacy in community mean
to women? D'Ann Campbell has suggested that celibacy in Shaker societies
enabled nineteenth-century women to avoid debilitating and repeated childbearing and could, therefore, have been a liberatory alternative for some
women (Campbell 1978). Still, we have learned very little from Shaker sisters' writings about whether they chose a Shaker life with this motivation
in mind. The indomitable John Humphrey Noyes criticized Shakers for *not*
reproducing, arguing that they were among the finest American (spiritual)
stock, and just the sort of people to produce excellent citizens. He commented further: "[Celibacy] is exactly adapted to the proclivities of women
in a state of independence or ascendancy over man. Love between the sexes
has two stages; the courting stage and the wedded stage. Women are fond
of the first stage. Men are fond of the second. Women like to talk about
love; but men want the love itself" (Dixon 1868, 180–81).

Even for the nineteenth century, would we agree that celibacy insti-
tutionalizes woman's "independence or ascendancy over man"? Historians
generally conclude that middle-class, nineteenth-century American women
developed and supported notions of women's "passionlessness," "purity,"
and "voluntary motherhood" in order to enhance their control of male sexuality and of their own fertility (Cott 1978; Gordon 1973). Citing the precipitous decline in white women's fertility across the nineteenth century,
Daniel Scott Smith has labeled it an example of "domestic feminism" (Smith
1973).

Yet recent feminist theory emphasizes instead woman's right to choose
her sexual identity, including a lesbian identity; her definition and control
over her sexual pleasure; her access to safe birth control; and her decision
if and when to have children and under what conditions (Davis 1988). Have
contemporary communes been successful in meeting this feminist definition of sexual and reproductive freedom? We suspect that many communal
efforts of the 1960s and 1970s resulted not in liberation but in new forms
of heterosexual conformity and exploitation of women.

In summary, some of the topics we recommend for further feminist
analysis include sexuality and procreation, female apostasy, community as

sanctuary from family abuse, women's spirituality, and a feminist perspective on community itself. We would encourage women who have lived or who continue to live in communities to write their memoirs. In addition, many historic communal societies need new study from a feminist perspective. We know of no feminist studies, for example, of Amana, Zoar, Icaria, Bethel, Aurora, the Moravians (nineteenth century), or of Llano del Rio, Koinonia, Rajneesh, Jonestown, or Hare Krishna (to name but a few from the twentieth century).

We would particularly encourage more focus on communities founded by women and on women-only communes. Many women, including lesbian-separatists, founded women-only communities in the 1970s and 1980s, but we have not learned nearly enough about their experiences. Lillian Faderman discusses briefly the experiences of rural, lesbian-separatist communities of the 1970s (Faderman 1991, 238–40). In the 1990s, lesbian women continue to form rural communities; Lesbian Connection (c/o Ambitious Amazons, P. O. Box 811, East Lansing, Mich. 48826) publishes a directory of groups of women's land communities in the United States. Regrettably, we have learned very little about contemporary women-only communities in U.S. *urban* areas, although Davis and Kennedy's oral history of the lesbian community of Buffalo, New York, provides a model for further scholarship (Davis and Kennedy 1986).

We believe that women of color have a rich community history; we want to know more about their experiences. Elsa Barkley Brown's study of the Independent Order of Saint Luke of Richmond, Virginia, gives us an especially creative model for understanding African-American women's efforts to promote community. At the beginning of the twentieth century, led by Maggie Lena Walker (the first woman bank president in the United States), black women in Richmond founded the Penny Savings Bank and the Saint Luke Emporium (a department store that provided economic development within the African-American community and gave gainful employment to many women and men). Brown stresses that "a well-organized set of institutions maintained community in Richmond; mutual benefit societies, interwoven with extended families and churches, built a network of supportive relations" (1990, 212). She concludes: "Walker and the Saint Luke women demonstrated in their own day the power of black women discovering their own strengths and sharing them with the whole community. They provide for us today a model of womanist praxis" (1990, 218).

In her analytical essays on contemporary black women's fiction, Susan Willis raises similar themes of African-American women's utopian visions of "community much larger than a household" and of alternatives to prevailing capitalist economic and social models. Willis believes that African-

American women writers offer unique insights into U.S. history as both chronological period and as process. "Journeying along motherlines," black women writers conjure up their experiences of migration, work, community, and motherhood with images like Paule Marshall's mother's "kitchen community" (*Brown Girl, Brownstones,* 1959), Toni Morrison's Shalimar (*Song of Solomon,* 1977), and Zora Neale Hurston's "black community where work is a pleasurable communal experience" (*Their Eyes Were Watching God,* 1937) (Willis 1987, 3–25).

We hope that interpretations like Brown's and Willis's will encourage more scholarship on black women's experiences with community. We wonder, for example, about women in the Canadian communities founded at the end of the Underground Railroad routes of the 1850s; about the women's community in Zora Neale Hurston's hometown of Eatonville, Florida; about women in the contemporary Sisterhood of Single Mothers of Brooklyn, New York, and about the women of MOVE, who were killed along with their men and children when the city of Philadelphia ruthlessly destroyed their communal home in 1985. We need more studies of African-American women's communities like the White Rose Mission of New York City, which was founded in the early twentieth century to help southern black women who migrated north to find jobs. Clearly, we have a great deal of scholarship still to do in order to uncover the range of communal efforts undertaken by women of color. It is very likely that, in the process, we will enrich and broaden our understanding of the many meanings of *community* for women.

Although, as we have attempted to indicate, there is a need for further research, examples exist of recently published work on women and communal societies whose authors incorporate a feminist analysis. Carol A. Kolmerten's (1990) study of women in Owenite Communities is one example; Jean M. Humez's (1981) edition of black Shaker Eldress Rebecca Jackson's visionary experiences is another. Marjorie Procter-Smith's (1985) book on women in Shaker community and worship employs a feminist analysis of religious symbolism. Dolores Hayden's (1976) study of the architecture of communitarian socialism gives an excellent model of how a feminist perspective can inform and enrich scholarly investigation. In particular, Hayden's chapter on the socialist-feminist plans of self-taught architect Alice Constance Austin at Llano del Rio, California, illuminates Austin's critique of the ways in which "the political problems of women were reinforced by the design of traditional dwellings." Similarly, Hayden's examination of utopian feminists' campaigns for kitchenless houses analyzes living space and women's needs (Hayden 1978). A special issue of *Signs: Journal of Women in Culture and Society* (10 [Summer 1985]), examines communities of women, broadly defined—for example, women reformers of Chicago's Hull House in the 1890s and African-American women in the twentieth-century Sanctified church. A contributed volume edited by Ruby Rohrlich and Elaine Hoffman Baruch (1984) includes articles on women in some ancient, historic, and contemporary communities, as well as poetry, essays on literary utopias, and women's visioning of the future.

In summary, we believe that the fields of communitarian studies and women's studies will be enriched by scholarship that focuses on gender and the needs and experiences of women in community. The possibilities are numerous. We offer this anthology as a beginning, rather than as an end. We hope that the articles and the ideas they generate will enable us to reclaim women's experiences and perspectives in the rich history of U.S. communalism.

Works Cited

Adler, Margot. 1986. *Drawing Down the Moon: Witches, Druids, Goddess-worshippers, and Other Pagans in America Today.* Boston: Beacon.

Braude, Ann. 1989. *Radical Spirits: Spiritualism and Women's Rights in Nineteenth-Century America.* Boston: Beacon.

Brown, Elsa Barkley. 1990. Womanist Consciousness: Maggie Lena Walker and the Independent Order of Saint Luke. In *Unequal Sisters: A Multi-Cultural Reader in U.S. Women's History,* ed. E. C. DuBois and V. L. Ruiz, 208–23. New York: Routledge.

Campbell, D'Ann. 1978. Women's Life in Utopia: The Shaker Experiment in Sexual Equality Reappraised—1810 to 1860. *New England Quarterly* 51 (Mar.): 23–38.

Cott, Nancy. 1978. Passionlessness: An Interpretation of Victorian Sexual Ideology, 1790–1850. *Signs: Journal of Women in Culture and Society* 4 (Winter): 219–36.

Davis, Madeline D., and Elizabeth Lapovsky Kennedy. 1986. Oral History and the Study of Sexuality in the Lesbian Community: Buffalo, New York, 1940–1960. *Feminist Studies* 12, no. 1 (Spring): 7–26.

Davis, Susan, ed. 1988. *Women Under Attack: Victories, Backlash and the Fight for Reproductive Freedom.* Boston: South End.

Dixon, William Hepworth. 1868. *Spiritual Wives.* London: Hurst and Blackett.

Faderman, Lillian. 1991. *Odd Girls and Twilight Lovers: A History of Lesbian Life in Twentieth-Century America.* New York: Columbia Univ. Press.

Gordon, Linda. 1973. Voluntary Motherhood: The Beginnings of Feminist Birth Control Ideas in the United States. *Feminist Studies* 1, nos. 3/4 (Winter/Spring): 5–22.

Hayden, Dolores. 1976. *Seven American Utopias: The Architecture of Communitarian Socialism, 1790–1975.* Cambridge, Mass.: MIT Press.

———. 1978. Two Utopian Feminists and Their Campaigns for Kitchenless Houses. *Signs: Journal of Women in Culture and Society* 4 (Winter): 274–90.

Humez, Jean M., ed. 1981. *Gifts of Power: The Writings of Rebecca Jackson, Black Visionary, Shaker Eldress.* Amherst: Univ. of Massachusetts Press.

Kolmerten, Carol A. 1990. *Women in Utopia: The Ideology of Gender in the American Owenite Communities.* Bloomington: Indiana Univ. Press.

McConnell-Ginet, Sally, Ruth Borker, and Nelly Furman, eds. 1980. *Women and Language in Literature and Society.* New York: Praeger.

Nochlin, Linda. 1973. Why Have There Been No Great Women Artists? In *Art and Sexual Politics,* ed. E. Baker and T. Hess, 1–39. London: Collier Macmillan.

Olsen, Tillie. 1979. *Silences.* New York: Delacorte.

Procter-Smith, Marjorie. 1985. *Women in Shaker Community and Worship: A Feminist Analysis of the Uses of Religious Symbolism.* Lewiston, N.Y.: Edwin Mellen.

Rich, Adrienne. 1979. *On Lies, Secrets, and Silence.* New York: Norton.

———. 1980. Compulsory Heterosexuality and Lesbian Existence. *Signs: Journal of Women in Culture and Society* 5 (Summer): 631–90.

Rohrlich, Ruby, and Elaine Hoffman Baruch, eds. 1984. *Women in Search of Utopia: Mavericks and Mythmakers.* New York: Schocken.

Signs: Journal of Women in Culture and Society. 1985. 10 (Summer): special issue, *Communities of Women.*

Smith, Daniel Scott. 1973. Family Limitation, Sexual Control, and Domestic Feminism in Victorian America. *Feminist Studies* 1, nos. 3/4 (Winter/Spring): 40–57.

Smith-Rosenberg, Carroll. 1975. The Female World of Love and Ritual: Relations between Women in Nineteenth-Century America. *Signs: Journal of Women in Culture and Society* 1 (Autumn): 1–29.

Washington, Mary Helen. 1987. *Invented Lives: Narratives of Black Women, 1860–1960.* Garden City, N.Y.: Doubleday.

Welter, Barbara. 1966. The Cult of True Womanhood, 1820–1860. *American Quarterly* 18 (Summer): 151–75.

Willis, Susan. 1987. Histories, Communities, and Sometimes Utopia. In *Specifying: Black Women Writing the American Experience,* by Susan Willis, 3–25. Madison: Univ. of Wisconsin Press.

Wright, Sue. 1989. Women and the Charismatic Community: Defining the Attraction. Unpublished manuscript, Graduate Department of Sociology, Univ. of Oregon.

PART ONE

Women's Search for Community
Religious, Secular, Feminist

Introduction

THIS SECTION PRESENTS three views of women searching for and creating intentional communities that would meet their specific needs. In the first article the author explores Sojourner Truth's search through several intentional communities for a congenial and appropriate setting. The author of the second article delineates several women's experiences and observations about Owenite communities in the second quarter of the nineteenth century. In the third article the author relates the history of an all-female community in late nineteenth-century Texas.

The Kingdom (1832(?)–1835) was first based in New York City and then in Ossining, New York. It was headed by Robert Matthews, who believed he was an incarnation of the Messiah. Elijah Pierson, a religious and wealthy city businessman, had many conversations with Matthews in which they sought to recognize each others' claims to divinity. They must have come to some agreement, as they soon set about making arrangements for The Kingdom and attracting other members. Sojourner Truth worked for Pierson as a domestic. She was impressed with the piety of the household and stayed to become part of The Kingdom.

Theoretically egalitarian as to race and class, The Kingdom welcomed two freedwomen, a working-class family, and wealthy merchants. The original philosophy of The Kingdom legitimized Matthews as the head of the community, with everyone else an equal member. Although members gave their possessions to form communal property, it was clear from the beginning that Pierson and other wealthy patrons kept the community alive by purchasing goods and property.

Sexual scandal, embezzlement, charges of murder, and religious eccentricity ended The Kingdom. In 1835, Elijah Pierson died of a stomach complaint. His friends and family outside The Kingdom believed that Matthews had poisoned him. The ensuing trial of Matthews on charges of murder and insanity revealed The Kingdom as a community of people who had experimented with communal property ownership, work patterns, and sexual reltionships. Sojourner Truth was named as the only accomplice of Matthews in the murder trial. She was acquitted, as was Matthews himself. The Kingdom fell apart under the stress of all the accusations. Recommended contemporary sources on The Kingdom are William L. Stone, *Matthias and His Impostures* (1835), and Gilbert Vale, *Fanaticism; Its Sources and Influences* (1835).

The Northampton Association of Education and Industry (1842–1846) was the next intentional community that Truth entered. Begun by David Mack, Samuel Hill, George Benson and other reformers, it was an attempt to integrate various social reform and utopian philosophies of the period. The Association was located near the village of Northampton, Massachusetts. The founders of the community purchased five hundred acres of land and the buildings of a former silk factory. The silk factory was to provide paid employment and income for the workers of the Association. Families and individuals joining the community purchased stock in the community; these funds were to pay off the original debt for the property and the factory.

The reform-minded founders of the Northampton Association wrote the Articles of Faith, which listed all the rights and privileges members of the community could expect. The articles stated that rights of women and of people of color would be the same as those of white men. Women were also compensated equally with men for the work they performed in the silk factory. Some domestic work was considered labor to be compensated in the same way as the factory work. However, only women performed the paid and unpaid domestic work and child rearing. The Northampton Association finally collapsed in 1846 as a result of economic mismanagement and lack of support. The two most complete sources on the Northampton Association are Charles A. Sheffield, *A History of Florence, Massachusetts* (1894), and Alice Eaton McBee, *From Florence to Utopia: The Story of a Transcendentalist Community in Northampton, Massachusetts, 1830–1852* (Northampton, Mass.: Smith College Council of Industrial Studies Series, no. 8 [1947]). For further information on Sojourner Truth, Frances Titus's *Narrative of Sojourner Truth, a Bondswoman of Olden Time . . . and Her Book of Life* (1878) provides background from contemporary sources, including Truth herself. More recent biographies include Jacqueline Bernard's *Journey toward Freedom—The Story of Sojourner Truth* (1967) and Hertha Pauli's *Her Name Was Sojourner Truth* (1962).

The Owenite communities (1825–ca. 1828) were first organized by Robert Owen, a British factory owner, philanthropist, and utopianist. Owen had successfully established a planned community for his employees and their families at his textile factory in New Lanark, Scotland. He arrived in the United States in 1824, enthusiastically ready to create Communities of Equality in the New World. Owen's ideas on secular communalism, advanced technology, and equality of all adults appealed to his audiences.

The most famous Owenite community, New Harmony, was established in Indiana in 1825. More than one thousand people arrived at New Harmony to participate in the new community experiment. A number of other Owenite communities sprang up within the next few years. Most of them tried to institutionalize political equality and equal access to education for all members. In actual practice, many communities were not able to live up to these ideals. By 1828, all the Owenite communities in the United States had closed, although the Queenwood community in England lasted until 1845. However, Owen's ideals influenced other intentional communities for several decades. Many members of Owenite communities in the United States went on to join or found intentional communities of their own. Recommended sources include Carol A. Kolmerten, *Women in Utopia: The Ideology of Gender in the American Owenite Communities* (1990), and J. F. C. Harrison, *Quest for the New Moral World: Robert Owen and the Owenites in Britain and America* (1969).

The Woman's Commonwealth (ca. 1867–1983), also known as the Sanctified Sisters, was begun in Belton, Texas, as a ladies' Bible class whose members disagreed with local ministers over theological doctrine. The Commonwealth later grew into a Christian socialist and feminist community. The dreams and revelations of the community's founder, Martha McWhirter, and of her followers led the women to adopt celibacy. Many husbands were unwilling to continue marriage with celibate wives, and thus the women turned to each other for economic and emotional support. By the early 1880s a group of approximately fifty women lived together, running their household and several businesses communally. The women were financially successful, owning two hotels, a laundry, and several farms. By the time the group left Texas in 1898 their estimated worth was over $200,000.

The Woman's Commonwealth moved to Washington, D.C., where its members continued as a communal group well into the 1920s. In 1902 they incorporated and wrote a community constitution that stated their joy and belief in the communal lifestyle. Martha McWhirter, the founder, died in 1904, but the remaining women maintained the community in Washington and a farm in the suburbs of Maryland. The last member of the community died in 1983. Recommended sources on the Woman's Commonwealth are George Garrison, "A Woman's Community in Texas" (1893), and Sally Kitch, *Chaste Liberation: Celibacy and Female Cultural Status* (1989), which includes a discussion of the Woman's Commonwealth.

1

Sojourner Truth

Utopian Vision and Search for Community, 1797–1883

WENDY E. CHMIELEWSKI

SOJOURNER TRUTH IS WELL KNOWN as an African-American heroine, abolitionist, and lecturer for woman's rights. Her communal vision and involvement with utopian communities is less familiar to modern feminists and scholars. An examination of Truth's life and work will illustrate both her vision of a new type of life for women and for all African-American people and her personal search for a community. As a woman deeply committed to social reform, she turned her attention to the burning issues of her day: problems of economic inequality, disruption of older social patterns, changing gender roles, and questions of gender and racial equity. Truth combined her desire for a more equitable society with her personal experience in communities that experimented with social change. In the process of her search for a congenial community, Sojourner Truth questioned patriarchal authority by resisting many of the traditional roles assigned to her race and gender. This search took Truth through various utopian communities or experiments. She tried to find answers and new ways of living for herself by recharting familiar paths and attempted to extend what she had learned to other women and black people by her speeches, lectures, and the example of her life. Always, Truth contributed her own ideas and conceptions about the creation of a new world.

Truth was born a slave in Ulster County, New York, in the last years of the eighteenth century. Until early middle age she was owned by a series of masters and often separated from family, friends, and community. She was called Isabella for the first forty-six years of her life; the name Sojourner Truth was divinely inspired and communicated to her in conversations with God.

For the first half of her life, Isabella turned to religion to answer her questions about the reason for the horrors of slavery, the poverty of many free black and white people, and what seemed like the general immorality of the world. Later, she found in religion inspiration and encouragement for her reform work and her search for alternative ways of living. Religion was the framework upon which, once free, she felt able to build a new life.

Isabella's early religious faith was mingled with cherished memories of her mother and father. Whatever secure and happy family life Isabella remembered with her parents was connected with this sense of the religious and the promise of a better life. Religion also had an early utopian cast for Isabella. Early religious instruction had come at her mother's knee. Mau-Mau Bett told her children that God would protect them against the harsh realities of slavery. She also taught them that there was a better world to come in heaven.

The idea of a perfect world or ideal state of being, a world to be wished and hoped for, was part of Isabella's worldview from childhood onward. Like many in slavery, she formed this hoped-for world in terms of her religious experience and her knowledge of Judeo-Christian iconography and of African religious practices learned from parents and other slaves.

When Isabella escaped from her last master, John Dumont, in 1827, she worked for Isaac and Maria Van Wagenen, whom she had known since infancy (Vale 1835, 3). They protected her from Dumont and provided her with secure surroundings. The Van Wagenens were Quakers who were early models for Isabella. During this period she took the name Van Wagenen. While living and working with this pious Quaker family, Isabella attended Methodist camp meetings.

Methodism, with its emphasis on God's concern for all souls, black and white, and on the connection between the individual and God, appealed to many African-American people, both slave and free. At Methodist camp meetings Isabella felt encouraged to speak out concerning her messages from God. In this atmosphere she gained her first experience in speaking publicly of her faith and beliefs. Possibly she spoke before mixed audiences of men and women, blacks and whites. For Isabella, preaching provided not only a release from her condition as slave and former slave but a way to form a new identity, that of "zealous exhorter" (Vale 1835, 21), in her first few months of freedom.

In 1829, two years after Isabella Van Wagenen claimed her freedom, she decided to move to New York City. She correctly believed that employment opportunities for domestic workers in rural communities were diminishing. The U.S. economy was becoming more industrialized. For many rural families, this meant a decline in the amount of time women spent on household manufactures, both for their families' own use and for market. This did not mean the farm wife labored less, but it did mean that extra female help in the form of a hired girl was not always necessary to the rural household (Kessler-Harris 1982, 27). At the same time, the farm family began to need more cash to pay for the essential household goods it was no longer profitable to produce in individual households. Money now needed for family subsistence could not be spent on extra household help, the kind of work Isabella depended on for her living. A Methodist friend told her of greater opportunities for domestic servants in New York City, and she was convinced that an urban environment would provide more economic and cultural opportunities.

New York City, a rapidly growing population center, embodied all the problems of urbanization in the first four decades of the nineteenth century. Seasonal unemployment for many of the unskilled members of the working class, overcrowded living conditions, poverty, and the failure of the municipal government to keep abreast of the growing population combined to create squalid living quarters, unsanitary conditions, and periodic epidemics.

Similar to the work roles of their rural sisters, the work roles of working-class urban women were changing throughout this period. Centralized production in factories was replacing home-based manufacturing. Some women continued to contribute to the family income by accepting "given-out work" that could be completed in the home (Mohl 1971, 3–13). Many of these industries, whether organized into factory production or supplying "given-out work," often provided only seasonal employment. By the mid-1820s much of the cottage industry of the city and surrounding areas had been replaced with the more profitable factory system, eliminating traditional employment for some women in their family homes. For some working-class women, occasional prostitution became a way to combat homelessness, poverty, and this lack of adequate employment.

African-American women were excluded by their gender from skilled jobs and by their race from available urban manufacturing. White women refused to work alongside their black sisters in factories. Black women filled the urban domestic jobs abandoned by the white women who moved West or entered New England factories (Harley 1978, 8). Free black women and newly freed slaves most often found jobs as cooks, washerwomen, and seamstresses (Kessler-Harris 1982, 47). The washing and sewing work was similar to that done in the factories, but the wages were far lower (Harley 1978, 11). Often seen by white men and white women as workers who competed in the marketplace by accepting low wages, black women were excluded from the antebellum labor movement by reason of their race and gender.

Nevertheless, New York had great attractions for Van Wagenen. We may assume, from the activities in which she became involved, that economic opportunities were not the only reason for her move. The black community in New York was a large and varied one. In the 1830s and 1840s, European visitors noted that African-American inhabitants "constituted an established and accepted ingredient in the city's cosmopolitan society" (Still 1956, 89). This was the New York Van Wagenen and her son Peter faced in 1829.

In New York City religion continued to play a large role in Isabella Van Wagenen's life. Like many other women, Van Wagenen found religious activity gave her a focus and a purpose outside of the daily harsh routine. In her first years in New York City Isabella attended many camp meetings and was well known at Methodist meetings for "her long and loud preaching and praying, remarkable . . . influence in converting; and while amongst [the Methodists] . . . was much respected by them" (Vale 1835, 21).

Van Wagenen was introduced to the Latourettes, a family of white, middle-class Methodists, all of whom were active in the religious moral reform movement. They appreciated her power as a preacher and invited Isabella to meetings held in the Latourette home. The Latourettes asked her to accompany the women of the family and others interested in reform into brothels and homes for prostitutes in attempts to save souls (Titus [1878] 1978, 87). Moral reform of society through religious channels was an idea that appealed to many in this period. The middle-class population of New York began to feel threatened by an ever-growing underclass, fearing the intrusion of urban problems into their homes. Middle-class women believed the home to be their special sphere of power and influence. For many of these women, saving the home from the intrusion of urban chaos became an issue of moral control for both the working class and their own middle-class families.

These women came to believe that their own homes were the places to begin their reform efforts. Uncontrolled sexuality – that is, sexuality outside of marriage – seemed one of the most troubling aspects of city life. These reform-minded women were concerned not only with the fate of their fallen sisters but also with saving middle-class daughters, sons, and husbands from the corruption associated with prostitution. The methods they chose to accomplish these ends were to reform their own families both materially and morally. Women were taught and believed that they had more direct control over their families and households than over society at large. Religion was viewed as an acceptably feminine way to take an active role in protecting homes and families from the corrupting influences of city life.

Some of the middle-class white women Isabella Van Wagenen met in

New York religious reform circles decided a simpler life would lead to a more moral life: plain food, furniture, and clothing replaced ostentation and over-abundance in their homes. For these women, the simpler life also came to symbolize a rejection of the expanding materialism that was associated with men and with the dangerous world outside the home. They connected male sexuality and a male business world with a world beyond the control of women. These factors continued to be seen as factors dividing the sexes into separate spheres (Smith-Rosenberg 1985, 109–28).

Isabella Van Wagenen believed in the need for social reform. She had to face daily the effects of urban problems, and she searched for solutions to the poverty, hunger, and exploitation surrounding her. There is no evidence that Van Wagenen adopted the stringent antimaterialistic bent of her reforming acquaintances. However, for the time being she did espouse their methods of reforming society. The women with whom Isabella associated based their philosophy of reform firmly on their religious beliefs. This moral position and the religious basis for reform of society, rather than the material asceticism, attracted Van Wagenen.

She found both white and black religious communities necessary to her. In the black community she located people with life experiences similar to her own; these contacts gave her much-needed support. She joined the African Methodist Episcopal church, which was an important religious focus for the community. Through the Zion church she was reconnected with her sisters and brother, who had been sold away from the family as young children.

Despite an initial reluctance, Isabella became more involved with the reform groups of her white acquaintances. Through her domestic work she met Sarah and Elijah Pierson, a couple who ran the Magdalene Asylum for repentant prostitutes near the Bowery Hill area. The Piersons were part of a loosely formed community of several households. They and their reform-minded neighbors believed in the need for a simpler and more spiritual approach to life.

Frances Folger, a longtime leader of reform in New York City, was also a leader of the Bowery Hill community. She was the author of several religious tracts and a strong influence on women involved in local evangelical churches. In 1829 she founded and led an organization known as the Retrenchment Society, whose women members attempted to rid their lives of excess material possessions. They "disposed of elegant furniture," ate only plain food, and wore clothing without ornament (Vale 1835, 25). By simplifying their living arrangements, they hoped to add more moral and spiritual meaning to their lives (Stone 1835, 49–51; Vale 1835, 25).

Isabella Van Wagenen was not part of the household on Bowery Hill while Frances Folger was leader of the community. Her connection with Elijah Pierson began after Pierson started receiving divine messages electing him to leadership of the community. With the death of his wife, it seemed to his friends and relatives that Elijah had become excessive in the religious aspects of his life. He came to believe he was inhabited by the regenerated spirit of Elijah the prophet, and that he was called by God to be a leader amongst his friends on Bowery Hill.

The diversity in background of the members of the communal experiment led by Pierson was attractive to Van Wagenen. Members included several wealthy businessmen, white working-class men and women, a Jewish woman, and two former slaves. Wealth, class, status, and race were not ostensibly the criteria for status within the community. Theoretically, all members pooled their personal goods and put them at the disposal of the group. However, the community was financially supported by the two or three wealthy members and backers. The existence of such a community, believing it could be the basis for the reformation of society and could provide a spiritual example for the rest of the world, was an achievement in and of itself.

Soon after Isabella Van Wagenen went to work at the Pierson house, a white itinerant street preacher named Robert Matthews contacted Pierson. Matthews had also received certain revelations. He claimed God had told him he was to be renamed Matthias and would be God's representative on earth. He would lead the faithful to the coming kingdom of heaven on earth. Pierson welcomed Matthias as a fellow mystic and as the coming Messiah. Isabella, then working as a domestic for Pierson, was present at many of the early conversations between the two men.

Matthias soon became a part of the Pierson household. Several interested people joined them: the wealthy Mr. Mills; Benjamin and Ann Folger and their two daughters; a young widow, Catherine Stimson; and two former slaves, a woman named Katy and Isabella Van Wagenen. Besides the Pierson home in Bowery Hill, the community, now known as The Kingdom, also purchased a farm in Ossining, New York. Many of the Bowery Hill neighbors, once in sympathy with Pierson's reform efforts, dropped away when a more serious form of community was envisioned. Pierson, Benjamin Folger, and other wealthy backers made available to the community, and to Matthias personally, large amounts of property and credit. As a show of faith and confidence in the endurance of the group, Isabella also placed her furniture, belongings, and savings at the disposal of the community.

Gender divided members with status and a public voice in The Kingdom from members who were kept silent. Although Isabella was herself a mystic, a receiver of divine revelations, and an acknowledged preacher, she was not accorded the same respect or status as Matthias. The women in the community believed Matthias to be the Messiah, but they cannot have been happy with the religious role he expected them to play. Matthias feared the religious power of women and believed them to be the cause of much evil: "They who teach women are of the wicked. . . . [Depart] all females who lecture their husbands, their sentence is the same. Everything that has the smell of woman will be destroyed. Woman is the capsheaf of the abomination of desolation–full of deviltry . . . all women, not obedient, had better become so as soon as possible, and let the wicked spirit depart. (Titus [1878] 1978, 93–94).

All the women in The Kingdom had been part of the very influential and well-organized religious reform circles in New York City. Sarah Pierson and Ann Folger were both members of the Retrenchment Society, the female-headed precursor of The Kingdom (Vale 1835, 24–25). Even after the usurpation of leadership of the Bowery Hill group by Pierson, the women members still "exhorted and gave their experiences" (Vale 1835, 43). Isabella had been quite active in Methodist circles, where she had led class meetings and converted many by her zeal and verbal exhortations at the camp meetings she attended. After the appearance of Matthias the women of the community stopped their public speaking. Certainly, a leader like Isabella Van Wagenen must have found it difficult to remain in a community where the charismatic leader believed the only role for women was an inferior one.

Believing that she had found a new way of life in The Kingdom, Isabella was disappointed to learn that racial and gender stereotypes had a place in the community. Not only were all women relegated to a position of inferiority, Isabella learned that she and the other black member, Katy, were assigned to do the heavier and dirtier domestic work (Pauli 1962, 77).

Van Wagenen's acceptance of the conditions in The Kingdom had several bases: faith in Matthias as God's representative on earth, willingness to experiment in social reform, and personal economic need. Like many others in this period, Van Wagenen believed that communal groups would prove successful economic and social alternatives to the outside world. She entered The Kingdom with the hope that her labors would guarantee a secure and pleasant home for the rest of her life and, at the same time, that she would be an active laborer in the reformation of society, a living example for the rest of society.

Whatever Matthias's expectations of the women in The Kingdom community, both the men and women very quickly etched out their own roles and positions. Matthias, and at the start of the community, Pierson, were recognized as the religious leaders. They did little beyond philosophize about the coming kingdom of heaven on earth. As Elijah Pierson and other supporters of the community were quite wealthy and willing to support Matthias, the new Messiah, other financial considerations were unnecessary. The women were responsible for all the domestic work for the entire community, with Isabella and Katy performing the heavier work. When the household was moved to Zion Hill in Ossining, the men worked outdoors on the farm; the women remained domestic workers but performed some outdoor tasks as well.

Some of the women, however, did play an active role in community affairs. Isabella often spoke of her religious opinions but for many months was so loyal to Matthias that her views differed little from his. Ann Folger, another community member, began to discuss religious topics with Matthias, much to the astonishment of Isabella, who knew his views on teaching women. At first Ann Folger echoed Matthias's opinions, but soon the conversation between the two turned toward the topic of spiritual mates, those matches made in heaven despite earthly marital connections. Benjamin Folger was convinced to renounce his claims on his wife, and Pierson performed a ceremony that joined Ann Folger and Matthias as husband and wife on earth, as they now believed they had already been joined in heaven.

Charges of insanity, religious fanaticism, and undue influence on unstable (and wealthy) members of the community brought The Kingdom time and again before the New York public. The suspicious circumstances surrounding the death of the community founder, Elijah Pierson, finally brought The Kingdom to an end. Matthias was charged with insanity and with the murder of Pierson. Isabella Van Wagenen was charged with conspiring with Matthias in the Pierson death. Both were found innocent of any wrongdoing, but the facts of sexual impropriety and other aspects of Matthias's misconduct entertained New Yorkers for days and struck the final blow to The Kingdom.

The ending of the community sent Isabella back to private domestic service. With the loss of most of her savings and household goods in the breakup of The Kingdom, she once again needed to support herself. Although she gained some financial reparation from a court battle with the Folgers, she found herself in need of more money. She soon came to the conclusion that the social and economic conditions of New York City were at fault. She had worked as hard as she could but could neither save any money nor gain any security.

Isabella believed she had been insensible to the conditions of the city that kept the poor impoverished. Although her attempt to remake society began with participation in religious reform efforts and continued with her role in The Kingdom, this was the first indication that Van Wagenen recognized the greater social forces at work in the large urban areas during the 1840s. She began to make plans to leave New York, the source of her troubled spirit, and to attempt to create a better kind of life for herself and others in the smaller towns and rural areas of the northeast. Like many other utopian experimenters of the period, Isabella came to believe that reformation of society could only take place in a pastoral setting.

Isabella Van Wagenen's next reform effort began with a personal transformation. In 1843, several years after the breakup of The Kingdom, Isabella received communications from God, who directed her to leave the city and travel east, preaching as she went: "The Spirit calls me there and I must go" (Titus [1878] 1978, 98). For Van Wagenen her own spiritual purification seemed the way to begin helping other people and creating a better and less selfish world. In the same message God also gave Isabella Van Wagenen a new name: *Sojourner* to indicate her traveling and *Truth* to tell of her message.

Sojourner Truth had attended camp meetings and had exhorted the crowds many times before. Now, however, preaching was her primary work and the way Truth hoped to spend the rest of her working life. Throughout her travels Truth searched for a place in which she could settle. Although she had experienced great difficulties and disappointment in The Kingdom community, Truth knew that a community that was experimenting with new social relationships might give greater scope to an African-American woman. She was looking for a congenial community in which a woman of her abilities would be accepted. Friends in Springfield, Massachusetts, suggested various experimental communities that might suit Truth and her work. She intended to visit the Shaker village in Enfield, Massachusetts, but was convinced to try the Transcendentalist Northampton Association instead.

The Northampton Association of Education and Industry, located in Florence, Massachusetts, was an intentional community based on some of the social philosophies of Robert Owen and Charles Fourier. The founders were New England men and women interested in translating their interest in Transcendentalism into social reality. The principles of Northampton were far different from what Truth had experienced during her participation in The Kingdom. The constitution of the Massachusetts community comprised seven basic by-laws that the originators of Northampton believed could make life more equitable for all members (Sheffield 1894, 69–72).

At the Northampton Association Truth would theoretically have the same rights and opportunities as any white, male member of the community and would live in an atmosphere of mutual respect and morality. The founders of the community believed they had designed a community that would "establish equality of rights and interests, to secure . . . freedom from care, anxiety, dependence, and oppression – to recognize the perfect brotherhood of the human race" (Gove Nichols 1844, 275). Unlike The Kingdom, there would be no self-appointed leader or restrictions beyond the ones necessary to the by-laws and the maintenance of the community.

Economically, Northampton seemed assured of a sound financial future. The original members of the community purchased an abandoned silk mill and refurbished the factory. All the members of the community were required to buy stock or shares in the Association. In return for their investment, stockholders would receive all food, clothing, shelter, education, a small wage, and a financial return on their investment from the silk mill. The original sum thought necessary for the maintenance of the community was never raised, however, and this lack added to the many problems that plagued the Northampton Association. Community members believed dissention and economic troubles caused the collapse of Northampton: "Many troubles were constantly growing out of the pecuniary difficulties in which the Community was involved. Many sacrifices were demanded, and much hard labor was required. . . . Some spoke of the want of that harmony and brotherly feeling which were indispensible to the success of such an enterprise. . . . So the Association ceased to exist" (Noyes [1870] 1966, 158–60).

Sojourner Truth was one of the people who left Northampton before its final collapse. She had sought out the community in hopes of finding a congenial home where she could work on reform efforts and where her basic needs would be supplied. She found the community overcrowded and so unorganized that it was difficult to live at all comfortably. Nevertheless, Truth was able to overcome her initial distress over the living conditions of Northampton and to gain a real affection for the community: "She gradually became pleased with, and attached to, the place and the people. . . . It must have been no small thing to have found a home in a 'Community composed of some of the choicest spirits of the age,' where all was characterized by an equality of feeling, a liberty of thought and speech, and a largeness of soul" (Titus [1878] 1978, 120). Truth, often named a community favorite for her hard work, cheerful spirit, wisdom, and religious faith, came to be regarded as one of the "choicest spirits of the age."

The issue of woman's rights was considered important at the Northampton Association. One female community member remembered equality of the sexes "was accepted as one of our fundamental principles" (Sheffield 1894, 117). However, the same woman also commented that the issue was never discussed at the Association. Some of the women and men who would go on to become leaders in the woman's rights movement were directly or indirectly involved with the Northampton Association. The abolitionists and feminists Sojourner Truth met and heard speak at the community played a part in her decision to work in the radical reform movement.

The Northampton community made an effort to bring new social relationships to the family. Men and women had equal economic shares in the corporation, and all adults worked for a wage. Some women worked in the domestic department, others taught community children in the classroom, and a large number of women worked in the silk factory. Some of the work burdens that the housewife experienced in an isolated nuclear family were alleviated in the community. Cleaning, laundry, and cooking were done by workers from the domestic department. However, all the workers in this department were women. Each family was also responsible for its own sewing. This meant that the women in each family had the task of making and mending clothing as well as working a twelve-hour day in the factory or domestic department.

Although the founders of the community believed in a stock company in which the adult members would all have shares, they failed to take into account the economic inequalities this could generate within the Association. Nuclear families that joined the Association together certainly had larger economic benefits from the community. However, half the members were single men and women or women with children (Sheffield 1894, 103–5). These members were at a disadvantage as they could rely on only their own share in the community wealth, rather than on a part of a family's portion.

Few women became community leaders, but several were especially respected for their abilities. Truth was mentioned by several community members, who remembered her fine speeches and clever repartee. Although Truth's work was in the domestic department of the community, where she was chief laundress of the association, her intellectual gifts were also well respected (Sheffield 1894, 96, 121).

The collapse of the Northampton Association once again left Sojourner Truth without funds and a home, so in 1856 she moved her headquarters to Battle Creek, Michigan. Truth's connection with the spiritualist Quaker seminary and community near Battle Creek was possibly her third experiment with an alternative living situation. Harmonia no longer exists, but records show that the village was built around a community and private seminary begun by a group of Quakers turned spiritualists (Lowe 1956, 132). The seminary was managed and taught by Reynolds Cornell and his son Hiram. Although not much is known about the Cornells, it is certain they had connections with the antislavery movement. An antislavery worker, J. W. Walker, visited the school in 1852; and the following year Parker Pillsbury also toured the institution. The school was successful for several years but definitely had been abandoned by 1873 (Lowe 1976, 55–56). For ten years, from 1857 to 1867, Sojourner Truth owned the house on the lot next to the seminary. It is possible that Truth never joined the spiritualist community, but we do know that she rested there between her many trips away from the Battle Creek area (Pauli 1962, 187). Truth's grandson, Sammy Banks, attended the seminary in 1859.

We may speculate, however, that Sojourner Truth would have found great value in the spiritualist philosophy of communication with the supernatural, and the promise of a better life in the next world. Truth may have found connections between her own mysticism and communication with the divine, and the practices of spiritualists. Spiritualistic mediums underwent trance states in which they received messages from a source beyond the reality in which most people lived. These messages were usually sought as answers, inspiration, and aid for the questions and problems that a rapidly changing world presented (Moore 1985, 6–7).

The bond between spiritualists and antebellum reformers was a close one. Many abolitionists and feminists were involved to one degree or another with spiritualism. Truth herself had encountered an early aspect of spiritualist theory at The Kingdom. Matthias's doctrine of spiritual mates, the belief that each person had a perfect mate either on earth or in heaven, was a tenet in which many later spiritualists also believed. Truth probably knew of the connection between spiritualism and the reformers who were her friends and colleagues (Moore 1985, 71–76, 83–84). Many reformers were attracted to spiritualism because it combined "the push for the immediate purification of the nation's morals" and the "betterment of social conditions of humanity" (Moore 1985, 72–73).

Whether Truth attempted to join the Harmonia community or only found friends there during her visits home is not known. By 1860 Truth was still living in Harmonia with her daughter Elizabeth and two grandsons (Lowe 1976, 152).

Although after moving from Harmonia Truth did not search for a communal experiment in which she could live, she did not retreat from her beliefs in social reform. Just the opposite—her work in abolition, woman's rights, and later the rights of freed slaves seemed to take up all of her energies and time. Perhaps Truth had come to believe that the work she did in convincing others of her program for social reform as she traveled across the country had become more important than her search for personal perfection.

While she lived at Northampton, Truth had met people famous for their work in the abolitionist movement who would become the moving spirits in the woman's rights movement. Already experienced as a speaker at religious gatherings and at Northampton community meetings, Truth found lecturing another field for her talents. Working for the abolition of slavery and for the rights of women proved to be powerful incentives. Friends who recognized Truth's talent and understood the propaganda value of an eloquent former slave speaking for the cause of abolition helped convince Truth to embark on her lecturing career.

Truth spoke at reform conventions, camp meetings, and churches. Between the years 1850 and 1875 she traveled thousands of miles by herself, attending meetings and lecturing in twenty-one states and the District of Columbia. Truth traveled not only in the northeast, but as far west as Minnesota, and through the border states and upper South.

The two causes nearest Truth's heart, and the two she believed the most important for the reformation of society, were abolition and woman's rights. The years between leaving the Northampton Association and the Civil War Truth spent lecturing on these two issues. As in her speeches and lectures on rights for women, she was eloquent on the need for the abolition of slavery and on the rights owed to her race. Without freedom for all people the golden future that Truth believed possible could not be created.

During the last thirty-three years of her life, Sojourner Truth became a nationally known figure and heroine to many people. In 1863 Harriet Beecher Stowe wrote an article about Truth for the *Atlantic Monthly,* extolling her piety, religiosity, and mysticism. During the Civil War, Truth was invited to the White House to meet Abraham Lincoln (Colman 1891, 50). Her work with the freedmen and -women in Washington, D.C., and her political work attempting to gain land for former slaves during Reconstruction did much to expand her fame among people of her own race. Even before the war years, workers in the abolitionist cause and the woman's rights movement had claimed Truth as their own. Truth's appearances at various reform conventions were extolled in the radical press and in correspondence between reformers.

During the last year of the Civil War, Truth traveled to Washington, D.C., to work with the various agencies that were aiding the newly freed slaves pouring into the nation's capital. While there, Truth raised money for the Colored Soldiers' Aid Society and for black soldiers from Battle Creek and worked at the Freedmen's Hospital and at the Orphan's Home in Georgetown (Titus [1878] 1978, 173, 177, 183).

The largest part of her work was with the creation of the Freedmen's Village in Arlington, Virginia, just across the Potomac from Washington. The village was an encampment for those who had escaped from southern states after the Emancipation Proclamation in 1863. Located on a tract of land that George W. P. Custis had deeded to his slave daughter, Maria Syphax, the village was a model camp that became self-supporting soon after the

1. Sojourner Truth (ca. 1797–1883), "I Sell the Shadow to Support the Substance." Truth sold copies of this photograph at antislavery and woman's rights conventions to support herself. *Courtesy of Friends Historical Library of Swarthmore College.*

war (Federal Writers' Project 1937, 75, 88). It included a hospital, an industrial school, shops, a church, and a home for the aged. The men worked on the abandoned Confederate farms in the area, or as blacksmiths, wheelwrights, carpenters, tailors, or shoemakers (Leech 1941, 251–52). The women also worked on the land.

Sojourner Truth was appointed a counselor to the village by the National Freedmen's Relief Association. She was to promote "their intellectual, moral, and religious instruction" (Titus [1878] 1978, 182). Truth reported that most of her work in the village consisted of teaching the women household duties, as they all wanted to learn "the way we live in the North" (Titus [1878] 1978, 179). She also served as a preacher to large audiences at Sunday meetings.

Although not planned as a communal society where all goods were shared, Freedmen's Village was a community where the inhabitants worked and learned together. Truth was an important asset for the community. The women of the village thought a great deal of her, and she helped them make the transition to freedom: "Her electrifying words seemed to inspire them with new life. The manhood and womanhood of these crushed people now asserted itself" (Titus [1878] 1978, 183). Truth was a woman of heroic proportions to the inhabitants of Freedmen's Village. A former slave herself, she proved that an African-American woman could begin her life in bondage and yet become well respected by both blacks and whites.

Her experiences with the newly freed people in Washington, D.C., convinced Truth of the need for black people to become self-reliant and self-supporting. After the Civil War she began to find employment in the North for various freedmen. She soon realized, however, that her efforts could not reach enough people. Like many other reformers Truth set her sights on the public lands in the West for the former slaves. She believed that the federal government should set aside specific land for the freed people and financially support their settlement. Under this plan former slaves could become self-sufficient as soon as possible, using farming skills they had learned on the plantations and farms of the South.

The Freedmen's Bureau, established in 1863 to aid newly freed slaves all over the South, had attempted to have certain public lands there set aside for homesteading. However, a combination of poor planning, mismanagement, corruption, inconsistent support from the federal government, and opposition from southern whites combined to prevent the establishment of a large, permanent, black farm-owning class (Oubre 1978, xiv–xv). Soon after the dismantling of the Freedmen's Bureau in 1869, Sojourner Truth began traveling around the country gathering signatures for a petition to

Congress that would grant land and financial support for a "Negro State" in the West.

Throughout the 1870s, Truth traveled in the Northeast and Midwest lecturing on the plight of the freed people. She tried to get individuals to sign her petitions, which she hoped would convince Congress to vote for the land and money. She could not believe that a nation that had fought a war to free the slaves would turn its backs on the freed people.

In 1879 Truth traveled to Kansas where a large number of black immigrants had arrived from the South. She hoped that these settlers would be able to form at least a shadow of the great community she had envisioned for the people of her race. Truth had great faith in the ability of former slaves to create the future: "There will be, child, a great glory come out of that. I don't expect I will live to see it. But before this generation has passed away, there will be a grand change. This colored people is going to be a people" (Bernard 1967, 248). Her vision of a western "Negro State" where self-sufficient black families could become landowners and respected citizens never materialized.

Truth worked for many years to create a world in which all women and black people would be able to live in freedom and equality. She attempted to live her vision of a new world. Like many other reformers of the antebellum period, she believed she had to reorganize her own life as an example for the rest of the world. She never found a community that could satisfy her varied needs, a lack that drove her back out into the world to work even harder to create a world that would contain places for all people.

Sojourner Truth often claimed that she would not be ready to go to heaven until she had been able to vote at least once. She never got her wish. The Fifteenth Amendment in 1870, while granting the franchise to black men, specifically denied her and all other women the right to vote because of their gender. Many other women carried on the fight for the rights of their sex, but with the death of Sojourner Truth in 1883, the movement lost a fighter with great boldness of vision.

Works Cited

Bernard, Jacqueline. 1967. *Journey toward Freedom—The Story of Sojourner Truth*. New York: Norton.
Colman, Lucy N. 1891. *Reminiscences*. Buffalo, N.Y.: H. L. Green.
Fauset, Arthur. 1971. *God's Faithful Pilgrim*. New York: Russell and Russell.
Federal Writers' Project Works Progress Administration. 1937. *Washington: City and Capital*. Washington, D.C.: U.S. Government Printing Office.
Gove Nichols, Mary. 1844. Northampton Association. *Phalanx* 7 (Sept.): 275.

Harley, Sharon. 1978. Northern Female Black Workers: Jacksonian Era. In *The Afro-American Woman: Struggles and Images,* edited by Sharon Harley and Rosalyn Terborg-Penn, 5–16. Port Washington, N.Y.: Kennikat.

Kessler-Harris, Alice. 1982. *Out to Work: A History of Wage Earning Women in the United States.* New York: Oxford Univ. Press.

Leech, Margaret. 1941. *Reveille in Washington, 1860–1865.* New York: Harper Bros.

Lowe, Berenice. 1956. Michigan Days of Sojourner Truth. *New York Folklore Quarterly* 12 (Summer): 127–35.

———. 1976. *Tales of Battle Creek.* Battle Creek, Mich.: Albert and Louise B. Miller Foundation.

Mohl, Raymond. 1971. *Poverty in New York, 1783–1825.* New York: Oxford Univ. Press.

Moore, Lawrence. 1985. *In Search of White Crows: Spiritualism, Parapsychology, and American Culture.* New York: Oxford Univ. Press.

Noyes, John Humphrey. [1870] 1966. *History of American Socialisms.* Reprint. New York: Dover.

Oubre, Claude F. 1978. *Forty Acres and a Mule.* Baton Rouge: Louisiana State Univ. Press.

Pauli, Hertha, 1962. *Her Name Was Sojourner Truth.* New York: Appleton-Century-Crofts.

Sheffield, Charles A. 1894. *A History of Florence, Massachusetts.* Florence, Mass.: Author.

Smith-Rosenberg, Carroll. 1985. Beauty, the Beast, and the Militant Woman. In *Disorderly Conduct: Visions of Gender in Victorian America,* edited by Carroll Smith-Rosenberg. New York: Knopf.

Still, Bayrd. 1956. *Mirror for Gotham.* New York: New York Univ. Press.

Stone, William Leete. 1835. *Matthias and His Impostures.* New York: Harper Bros.

Stowe, Harriet Beecher. 1863. Sojourner Truth, Libyan Sibyl. *Atlantic Monthly,* Apr., 476–81.

Titus, Frances. [1878] 1978. *The Narrative of Sojourner Truth, a Bondswoman of Olden Time . . . and Her Book of Life.* Reprint. New York: Arno.

Vale, Gilbert. 1835. *Fanaticism; Its Sources and Influences, Illustrated by the Simple Narrative of Isabella.* New York: Author.

2

Women's Experiences in the American Owenite Communities

CAROL A. KOLMERTEN

"I acknowledge the theory is beautiful but I sometime fear for the practice."
—Hannah Fisher Price,
a New Harmony resident

WHEN WE READ THE LETTERS from the women who lived in the American Owenite communities, we hear a story of betrayal. The promises of Owenite theory—for economic, social, and sexual egalitarianism—are turned inside out in the women's letters. Their anguish is palpable.

For many who have studied the Owenite communities, the complaining women are simply troublemakers who did not understand how an intentional community had to function. Certainly most of the leaders of the communities besieged by "woman problems," as they called them, found the women's complaints simply exasperating. Even I, who have spent over fifteen years studying the Owenite communities, for many years commiserated with the husbands and male leaders. I had absorbed, without thinking, the patriarchal view of complaining women. Oblivious to their pain, ignoring the voices I heard, unable to understand their silences, I placed their misery within the only framework I knew: if they did not like the communities, something was wrong with the women. It took me years to learn to trust my own ears, to hear that these women's misery was real and justifiable, and to realize that the "something wrong" was with the communities, not with the women.

In the Owenite communities, being a woman meant serving everyone, not just one's individual family. For women who came to the communities believing in the Owenite tenets, such service might be given with reasonable goodwill. Or, for young women who came to the communities to attend school or to remove themselves from a failed love interest, life could be "quite gay." At New Harmony, the largest and best known of the Owenite communities and the one populated by the most single people, a plethora of advantages mitigated required work assignments of milking cows early in the morning. The community offered a life of weekly balls and concerts and all sorts of interesting, idealistic young men with whom to enjoy them. As one woman wrote from the community, "there are many youth of both sexes that are very happy in the variety of each other" (Hannah Fisher Price to Joseph Warner, Mar. 10, 1826).

Though New Harmony did include a significant number of single young women who enjoyed a version of a collegiate experience in the communities, most of the Owenite experiments attracted married men and their wives and children.[1] Certainly, a number of married people joined the communities because they believed in Owen's socialistic tenets and his plans for a New Moral World based on egalitarianism, but recent evidence shows that probably more people joined an Owenite community because it offered a new start in life. Robert Owen preached an appealing secular message that promised an eight-hour working day and a community of mutual help. The economic benefits associated with Owenism attracted numbers of people who had no interest in Owen's notion of utopian reform or in his attacks on the priesthood. It is the women who joined an Owenite community as the wives of men who wanted to start life over again who felt the most betrayed in their experiences in the communities. The work they had to perform for the community supported ideas they did not necessarily believe. What happened, as I have explained elsewhere, was that culturally accepted ways of thinking about Woman, what I call an ideology of gender, hardened in the communities into cultural practices that few of the married women could escape (Kolmerten 1990, 170–76). As in the mainstream culture, married women were expected to live out their roles as helpmates, to practice self-sacrifice. Whether they liked it or not, the married women in the communities were considered to be the servers of everyone, to belong to the community. Believing in the community's tenets was beside the point for the married women, who were expected to *be* the community's wives.

To married women who followed their husbands to the communities, the Owenite experiments offered too much hard work, while the existence of the communities threatened their power. Because part of the communities' egalitarian goal was to turn the domestic province from a private into a public one, these women felt deprived of the only sphere of influence— the home–open to them in the United States of the 1820s.

Sarah Pears, arriving in New Harmony with her optimistic husband and

their seven children in the spring of 1825, is a perfect example of a threatened married woman. She left, along with her husband, an epistolary record
of her year in New Harmony, ironically now anthologized as *New Harmony:
An Adventure in Happiness*–perhaps the most misnamed collection of letters in U.S. history. While she began her "adventure in happiness" with
faint hope ("we feel perfect confidence in Mr. Owen's sincere desire to promote the happiness of all," she wrote her aunt in her first letter home), Sarah
quickly changed her mind when she understood her and her daughter's role
in the community. Her oldest daughter she described as "poorly" because
of an illness she had caught washing clothes for the community. Sarah lamented that "all the hard work falls upon her and it is more than she can
bear. We had hoped she would have been rather relieved from her heavy
labor than otherwise by coming here, but at present it is far from the case"
(Pears 1933, 18). Interestingly, the complaint came not from eighteen-year-
old Maria, the person doing the heavy labor, who nonetheless found community life to be "quite gay" (Pears 1933, 33); rather it came from her
mother, a person without a place in community life.

    Sarah Pears quickly dismissed any hope that communal life would im-
prove her life, and her letters record her growing disillusionment and depression. As Carroll Smith-Rosenberg found in her study of the ailments
of nineteenth-century American women, illness often represented the only
legitimate rebellion women could engage in to escape from their prescribed,
heaven-ordained "duties."[2] Set in a foreign environment with few ameni-
ties and an abysmal climate, given more work to do than in her previous
life in Pittsburgh, Sarah Pears rebelled in the only way available to her.
She became ill, too ill to "take her turn" at the cooking or washing, and
she complained not to the hierarchy of the community, with positive suggestions for improving communal life, but to her aunt, safely removed in
Pittsburgh.

    At first Sarah Pears told her aunt that, "sick and debilitated in body,
distressed and disappointed in mind, oppressed by extreme heat night and
day such as I never before experienced, I felt utterly incapable of writing."
She complained that she could hardly get enough sleep. Then she wrote
of feeling "excessively stupid and dull," and finally, "hopeless" (Pears 1933,
33, 41, 52). As she herself felt worse, she viewed the events of the community from an increasingly pessimistic perspective. New Harmony had taken
away all the comforts of her life and replaced them with a rhetoric of equality but with a practice of inequality. Because New Harmony had none of
the technological advances that Robert Owen had advocated for doing what
he termed "the drudgery," women like Sarah and her daughter were to perform this work.

In accordance with Robert Owen's theory that women would not be economically dependent upon men if they had livelihoods themselves, women in the communities were offered "regular employment." In theory, Owen's ideas sounded liberating for women, but in the patriarchal Owenite communities, what happened in practice was that women who did work in community industries then had to spend their "free" time doing traditional female work. For example, working women in New Harmony had to spend Sunday, the day the men and young people relaxed, doing the washing, ironing, and other nominally female tasks for their families. As Sarah Pears reveals in one of her letters home:

> Indeed the day [Sunday] here is only used as a day of recreation, visiting and amusement, military operations, and with some few of work. Those ladies who are in regular employment, having no time allowed them, have some excuse for washing, ironing, and doing their own sewing on the Sabbath. Every Sunday evening there is a meeting at which Mr. Owen reads over the particulars of the expenditures of the Society, and the amount of work performed by each occupation, and also the names of the workmen and women, with characters attached to each. (Pears 1933, 83)

Whereas the men needed to perform only one service for the community, the women who worked "equally" alongside the men in communal enterprises discovered that their work was not over at the end of the working day or week. They were still responsible for their family's food, clothes, and dwelling place.

The letters of other Owenite women reveal the cultural practices of community life that illustrate how gender differentiated the expectations for women and for men. Dedicated, single Marie Fretageot, a teacher in the New Harmony schools, was in many ways the complete opposite of Sarah Pears. In the early 1820s, Fretageot had established one of the first Pestalozzian schools in the United States in Philadelphia. Inspired by Owen's speeches in Philadelphia, Fretageot decided to join his experiment because she agreed with many of his theories, particularly the notion of joining forces to create the most advanced schooling in the country. Her description of her subsequent hectic life at New Harmony helps to illustrate that it was women to whom the bulk of the work fell. In one of her many letters to her educational colleague William Maclure, Fretageot listed her daily activities: "My school is going on pretty well. . . . I get up regularly at four o'clock." Her duties combined her professional pursuits as well as her "female duties," so that she was the busiest teacher in the community. From 4:00 until 6:30 A.M. she taught "twelve young men" who boarded with her; from 9:00 to 11:00 A.M. she instructed all of the children under twelve. After dinner she taught the smaller children again from 2:00 to 4:00 P.M. and once more received her twelve young men plus all the children above twelve from 6:00 to 8:00 P.M. The other hours, she wrote, "I am occupied cooking for the whole family. I may say that I have but very little the occasion of wearing out the chairs of the house, having not a single female to help me" (Fretageot to William Maclure, Mar. 2, 1827).

While her male colleagues were responsible for only a select group of older students, Fretageot taught all of the younger children as well as her "twelve young men," for whom she also had to cook and clean. The male teachers in the school—Robert Dale Owen, William Maclure, Paul Brown—write of their casual days at New Harmony and of their many trips away from the community, but Fretageot left no comparable carefree epistles. She was continually in New Harmony working in some capacity "like a slave" (Maclure to Fretageot Jan. 3, 1827) and remaining to direct the schools until 1831, long after Owen's communal enterprise had been abandoned.

Equally busy was another married woman who came to New Harmony because of her and her husband's dedication to Owen's theories. Hannah Fisher Price, also from Philadelphia, had married a Philadelphia physician, William Price, who was interested in Owen's theory about the importance of "united efforts." Both Hannah and William wanted what Owen did: to change the habits of people to effect a new, moral world. Thoroughly dedicated to Owenite reform, Hannah arrived at New Harmony in the early spring of 1826 with her husband and three small daughters. Her first sentence in her first letter home aptly summarizes her exhaustion: "It is so long since I had a pen in my hand I hardly know how to use it" (Hannah Fisher Price to Joseph Warner, March 10, 1826). Though dedicated in ways Sarah Pears never was to Owen's notion of reform, Hannah soon responded to the town's overcrowding and lack of order: "We found things here in a very confused state and much time has been spent in legislating. . . . At present we are not situated at all comfortable. . . . The town is so crowded, and the buildings not made the most commodious, that we suffer many inconveniences that might be avoided were proper buildings made ready for our reception. We sometimes get quite out of heart" (Mar. 10, 1826).

Women worked hard in the other Owenite communities as well because of gender-based assumptions. In the Franklin Community, in upstate New York, Eliza M'Knight worked harder than her husband, who was always too ill to take part in the field work. As her husband relates: "Twelve members boarded at our house and my wife, though a delicate woman, cooked for them, until she became so worn out with fatigue that I was obliged to hire a girl to assist her. She was told this problem would be over as soon as the public dining room could be finished" (M'Knight 1826, 9). However, when the room was completed the president of the community then instructed Eliza to "go to the public kitchen" and cook for everyone, despite his promises to her for a "resting spell."

But it was not just hard work that bothered the community women; they were also distressed about the kind of work they were required to do and the fact that they had no free time. As Sarah Pears wrote about her duties at New Harmony: "My strength, which never was great and is much diminished since I came here, is unequal to taking my turn in the kitchen, which I find it is required that all should do by turns for six weeks together. No one is to be favored above the rest, as all are to be in a state of perfect equality" (Pears 1933, 60). Sarah's ironic restatement of Owen's theory that "all are to be in a state of perfect equality" gained its force from her own knowledge that the "all" required to take turns in the kitchen were only the women of the community, not the "all" who would be in the state of perfect equality.

This rather specious notion of equality necessarily threatened the women of the communities, particularly the married women of the upper and middle classes who came to community life, as did Sarah Pears, because their husbands wished to make a fresh start under the economic benefits Robert Owen promised. These women did not want to do menial work for the community at large. Believing that their sacred sphere was being violated, they vociferously rebelled. For these women their deprivation was relative; in their former lives they had been much better off with only domestic duties. Helen Fisher, a widow who was the sister-in-law of Hannah Price, explained in a letter to her brother-in-law that the only reason she became a teacher in the New Harmony schools was "the fear of being put to the wash-tub or the kitchen, of which I understand nothing" (Helen Fisher to Redwood Fisher, Aug. 11, 1826). In Owenite communities women like Helen Fisher had more work to do—and usually of a kind their social position had dictated that servants perform—and less power.

Thus, for many of the women in the communities, community life was inimical to good living and common sense. Women complained of the overregulation of their days and their time, and of their lack of power to do as they wished. Helen Fisher wrote to her brother-in-law shortly before leaving New Harmony that "every thing will appear delightful after Harmony" (Aug. 11, 1826). Lydia and Alma Eveleth wrote to Sarah Pears just as New Harmony was breaking up in 1827 to tell her, with glee, that "now we can do as we please" (Pears 1933, 88).

Some of the women of the Franklin Community in New York once inquired whether they could go to church on Sunday morning but were told that "we have church in the dining room, every Sunday morning, at the usual hour." The required Sunday morning services consisted of a public recounting of work that had been accomplished during the week. "The members' names are first called over, beginning with the ladies. 'Well, Mrs. A. How many pairs of stockings have you knit during the week? Mrs. B. What sewing have you done? Mrs. C. What members have you washed for?— how many dozen clothes in all? Mrs. D. how much wool have you spun?' This is the way *ladies* are obliged to spend the Sabbath morning," wrote one disgruntled member of the community (M'Knight 1826, 14).

Married women, especially those with children, had much to feel powerless about in the communities. The conditions in "the West" were difficult, at best, with little fresh food and dwindling commodities, including medical supplies and milk. As a mother of a fourteen-month-old when she came to New Harmony, Sarah Pears watched helplessly as the infants of two of her friends died—"young Mrs. Grant" lost her five-month-old baby, Sarah wrote to her aunt (Pears 1933, 34), and at the same time Mrs. Pearson's seven-month-old died while living at the Pears's house. Her striking imagery reflects her helplessness and subsequent alienation. She wrote that she heard "very little more of the old world than if I were an inhabitant of a different planet." Another time she wrote of being "out of humanity's reach" (Pears 1933, 53, 41). Even women devoted to Owen's tenets reflected the despair that accompanied being so far from loved ones, especially during times of crisis. When Hannah Fisher Price heard of her brother-in-law's death she wrote in misery that she was "a thousand miles from you all," her unhappiness magnified because of "the time that must intervene before I shall again see any of you" (Hannah Fisher Price to Joseph Warner, May 3, 1826).

For women like Sarah Pears, the hardships caused by frontier living coupled with excessive hard work led to depression and sickness. But the final blow that caused them to convince their husbands to leave the communities was losing power in their sphere of influence to raise their children. Sarah Pears was unhappy in New Harmony because of the magnitude and type of work she was expected to perform, but when Robert Owen proclaimed that children needed to be removed from their parents and housed together, Sarah rebelled. She wrote her aunt with horror: "All our elder children . . . are to be taken away from us, [and] are to be placed in large boarding houses. . . . Instead of our own dear children each housekeeper is to receive two more families, one of which will have a child under two years old. The rest will be at boarding school." Sarah realized that when her children left her, her role, her purpose would be gone and she would no longer be able "to tell them anything. They will be completely taken from under my control." The thought of having someone else, someone "wrong," taking her children from her and raising them caused her great distress. As she said to her aunt, "It is impossible to express how completely miserable I am. . . . I know were I to consider this world only, I would rather, far rather, that Mr. Owen would shoot me through the head." Reacting intensely against the imminent breakup of her family, Sarah Pears implored her aunt: "Can you . . . conceive of anything so absurd as breaking up and dividing families in order to make them more comfortable? Comfort! Name not the word in Harmony, or at least in the Community of Harmony. And Equality!—It would be a total anomaly!" (Pears 1933, 72–74).

In the Franklin Community, Eliza M'Knight felt the same passion as Sara Pears's that someone "wrong" would be raising her children in a community where her only value was that of a cook and domestic worker. When Eliza was teaching her son his Bible lessons one Sunday, one of the leading reformers at the community told her "how ridiculous it is to be teaching children such *a bundle of lies.*" This conversation affected the M'Knight's son, who the following day asked "what use is there in my learning the Bible, if it is all lies?" (M'Knight 1826, 14). The outraged Eliza confronted the president of the community, asking him about Bible teachings. The president, an Owenite reformer who had previously edited the *New Harmony Gazette*, replied that the Bible was full of "superstitious notions" and that children had to be separated from other children and parents who might give them "erroneous notions" because they had been deluded by the "priestcraft and foolish creeds." Eliza, desperate, told him: "I have heard enough. . . . I see you are determined to destroy the youth with your infidelity. But I can assure you that you will not have *my* children to corrupt" (M'Knight 1826, 12). True to her word, Eliza convinced her husband to leave the community immediately, even though he was hesitant to depart before he received pay for the work he had done. Eliza, adamant, told him she would rather beg for her bread than remain in Franklin.

After the M'Knights left the community, the community's president, Robert Jennings, called James M'Knight "a fool" to have been "led away by your wife" (M'Knight 1826, 13). James M'Knight's explanation, that he did not wish to remain in a situation "where my wife was unhappy," caused Jennings consternation. Although he was a dedicated Owenite reformer, devoted in his Sunday lectures to "equality" in all its ramifications, Robert Jennings could not comprehend Eliza M'Knight's response. His own response illustrated quite aptly his view of the unimportance of women as anything but helpmates and servers of men: "As to *my* wife . . . I don't mind what she says, if she is not satisfied she may take herself away" (M'Knight 1826, 13).

Even at the most radical of the Owenite communities—Nashoba in southwestern Tennessee—the "women problem" plagued reformers who did not know how to deal with an unhappy married woman not committed to Owenite ideals. Created by Scotswoman Frances Wright, Nashoba was to provide a model by which the United States could end slavery. Wright adopted Robert Owen's communalism as the best way to combine interests so that slaves could work their way to freedom. Nashoba, from its inception, had the strongest constitutional guarantees of women's rights of any of the Owenite communities. The Nashoba constitution promised that its "one great end" was the "liberty and equality of all members" (*New Harmony Gazette,* Feb. 6, 1828). On paper, Wright created at Nashoba more explicit rights for women than existed at any other nineteenth-century community. Wright dictated that "no woman can forfeit her individual rights or independent existence, and no man [can] assert over her any rights or power whatsoever" (*New Harmony Gazette,* Feb. 6, 1828).

The constitutional promises for rights, though, did not influence Eliza Andrews Flower, a woman who had come to the community because of her husband's attraction to Wright's plan to end slavery. Eliza left no letters about community life that we can find, so we have to reconstruct her life from others' words, but nonetheless, her silences can indeed speak to us.

Eliza Andrews came to the United States from England in 1816, the year she was twenty-five. An unmarried daughter of a minister and considerably beyond marriageable age, Eliza quickly married fellow journeyer George Flower and settled down to having babies in the southeastern Illinois frontier town of Albion that they established. Separated from all the people she had known, Eliza made the best of difficult situations including wild animals, a lack of food and adequate shelter, and giving birth to her first child alone when George was back in England. By 1826, Eliza had made a home for her husband, for his children by an earlier marriage, and for their own children. A new friend noticed how much her affections were "entirely centered in her husband and children" (Camilla Wright to Julia Garnett, Jan. 10, 1826, Garnett-Pertz Collection).

When her husband decided to devote himself to Frances Wright's experiment in communalism at Nashoba, Eliza moved with her husband and children to Tennessee. George, long devoted to antislavery activities, had helped Wright establish the community by obtaining land and provisions for communal life. But less than a year after the Flowers moved to Nashoba they left, returning to Albion. Though we can never know for sure why they left an experiment that George helped establish and believed in so much, we can speculate.

Eliza Flower was the interloper at Nashoba, the one person who did

Print by Nagel & Weingaertner N.Y.

2. Frances Wright (1795–1852), founder of the Nashoba Community. Inscription on the original: "Humankind is but one family, the education of its youth should be equal and universal." *Courtesy of The National Portrait Gallery, Washington, D.C.*

not fit in. As her former friend Camilla Wright wrote shortly after the Flowers' departure, "she is not in any way suited to fill any situation in this establishment nor does she possess a mind calculated to enter into the views connected with it" (Camilla Wright to Julia Garnett, Dec. 8, 1826, Garnett-Pertz Collection). Eliza was in the same precarious position that Sarah Pears occupied at New Harmony and Eliza M'Knight at Franklin: that of an outsider who did not believe in the system and who had no power within it because she had joined communal life as an appendage to her husband. But Eliza Flower had an additional worry—her husband's attachment to Frances Wright. Wright's fervor, her altruism, and her energy were the sparks that ignited George Flower's own willingness to leave his comfortable home in Albion and venture into the wilds of Tennessee, with no comforts except intellectual ones. The primitive log cabins and the lack of food were problems to everyone at Nashoba, but all the white adult residents except Eliza Flower had gone there because of either their dedication to Wright or their belief in her system to end slavery or both. Only Eliza was present as a "wife."[3]

Frances Wright and George Flower did have a strong friendship built on common interests and aims. Wright, unlike Eliza Flower, was committed not to children and family but to an idea. Certainly, that idea held the interest and respect of George Flower also. Being devoted to family, Eliza could only view Nashoba as a threat to her—it made her give up her own home and her power within it. George was not her husband solely; he belonged to the community and to Wright as well—probably more to Wright than to Eliza. Having no place in Nashoba, Eliza's only recourse was to persuade her husband to leave the community. George's letter to Camilla and Frances Wright shortly after he left Nashoba depicts a man who did not leave willingly: "Just to hear the sound of yr voices and see the lines of yr countenances. . . . All these things you know are necessary to come to the heart of the matter" (George Flower to Camilla and Frances Wright, Oct. 3, 1827).

Dealing with unhappy women left most of the Owenite reformers perplexed as to what to do. Believing, as did Camilla Wright about Eliza Flower, that these women simply did not have the minds necessary to enter into communal living, the reformers assumed that the problem resided with the women and their inability to adapt. Most of the leaders thoughtlessly attributed the so-called woman problem to a variety of reasons residing within the individual women living in the communities. Robert Owen, for example, attributed the problems with such women as Sarah Pears at New Harmony to the fact that women "talk too much." Owen explained the problem from his perspective:

Female labor in a community would certainly under proper arrangements be lighter than it can ever be in individual society. Perhaps the true cause of the evil complained of, may be, that, when females who have heretofore been strangers to each other meet together in order to cooperate in some domestic labor, they spend time in talking, which should be devoted exclusively to work. Now they cannot talk and work too. . . . I can discover no other cause than the one assigned, why female cooperative labor should be more onerous than their individual unaided exertions in individual society have been. (*New Harmony Gazette*, Aug. 30, 1826)

In a community where true equality existed, female labor might indeed be "lighter than it ever could be in individual society," but in a community where equality meant that women could have full-time employment performing work that many of them believed to be the work of servants, their work was not lightened. Rather than being relieved of work, as was the communities' goal through the use of advanced technology, most women found their labor increased, and perhaps more important, they felt powerless to control their lives or their families.

By insulting the community women, as he must have when he attributed the women's problems to their "talking too much," Robert Owen only convinced them that communal life was not possible for them. His ideas, which included his wish to dissolve the nuclear family, threatened women's traditional sphere without replacing it with anything but more work to perform. Indeed, the woman problem at the communities stemmed not from "too much talking" but rather from not enough autonomy and from the expectation that women existed to be unquestioning servers of the needs of the community. Even married women who were dedicated Owenites, such as Hannah Fisher Price, within a short time gave up the "beautiful" Owenite theory to move back to the "old world." Though Hannah remained convinced of the benefits of cooperation and hoped someday "to see a modified community after [Robert Owen's] plan," she left New Harmony "quite cured of communities" (Hannah Fisher Price to Joseph Warner, Sept. 8, 1826). Recovering and listening to women's voices offers a new perspective on communal history. Utopia for women, it seems, has everything to do with empowering women with an authority to control their own lives and very little to do with communal cooking and housecleaning.

Notes

1. Although New Harmony is the most famous Owenite community, at least eight other Owenite communities were established in 1825 and 1826, and probably five times that many Owenite societies and pseudo-Owenite communities. In upstate New York, two Owenite com-

munities were formed in 1825 and 1826, the Franklin Community at Haverstraw, and the Forestville Community at Coxsackie. In Philadelphia, a third Owenite community, the Friendly Association for Mutual Interests, began in Valley Forge in late 1825. Also beginning in late 1825 was the Yellow Springs Community in Yellow Springs, Ohio. The sixth Owenite community, the Blue Spring Community, formed at the same time in Bloomington, Indiana, while the seventh community, the Kendal Community, was forming in northeastern Ohio. Though all historians might not label Frances Wright's Nashoba a strictly Owenite community, I am doing so here because Wright did pattern her community after Owen's New Harmony and the constitutions of both communities look similar in most respects. For a more through discussion of these other Owenite communities, see Kolmerten (1990), Bestor (1970), and Harrison (1969).

2. See Smith-Rosenberg (1971 and 1974) and Wood (1973). In looking for psychosomatic reasons for women's illness at the Owenite communities, we must also consider that some women who said they were sick were really sick. Helen Fisher, a chronic complainer, wrote to her brother on Aug. 11, 1826, from New Harmony, telling him that "my health is beginning to suffer from this climate. I have a very bad cough and continual head-aches, which make me rather uneasy." Indeed, Helen died in Cincinnati less than two years later, perhaps from tuberculosis, the symptoms of which include a cough and headaches.

3. At least one of Wright's friends, Frances Trollope, hinted that Wright and George Flower had an affair before Wright purchased Nashoba. Wright's recent biographer, Celia Eckhardt, assumes that Trollope is correct and cites the affair as the reason the Flowers left Nashoba. See Trollope's Dec. 7, 1828, letter to Harriet Garnett, and Eckhardt (1984, 133).

Works Cited

Bestor, Arthur. 1970. *Backwoods Utopias: The Sectarian Origins and the Owenite Phase of Communitarian Socialism in America*. Philadelphia: Univ. of Pennsylvania Press.

Eckhardt, Celia Morris. 1984. *Fanny Wright, Rebel in America*. Cambridge, Mass.: Harvard Univ. Press.

Fisher, Helen. Letters. Fisher-Warner Papers. Friends Historical Society of Swarthmore College, Swarthmore, Pa.

Flower, George. Letters. Theresa Wolfson Papers. Cornell Univ., Ithaca, N.Y.

Fretageot, Marie. Letters. Maclure-Fretageot Correspondence. Workingmen's Institute, New Harmony, Ind.

Harrison, J. F. C. 1969. *Quest for the New Moral World: Robert Owen and the Owenites in Britain and America*. New York: Scribner.

Kolmerten, Carol. 1990. *Women in Utopia: The Ideology of Gender in the American Owenite Communities*. Bloomington: Indiana Univ. Press.

M'Knight, Eliza. 1826. Quoted in James M'Knight, *A Discourse Exposing Robert Owen's System as Practiced by the Franklin Community at Haverstraw*. New York: J. Gray.

New Harmony Gazette. 1825–1829. New Harmony, Ind. and New York.

Pears, Sarah. 1933. In *New Harmony, An Adventure in Happiness: The Papers of Thomas and Sarah Pears*, by Thomas Pears. Indianapolis: Indiana Historical Society.

Price, Hannah Fisher. Letters. Fisher-Warner Papers. Friends Historical Society of Swarthmore College, Swarthmore, Pa.

Smith-Rosenberg, Carroll. 1971. Beauty, the Beast, and the Militant Woman: A Case Study of Sex Roles and Social Stress in Jacksonian America. *American Quarterly* 23: 562–84.

———. 1974. The Hysterical Woman: Sex Roles and Role Conflict in Nineteenth-Century America. *Social Research* 39: 652–78.

Trollope, Frances. Letters. Garnett-Pertz Collection. Houghton Library, Cambridge, Mass.

Wood, Ann Douglas. 1973. The Fashionable Diseases: Women's Complaints and Their Treatment in Nineteenth-Century America. *Journal of Interdisciplinary History* 4:25–52.

Wright, Camilla. Letters. Garnett-Pertz Collection. Houghton Library, Cambridge, Mass.

3

Heaven on Earth

The Woman's Commonwealth, 1867–1983

WENDY E. CHMIELEWSKI

ON THE TEXAS FRONTIER during the late 1860s, a group of women formed an experimental community around their religious values. They later incorporated socialist ideas and ideals found in the contemporary woman's rights movement into their experiment. The one ideal to which they remained steadfast was the centrality and immediacy of a woman-centered community. The women, who became known as the Woman's Commonwealth or the Sanctified Sisters, used the religious and moral behavior often associated with their sex to challenge patriarchal power.

The Sanctified Sisters began as a group of religious and zealous women who challenged authority in the Protestant churches of Belton, Texas. They went on to use their religious beliefs and sisterly support to build an alternative living situation in which women had power and direction over their own lives. Martha McWhirter, the charismatic leader, and her co-communalists all came from an evangelical religious tradition that emphasized individual choice and gave the women a framework from which to propose an alternative path in their spiritual quest for perfection.

The women who joined the Sanctified Sisters created their community in several ways. They challenged traditional female roles and experimented with new ideas about women's sexuality, the power relationships between husbands and wives, marriage, child rearing, work roles, and communal ownership of property. The women also formed new emotional bonds with each other and replaced the nuclear families from which they had come with a successful communal family based on equitable relationships.

The Sisters began their questioning of women's roles by assuming that, as Christian women, they had a right to interpret the Scriptures and to challenge the authority of the church on religious matters. The immediate and hostile response of the townspeople of Belton to the women's community was to remind the Sisters that women had neither the right, nor the duty, nor the power to challenge the male-controlled religious establishment.

In a society that dictated that women be directed by fathers, husbands, and strict social rules, establishing a community removed from male direction and control was viewed as either the action of crazy women or a direct challenge to male superiority and power. The men of Belton recognized the challenge the Sisters presented to traditional gender roles. They viewed the women as religious fanatics, crazy, and dangerous to social tradition. Not only did the women's husbands, as the men most directly affected by their actions, react violently to the women, but townsmen outside those families also responded with legal action, violence, and ridicule.

The Sisters made direct connections between their actions and the movement for woman's rights. They also voiced their connections with the woman's movement when they chose a social organization inspired by feminist literature and activities. They directly confronted the issues of women's roles in society in exactly the ways political and social feminists were doing in other arenas.

The history of the Woman's Commonwealth begins with the community leader, Martha McWhirter. After the Civil War, the McWhirters moved into Belton from a nearby farm. George McWhirter became a prosperous merchant, with interests in several stores, the Belton Flouring Mill, and a construction company (Sokolow and Lamanna 1984, 375; Tyler 1936, 270, 297). Contemporaries remembered Martha "as a moral, upright woman, and a natural leader" (Atkinson [1929] 1970, 81). In 1866 Martha McWhirter regarded the loss of two children and a brother as a chastisement from God and became determined to lead a better life.

In 1867 McWhirter attended many of the meetings of a Methodist revival held in Belton. While walking home alone one evening after a week of the meetings, McWhirter heard "a voice within [ask her] if she did not believe what she had seen in the meeting that week to be the work of the devil." The following morning McWhirter became convinced that the voice she had heard was from God. While preparing that morning's breakfast, McWhirter experienced "a kind of Pentecostal baptism" (Garrison 1893, 30). That McWhirter went through this baptism away from the church or camp meeting setting and away from the influence of her minister is significant. Even more significant is that McWhirter's baptism occurred in her own kingdom–the kitchen, while she was performing that most ordinary of female tasks–cooking for her family.

Ecstatic religious practices dominated the Texas frontier, particularly after the Civil War. Revival meetings, similar to the ones Charles Finney had held throughout the northeast several decades earlier, formed a large part of religious practice in such areas as Belton. The women who became the Sanctified Sisters all belonged to denominations that accepted an evangelical approach to religion. McWhirter soon communicated her beliefs and new interpretation of doctrine to the other women in her weekly prayer meeting (Atkinson [1929] 1970, 81). At first their churches welcomed these zealous women, but it soon became evident that the women from Mc-Whirter's prayer group had minds of their own. They censured the churches' formalities and proclaimed their own doctrine of entire sanctification (Hinds [1908] 1975, 435).

The sanctification experiences were common phenomena among Mc-Whirter's early adherents. The women received revelations that convinced them that McWhirter's new interpretations of their condition were correct. McWhirter and the other Sisters developed their religious doctrine through individual dreams and divine communications. Mystical guidance through these dreams and divine revelations continued to be important to the women throughout the whole life of the community and guided many beliefs and actions. While there is no evidence that in later years new members had to undergo sanctification to join the community, all members were expected to accept the community principles, which included divine guidance (*Constitution* 1902).

By 1874 the women of McWhirter's weekly prayer meetings began to recognize themselves as a separate group and held their meetings in the old Union Sunday school building, the original site of Martha's power in the religious community of Belton (James 1965, 68). It is likely that the religious zeal of these women and even their criticism of church authority would have been considered "the outpourings of silly females," but for the subversive quality of their dreams and pronouncements (Sokolow and Lamanna 1984, 378). While many husbands expected their wives to be especially interested in religious activity, they did not understand either the uproar in the churches or the adherence of their wives to the doctrines of the Sanctified Sisters. They also did not expect the rebellion of their wives to extend beyond the church and into their homes, which is exactly what happened after 1875.

The background of the women who joined the Sanctified Sisters is an important component of the history of the community and the subsequent philosophy they formed. The first generation of Anglo-American women on the Texas frontier often lived on isolated farms far from the towns that could provide them with manufactured goods. As farm wives they were responsible for producing food and clothing for their families, for many goods used in the household, and for helping with the raising of produce for market. Running a farm was often a partnership between husband and wife. Women on the frontier were faced with contradictory messages concerning their roles. Traditional nineteenth-century images of women's roles included passivity, emotionality, physical weakness, self-sacrifice, dependency, and submission to male authority. However, on the frontier, a different female stereotype appeared. The pioneer woman was still expected to submit to her husband's wishes, but she was also responsible for running the family farm when her husband was away, for bearing and raising her children in isolated areas, and for working many hours on the farm itself (Malone 1983, 23).

Although the almost mythological view of the pioneer woman continued to be admired, the image of the lady who aspired to embody the traits of true womanhood soon overtook that of the stalwart pioneer woman, who lost her place in the more settled areas of the frontier. Women were told that the feminine ideal was not the strong pioneer woman, but "A True Lady," the title of a Feb. 26, 1880, article in the *Belton Journal,* whose author explained: "Wildness is a thing which girls cannot afford. . . . It is the first duty of a woman to be a lady. . . . A man's ideal is not wounded when a woman fails in worthy wisdom; but if in grace, in fact, in sentiment, in delicacy, in kindness, she would be found wanting, he receives an inward hurt."

Many of the women who joined the Sanctificationists had arrived in Bell County, Texas, as settlers, and had begun their lives there on farms. These women found their lives disrupted, first by the Civil War, which placed more responsibility for family concerns on their shoulders while male relatives were away fighting, and second by the change from farm wives who contributed directly to the family economy to urban housekeepers who did not have as active or as visible a role in family production (Scott 1970, 45). Many frontier women must have been happy to trade the isolated and hard work of the farm for the relatively easier town life. The move could also have meant a rise in status. Some women were able to reassume the roles of true womanhood not easy to maintain on a frontier farm.

It is clear that the women who formed the Sanctificationist band were not satisfied with prescribed rules for their behavior. All the women but two came from households in which the family income had its source in a male relative's commercial or professional occupation (U.S. Bureau of the Census 1880). Martha McWhirter testified to her own dissatisfaction with her diminished role as housewife. Although most of the Sisters could expect substantial family incomes, their visible participation in the production of that income had diminished.

It was soon obvious that challenges to religious orthodoxy alone would not satisfy the group of women surrounding McWhirter. Increasingly, the women's dreams revealed their dissatisfaction with the lives they led. This dissatisfaction took the form of questioning the marriage bond and the role of sexuality in marriage. One of McWhirter's close friends, Josephine Rancier, reported that God told her in dreams that she should separate from her unsanctified husband (*Belton Journal,* Feb. 26, 1880). At first the Sisters publicly linked their stand on celibacy with their religious beliefs. For these women, sexuality was connected to carnality and therefore had no place in a spiritually perfected life. Sexuality was of the earth; spiritual passion was for those who had received God's divine call. It became obvious to the Sisters that their husbands did not view the issue in the same light. Sexuality became one of the first battlegrounds on which these women and men fought. The women demanded the right to determine the disposition of their own sexuality, and the men asserted the conjugal prerogatives of nineteenth-century husbands.

The Sisters soon realized that their stand on sexuality gained them some control over their own bodies, particularly in the area of reproduction, but not over other aspects of their lives. They attempted to replace disinterest in sexuality with celibacy in a radical attempt to gain self-determination. The fact that many of the husbands of Sisters were unwilling to stay within marriages that did not include sexual relationships only proved to the women that their unsanctified husbands equated sexuality with marriage. The husbands, without their traditional conjugal rights in the bedroom, felt a loss of control over the whole marriage.

The double standard of male and female sexuality and morality was familiar to all nineteenth-century women. The Sisters, particularly conscious about the issue of sexual control of women, challenged this male-defined concept of sexuality and selected alternative forms that gave them autonomous control of their own bodies. Rather than compromise their religious belief and secular independence, many of the Sisters took the difficult step of leaving or allowing their husbands to leave the marriage. In an era in which marriage was the main source of livelihood for many women, this was a precarious choice.

Although McWhirter stated that religious differences were the root cause of spousal desertion, in reality the differences in opinion between husbands and sanctified wives about individual sexual relationships were at least as important a factor. McWhirter also failed to mention the dissatisfaction many Sisters felt in their marriages, the physical and emotional abuse they endured, and the rebellion the women fomented against the traditional role of wife.

The physical and emotional abuse became evident in several divorce cases involving the Sanctified Sisters. Ada McWhirter Haymond, Martha's daughter, testified that her husband Ben "was always more or less disagreeable in the family," that they had disagreed over family finances, and that he had attempted to forcibly evict Ada from their home, finally deserting her and their children (Bell County 1887, 17; Kitch 1989, 105). Other wives recorded the mental and physical abuse they received before they joined the Sanctificationists. (Scheble, 110). Margaret Henry stated that her husband "treated her cruelly whether he was drunk or sober"; Agatha Pratt left her husband because he was chronically drunk and often abused her (James 1975, 184). Josephine Rancier legally separated from her husband because of his desertion of the family, his abuse, and his chronic indebtedness (U.S. Bureau of the Census 1880; Sokolow and Lamanna 1984, 379). McWhirter herself testified at her daughter's divorce trial that "there is no sense in a woman obeying a drunken husband" (*Belton Journal*, Feb. 26, 1880).

Many of the women who joined the community not only were dissatisfied with their own marriages but believed that the institution itself was disastrous for women. Some, concerned with the fate of their daughters or sisters, joined the community with their female relatives. The intergenerational aspect of the community is significant. From the available evidence, many of the second-generation daughters remained in the community and never married, or maintained ties with the community (U.S. Bureau of the Census 1900; U.S. Bureau of the Census, *Washington, D.C.* 1910). Belton mothers and daughters may have seen joining the Sanctified Sisters as a way out of a cycle of abuse. For mothers, the community meant an end to abusive marriage and a way to protect their daughters from the same fate. For daughters, it meant having an option for their lives not originally available to their mothers. It also meant that daughters could view their mothers as dignified women who had the courage to save themselves and their children from the tyranny of family violence.

The Sisters rejected nurturing their husbands but were anxious to retain their maternal nurturing. Many of the women joined the community with their children. Mothers gave up their individual responsibilities for their children, but all the women believed child rearing was a special community task. The Sisters maintained their own school for community children. Sanctificationist children were considered full members of the community (*Constitution* 1902, 10).

Many in Belton viewed the community of women as a threat to traditional gender roles. The men most directly challenged by the women's activities, their husbands and male relatives, tried several forms of action: divorce, deprivation of sources of livelihood, desertion, and physical abuse.

However, men outside the families of the Sisters also felt threatened by the women's community. Two incidents in particular illustrate their perceptions of the threat and what kinds of actions the men believed themselves justified in taking. In 1880, two male residents of Belton, Matthew and David Dow, received permission from McWhirter to join the Sanctified Sisters. The Brothers agreed to the religious and sexual strictures of the Sanctified Sisters. Other Belton citizens were horrified at the acceptance of adult men into the group (*Belton Journal*, Feb. 19, 1880; James 1965, 70). A mob dragged the Dow brothers from their home and beat them. The brothers were threatened with further violence if they did not leave town. They refused to be intimidated and stated that their "religion was good enough to live by and good enough to die by" (*Belton Journal*, Feb. 26, 1880). The brothers' refusal to leave town led the judicial authorities in Belton to bring the Dows to trial on the charge of insanity.

A number of the male witnesses against the brothers were husbands of women who had joined the Sanctified Sisters. Judge and jury found that the brothers were insane and that "their restraint [was] a duty to society and themselves" (*Belton Journal*, Feb. 26, 1880). Matthew and David Dow were conveyed to the state insane asylum in Austin, where the authorities refused to admit them, as they were obviously sane.

The charge of insanity to quell the rebellious women was raised a second time. In 1883 Sister Mary C. Johnson was tried and also sent to the asylum in Austin. At the death of her husband, John G. Johnson, Mary was to receive his two-thousand-dollar life insurance policy from the Knights of Honor. Johnson refused to take the policy. John had been unsanctified, and as Mary had refused to take money from him when he was alive, she did not wish to do so after his death (Garrison 1893, 39). Mary Johnson's brother then petitioned that she be tried for lunacy solely on the grounds of her refusal of the insurance money. A Bell County jury found her insane, and she was sent to the same asylum in Austin as the Dow brothers.

Unlike the case of Matthew and David Dow, the asylum authorities did not immediately deny the insanity charges against Johnson. Even though the charges of religious fanaticism against Mary Johnson had been the same as those charged to the Dow brothers, the asylum authorities were more willing to believe that a woman was likely to be a danger if left free in her community. Johnson had acted in ways that did not conform to notions of ladylike behavior. Nineteenth-century doctors frequently confused female acts of independence with emotional illness (Ehrenreich and English 1973, 42). The citizens of Belton had been made aware of the conditions at the state asylum in Austin in 1880: "Escaped lunatics create much trouble [in Austin] . . . one had the appearance of being half starved and was dangerous to women. . . . On approaching the cabin [he] saw a negro woman in the yard and immediately attacked her. . . . Neighbors conducted him to the asylum and turned him over to the attendants, who . . . appeared sublimely indifferent, and treated the whole matter as if . . . such acts by the inmates . . . were everyday occurrences" (*Belton Journal*, July 29, 1880). That the Belton jury was willing to send the widow of a prominent citizen to such an institution indicates the rancor they felt toward the Sanctified Sisters.

By the end of the 1870s the women realized that economic independence from their husbands was also necessary if they wished to control their own lives and to maintain their ties with other Sisters. In 1879 the Sisters began their first communal economic venture. Until this time the ties between them had been religious belief and emotional support for those women trapped in unhappy marriages.

The traditional nineteenth-century partriarchal family household was based on the economic ties between its members, with the male head providing and controlling the major portion of the income. For the urban families of Belton, money was more important than it had been on the farm, and the question of who controlled finances frequently became a source of contention between husbands and wives. In the late 1870s the Sisters demanded payment for the domestic work they provided as housekeepers, wives, and mothers (Mattox 1901, 167; Sokolow and Lamanna 1984, 380). They also wanted complete control over the funds they used in the household. Then Martha McWhirter refused to take money for household expenses from her husband when he threatened to withhold the money unless she accounted to him for its use.

The women began a communal fund with the twenty-dollar savings of a Sister who taught school in Belton. The women saved money from the sale of their own butter, milk, and eggs. It may be that because these were domestic sources of income, husbands had legal but not actual control over the production or sale. In some fashion the Sisters managed to save about fifteen dollars a week from the sale of these products. By the end of 1879 all the Sisters were able to be financially independent of their male relatives.

Sisters were not afraid of earning money in occupations that were tradionally male dominated. Margaret Henry directed the firewood business for the Sisters. The women bought wood at twenty-five cents a cord as it stood in the local cedar breaks, chopped it down, loaded the wood into wagons, and sold the firewood in town for three dollars per cord (James 1965, 73). Another Sister practiced dentistry, and still another repaired community shoes (*Temple Daily Telegram*, Sec. 2, Dec. 1, 1929).

By 1883 the Sisters entered a long period of great financial success. By that summer they were earning approximately six hundred dollars per month. The Sisters earned about six dollars a day from the sale of milk and butter, ten dollars a day from the sale of wood, and up to two hundred dollars a month from a communal laundry business they organized (Garrison 1893, 37). That same year Sister Margaret Henry gained control of her house through the death of her husband, John. The Sisters decided to live in the house and run it as a hotel. For the first year very few travelers stayed at the hotel. The women believed that the citizens of Belton worked against them and warned people away. After the first year, however, the hotel suddenly became popular. It is possible that the townsfolk were persuaded to change their tactics when McWhirter donated five hundred dollars in the Sisters' name toward bringing a railroad spur into Belton. Not only did this improve relationships between the Sisters and the rest of the town, but it was also good business sense on the Sisters' part, as the new railroad station was located across the street from their hotel (Wright 1974, 37).

By 1898 the Sanctified Sisters were not only a successful communal family but a financial success. McWhirter reported that the net income of the community was eight hundred dollars per month. The women owned the hotel, leased two more hotels in the nearby town of Waco, and collected rent from store houses, dwellings in Belton, and two farms outside the city (Fischer 1980, 174). The women of the Sanctified band realized that economic independence was an important component of the survival of their communal ideal. By earning and spending their own money, they relinquished the status they had as female dependents of prominent men but sought to gain an economic and social identity they had chosen and formed themselves. They were preeminently successful in their endeavor.

Once the Sisters began to live together in the same space after the mid-1880s, new features of the community began to appear. The women continued some of the patterns that they had practiced since the beginning of their band. They worked communally and managed to have large blocks of leisure time as well. By living together it became easier for the Sisters to live, act, and work communally.

From the beginning, the Sisters formed work patterns that supported their attempts to reorganize their lives. Much of their work, even before the opening of the Central Hotel, was communally organized. The laundry business, which they moved from house to house, provided the Sisters with a way to earn money with traditional female skills and created a time when the women could socialize as well. Most child rearing was done communally. The children also worked in the community hotel or on one of the farms. Like the adults, the children's lives combined work, learning, and play.

By 1891 the work patterns in the hotel and other property were all communal. There were thirty-two members then living in the community (Garrison 1893, 41). Ten members were required to run the hotel: four women did the cooking, three young girls waited on the tables in the dining room, one Sister and one young girl attended to the thirty-five bedrooms, and one of the male community members worked as the hotel clerk. Six of the Sisters worked in the laundry two days a week and at odd jobs for the rest of their work time. The Sisters also kept a farm; usually two women and four of the children lived there. The farm provided produce for the community and the hotel in the summer, and the inhabitants wove rag carpets in the winter. All jobs were changed around every month, and the cooks rotated every two weeks. The system worked so well that community members only worked about four hours a day and then were free to do as they chose.

Margarita Gerry reported that the Sisters she visited in 1902 were simple, unlettered country women. However, this was a romanticization on Gerry's part (Gerry 1902, 133). These were women who had reinterpreted theological doctrine for their own use, formed a women's literary club, begun Belton's first public library, and used parts of various contemporary communal, spiritual, and feminist philosophies they believed appropriate in the design of their own lives. The Sisters read the writings of Tolstoy, the works of single-tax advocate Henry George, the religious writings of Emanuel Swedenborg, the feminist *Woman's Journal,* and the utopian works of Edward Bellamy (Garrison 1893, 43).

The Sisters spent their leisure time in many different ways. They read a great deal; some of the Sisters played the piano, painted, and took music lessons from boarders. Like other women all over the United States during the 1890s, the Sisters formed a women's literary club. With the donation of 350 books the club created Belton's first public library in a small room of the hotel (Sokolow and Lamanna 1984, 390).

Some of the Sisters traveled, sometimes for pleasure but usually for the edification of the community. When the Sisters wished to improve their dairy farming techniques, two or three of them visited farms in Wisconsin (Wright 1974, 37). The Sisters also visited the Chicago Exposition in the mid-1890s (Sokolow and Lamanna 1984, 397). In the summer of 1890, the entire group of women traveled to New York City. While the primary reason for these trips was travel and to "see something of the world," the women were also searching for another location for their community. The Sisters were probably acting on dream directives in this search, as small groups also traveled to San Francisco and Mexico City to investigate sites (James 1965, 72).

While the group had increased its contact with the outside world, they were able to maintain community identity through private separate living quarters and a delicate sense of group dynamics. Although the Sisters spent their work hours and some leisure hours in the public space of the hotel, much of their time was spent in the more private atmosphere of the community's quarters. The Sisters had large buildings, separate from the hotel structure, that contained a sitting room, dining room, kitchen, work space, and bedrooms for each of the women (Wright 1974, 36).

Communal living space and communally organized work were not the only ways in which the Sisters maintained their group identity. Dreams, visions, and religious experiences, which had guided community members from the beginning, remained important. The Sisters discussed their experiences with each other and frequently obtained guidance for the entire group (Bell County 1887, 5). When interviewed, McWhirter often cited "revelations" as the reason for certain decisions on behalf of the community. However, beyond the mystical guidance of dreams and visions, McWhirter told historian George P. Garrison that the Sisters received "their greatest help from a delicate sense which belongs to the entire community rather than to any individual member" (Garrison 1893, 46). Religious mysticism remained a central aspect of guidance for community projects.

Without formally excluding men, the Belton community was formed by women as a female-centered organization. Any male members of the community were expected to conform to the new gender roles and forms the women had developed. Few men ever stayed for long with the Sisters; conflicts seemed to arise over traditional role expectations. The Sisters told a reporter that men were "'welcome if they are willing to live the life we do. But they never stay long. You see it is in the nature of men to want to boss – and – Well, they find they can't.' At which all the sisters nod their heads" (Gerry 1902, 139). On occasion the sense of community balance and harmony was disrupted. The community was disrupted when one Sister left to marry: "All felt a psychical disturbance due to her unfaithfulness," but this feeling disappeared after the woman left the community (Garrison 1893, 95).

The kin connections that most of these women had upon entering the community and the connections they went on to form with each other were an important aspect of the Woman's Commonwealth. The close emotional and often physical ties between women that Carroll Smith-Rosenberg found in her study of late eighteenth- and nineteenth-century women were usual forms of interaction. Female networks were frequently based on an "inner core of kin" – the relationships between mothers, daughters, sisters, sisters-in-law, cousins – and sustained by the everyday events of women's lives

(Smith-Rosenberg 1975, 11). The Sisters of the Belton community were able to live, work, and devote their lives to each other. The inner strength and durability of the community were formed by the kin and friendship networks already in place before the women began to live together. The women relied on the conventional bonds of female friendship to form the core of their community. The devotion that many of the Sisters felt for their leader, Martha McWhirter, was another factor in the balance of communal alliance. This devotion was demonstrated by the fact that at least four community members named their daughters after McWhirter. Gertrude Scheble, for example, named her youngest child Martha McWhirter Scheble.

Martha McWhirter and her family are a good example of multi-generational membership in the community. Two of McWhirter's children joined the community as adults, three of her grandchildren, and one great-grandchild. Margaret J. Henry, a close friend of McWhirter's and also a founding member, joined the group with her two daughters, Carrie and Ella. Other women joined with mothers or daughters.

Despite their eventual acceptance by the citizens of Belton and their success as a community, the Sisters decided to move their community to Washington, D.C., in 1898. It is not clear why the women moved away from their hometown. There were no new outbreaks of hostility against the Sisters. Rather their neighbors begged them not to leave Belton (Gerry 1902, 136). Some have speculated that dreams directed the Sisters to a new location. Others believed that the older Sisters wished to retire, and the younger Sisters wanted the more stimulating environment of a large city. The Sisters finally settled on a large house in the Mount Pleasant suburb of Washington.

The Sisters continued to live much as they had done in Belton. The house itself contained both private rooms and communal quarters. Occasionally, the Sisters opened the house to boarders, but mainly they lived on their savings (Hinds [1908] 1975, 441). The domestic work continued to be rotated every week among the members. All members of the community were required to perform some manual labor. The proceeds from this work were held for the common use of all the women (*Constitution* 1902, 3). As in the early days in Belton, the women sold garden produce, preserves, butter, eggs, and milk, and a homemade wine named Koumiss to their neighbors. Perhaps the number of orders increased beyond the household means of supply, because in 1903 the women purchased a 120-acre farm near the town of Colesville, in Montgomery County, Maryland (*Deeds,* 1903).

In 1902 the Sisters officially became known as the Woman's Commonwealth of Washington, D.C. They had always disliked the name Sanctified

3. Members of the Woman's Commonwealth, ca. 1904, in Washington, D.C. Martha McWhirter is seated in the center of the front row. *Courtesy of General Research Division, The New York Public Library, Astor, Lenox, and Tilden Foundations.*

Sisters and had only grudgingly accepted the name. With the assumption of the new title, the Sisters for the first time wrote down the rules and regulations by which they lived. They still believed that "ecclesiastical connections, and . . . set forms and ceremonies cause sectarian divisions and much dissension and unhappiness." In the preamble to their constitution the Sisters stated their beliefs on communal living: "That the communistic life produces in the fullest measure honesty, sobriety, spirituality, happiness and a keen sense of justice" (*Constitution* 1902, 3).

The constitution required that all property was to be held by the trustees for the benefit of the Commonwealth. All members were to live in a "combined household, [where] the members shall be mutually guaranteed by the services of the members, and by the entire resources of the organization, food, clothing, care in sickness and misfortune, in infancy and old age." As the women still cared for young children, their care was also mentioned in the Commonwealth constitution: "All children of the Colony shall be regarded as wards of the organization and special objects of its care and love" (*Constitution* 1902, 9–10).

The women lived a comfortable life. When reporter Margarita Gerry visited the community in 1902, she found them tranquil and happy. "This is living," one of the younger Sisters told her emphatically (Gerry 1902, 136). In 1900 there were twenty-three people living in the community. The Sisters received application letters daily from women who wished to join. Only a few women were ever accepted, as the Sisters wished to maintain their delicate sense of community. A few of the younger Sisters left to marry or to try jobs outside of the Commonwealth.

Martha McWhirter died in April 1904. Many prophesied that the Commonwealth would break up once the dynamic leader was no longer able to direct the group herself. However, the remaining women continued to live as a communal family for many more years. Some of the Sisters remained in Washington and occasionally opened the house to boarders. Other Sisters lived on the Commonwealth farm in Maryland (U.S. Bureau of the Census, *Maryland* 1910). By 1914 the house in Washington had been sold and community members moved to other Commonwealth property in Maryland and Florida.

In 1910, eighteen members remained in the community, evenly divided between the house in Washington and the Maryland farm (U.S. Bureau of the Census, *Maryland* 1910). The farm in Montgomery County, Maryland, remained the home to the surviving members of the Commonwealth for several more decades. During the 1920s and 1930s, after the house in the District was sold and all community members resided on the farm, the Sisters served meals on weekends to customers from Washington. It is said that many dignitaries visited the community for the superb food and stayed to play croquet on the lawns after dinner. Martha Scheble, the last surviving Sister, kept up the community tradition of opening up the house to guests and having boarders until she died in 1983.

The Woman's Commonwealth was one of the few intentional communities designed, controlled, and populated by women. It was shaped by the women inhabitants according to their needs and their beliefs. The Sisters demanded independence and self-determination and soon learned that this aspiration threatened traditional patriarchal society. By banding together the women could survive economically and fight against the hostility of the outside world. Believing that the communal life provided the best social family and environment for individuals, the women found that this mode of living fulfilled many of their needs.

Piety, submission to male authority, domesticity, and purity were the parameters that shaped most nineteenth-century women's lives. Like other utopian feminists and reformers, the Sisters found that they had to deal with the issues of marriage, sexuality, gender roles, and work that defined them as women. The women of the Commonwealth had the opportunity to re-shape on a small scale, and for a small number, matters that concerned many women. By choosing to reorder their lives around the issues of women's independence and self-determination, and by establishing a community devoted to women, the Sisters of the Woman's Commonwealth placed themselves firmly within a tradition of feminism and feminist utopianism.

Works Cited

Atkinson, Bertha. [1929] 1970. *History of Bell County*. Reprint. Belton, Tex.: Bell County Historical Society.

Bell County, Texas. District Court. 1887. Haymond v. Haymond. 3037.

Constitution and By-laws of the Woman's Commonwealth. 1902. Washington, D.C.: Crane.

Deeds to Woman's Commonwealth Farm. Montgomery County, Maryland, Colesville, Office of Deeds. Oct. 1903, Dec. 4, 1930, Liber 514, Folio 459; Jan. 13, 1943, Liber 899, Folio 432; Dec. 17, 1945, Liber 992, Folio 398; Oct. 24, 1984, Liber 6567, Folio 090.

Ehrenreich, Barbara, and Deirdre English. 1973. *Complaints and Disorders: The Sexual Politics of Sickness*. Old Westbury, N.Y.: Feminist.

Fischer, Ernest G. 1980. *Marxists and Utopias in Texas*. Burnet, Tex.: Eakin.

Garrison, George P. 1893. A Woman's Community in Texas. *Charities Review* 3 (Nov.): 28–46.

Gerry, Margarita Spalding. 1902. The Woman's Commonwealth of Washington, D.C. *Ainslee's Magazine* 10 (Sept.): 133–41.

Hinds, William Alfred. [1908] 1975. *American Communities and Cooperative Colonies*. Reprint. Philadelphia: Porcupine.

James, Eleanor. 1965. The Sanctificationists of Belton. *American West* 2 (Summer): 65–73.

———. 1975. Martha White McWhirter (1827–1904). In *Women in Early Texas*, ed. Evelyn M. Carrington, 180–90. Austin, Tex.: Jenkins.

Kitch, Sally. 1989. *Chaste Liberation: Celibacy and Female Cultural Status*. Urbana: Univ. of Illinois Press.

Malone, Ann Patton. 1983. *Women on the Texas Frontier: A Cross Cultural Perspective*. Southwestern Studies, monograph no. 70. El Paso: Texas Western Press.

Mattox, Captain A. H. 1901. The Woman's Commonwealth. *Social Science: A Review of Social and Industrial Betterment* 4 (Nov.): 166–70.

Sanctificationists—Unique Religious Group in Belton. 1941. *Belton Journal and Bell County Centennial Edition*.

Scheble, Adolphus. Diary. Private collection.

Scott, Ann Firor. 1970. *The Southern Lady: From Pedestal to Politics 1830–1930*. Chicago: Univ. of Chicago Press.

Smith-Rosenberg, Carroll. 1975. The Female World of Love and Ritual. *Signs: A Journal of Women in Culture and Society* 1 (Autumn): 1–30.

Sokolow, Jamie, and Mary Ann Lamanna. 1984. Women and Utopia: The Woman's Commonwealth of Belton, Texas. *Southwestern Historical Quarterly* 87 (Apr.): 371–92.

Tyler, George W. 1936. *History of Bell County*. Belton, Tex.: Dayton Kelley.

U.S. Bureau of the Census. 1880. *Tenth Census of the United States: Population. Bell County, Texas, City of Belton*.

———. 1900. *Twelfth Census of the United States: Population. Washington, D.C.*

———. 1910. *Thirteenth Census of the United States: Population. Montgomery County, Maryland.*

———. 1910. *Thirteenth Census of the United States: Population. Washington, D.C.*

Wright, Gwendolyn. 1974. The Woman's Commonwealth: Separatism, Self, Sharing. *AAO: Architectural Association Quarterly* 6:36–43.

PART TWO

Women's Creativity in Community

Introduction

THIS SECTION CONTAINS THREE ARTICLES that examine women's creativity in community. The first discusses the writings and artistic activities of three women who lived at Brook Farm as young women and who continued their productive creativity throughout their lives. Two articles on Shaker sisters examine, respectively, their fancy goods production and their literary expressions of gospel union and love for each other.

Brook Farm (1841–47) lasted only six years but has captured the imagination of Americans as a unique secular experiment where intellectual and manual labor could be combined in a communal setting, with sufficient leisure for members to pursue education, art, and the cultivation of their talents. It was an "American seedling–the child of New England Unitarianism." Brook Farm counted many prominent intellectuals among its friends and members, including Ralph Waldo Emerson and Margaret Fuller of the Transcendentalist Group of Boston and Concord. Neither joined, but many talented and dedicated people did.

Brook Farm was founded on two hundred acres of land owned by George Ripley, eight miles southwest of Boston (near Roxbury). It was Ripley's hope that Brook Farm would "be a place for improving the race of men. . . ; thought would preside over the operations of labor, and labor would contribute to the expansion of thought; we should have industry without drudgery, and true equality without its vulgarity" (George Ripley to Ralph Waldo Emerson, Nov. 9, 1840, cited in Sams 1958, 6). The community was originally organized as a joint stock company, with some members contributing money and others contributing labor.

Brook Farmers did not tamper with conventional marriage (many members were single) but did attempt to raise and educate their children communally. Married couples lived together and single people shared rooms. They ate communally prepared meals together and gathered in the evenings for cultural and educational programs. Members struggled with agricultural and gardening tasks and attempted some manufacturing ventures (for example, Marianne Dwight's lampshade manufacture) but never succeeded in putting the community on a sound financial footing. From the record, it appears that women did sex-specific work like laundry, cooking, sewing, teaching, and some crafts manufacture.

In 1844 the Brook Farmers adopted the administrative structure of the French utopian socialist Charles Fourier (1777–1837). During its Fourier period, the community published a periodical, *The Harbinger*, which promoted utopian socialism. As a Fourierist community, Brook Farm organized itself into departments of labor, agriculture, domestic industry, and the mechanic arts; built a workshop; and in 1844 began construction of a Fourierist phalanstery as a model dwelling place for all community members. Before it could be completed, however, the phalanstery burned to the ground in 1846. Brook Farm Phalanx never recovered from this disaster. In 1847 the farm was sold at a loss and the community disbanded. Although short-lived, Brook Farm enjoyed unusual support and publicity during its existence; its story is well chronicled by many distinguished visitors and members. Some sources on Brook Farm are Henry W. Sams, ed., *Autobiography of Brook Farm* (Englewood Cliffs, N.J.: Prentice-Hall, 1958), and Edith Roelker Curtis, *A Season in Utopia: The Story of Brook Farm* (1961).

The Shakers (the United Society of Believers in Christ's Second Appearing) began in North America in 1774 with the arrival of nine persons fleeing religious persecution in England. This small band of English mystics was led by Mother Ann Lee (1736–84), a middle-aged woman raised in the industrial blight of Manchester, England. Mother Ann's followers believed that she represented the second (female) embodiment of the Christ spirit (Jesus being the male embodiment), and that each believer could also experience personal reawakening. Mother Ann Lee called on her disciples to renounce earthly marriage and carnality and to join in gospel union with a family of Christian sisters and brothers. Named for their shaking dances during worship, the Shakers gradually gained converts and committed themselves to Christian communalism and separation from the world, to the confession of sins, to a belief in a dual (male and female) godhead, to celibacy, pacifism, and obedience to anointed spiritual and temporal leaders of both sexes. The Shakers believed in and received divine revelations and gifts of inspiration. Their worship services resounded with song and dance (in lines, similar to marching), as well as conversation, reading, and preaching.

In community the Shakers worshipped and ate together (they were vegetarians), but men and women entered the rooms by different doors and sat in separate sections. Their living arrangements were segregated by sex in dormitorylike buildings, and most work activities were sex-specific as well. Children came to the Shaker communities when their parents joined. Shakers also adopted orphans and abandoned children and provided them with nurture, education, and vocational training. At age twenty-one, children were given the choice of becoming members or making their way "in the world."

The Shakers began as agriculturalists. Throughout their history the products of their fields, orchards, dairies, nurseries, and gardens provided members with a wholesome diet and exceptional longevity. In addition to agricultural surplus, they sold garden seeds, dried vegetables and fruits, and medicinal herbs. The Shakers were also keenly interested in technology and industry and patented dozens of their own inventions—for example, a washing machine, a cheese press, a green-corn cutting machine, and an hydraulic water system. Among the many Shaker industries that provided income for the communities were businesses in tanning, machinery, furniture, brooms and brushes, textiles, clothing, milling, brick making, fancy goods, and cloaks (the latter, the Dorothy cloak designed by Sister Dorothy Durgin of Canterbury, N.H. and patented in 1901). Because of their moderation and simplicity in living and their extraordinary work ethic, the Shakers became prosperous and were sometimes envied by their neighbors. They employed hired help and, in the twentieth century, welcomed new inventions like electricity and radios.

The peak membership of Shakers occurred in the 1850s, when members numbered about six thousand in eighteen or nineteen communities located in the Northeast and Midwest. Yet over the course of the nineteenth century conversions declined and seceders increased; the number of Shakers began to dwindle. In 1965 the covenant was closed; thereafter, no new members were admitted. In many cases, the remaining members—primarily elderly women—made plans for the orderly transfer of their archives and properties to museums and historic preservation sites. Other communal sites were purchased by nonprofit institutions like schools and retirement communities. By 1992 only a few Shakers were left: one sister at Canterbury, New Hampshire, and a handful of Believers at Sabbathday Lake, Maine.

Judging from the number of years they have existed, the Shakers are the most successful communalists in U.S. history. Because of recent books, art exhibitions, and the restoration of communal sites, many Americans have come to admire the fine quality of Shaker architecture, furniture, crafts, and clothing. This appreciation of Shaker heritage is especially due to the efforts of Edward Deming Andrews and Faith Andrews, a husband-wife team who collected Shaker artifacts and wrote three fine books about the Shakers. Recent recommended sources are Priscilla J. Brewer, *Shaker Communities, Shaker Lives* (1986), Beverly Gordon, *Shaker Textile Arts* (1980), and June Sprigg, *By Shaker Hands: the Art and World of the Shakers* (Hanover, N.H.: Univ. Press of New England, 1975, reissued 1990).

Two more articles about the Shakers are included in part 3.

4

Creative Women of Brook Farm

LUCY M. FREIBERT

IN POPULAR MEMORY OF BROOK FARM, nineteenth-century men washed dishes and served at table and women wore bloomers and sometimes worked beside the men in the fields. The musical world knows Brook Farm as the sometime habitation of the distinguished music critic John Sullivan Dwight, who, with other members of his family, supported the communal venture to the end (L. Swift 1900, 160). Literary folk remember it as the scene of Nathaniel Hawthorne's "gallant attack upon a heap of manure" with the unfamiliar pitchfork and his discovery that "a man's soul may be buried and perish under a dung-heap or in a furrow of the field, just as well as under a pile of money" (Hawthorne 1907, 6, 20). They also recall his consequent departure for the customshouse and consulate and his use of Brook Farm in *The Blithedale Romance* (1852) as the backdrop for his dramatization of the dangers of being female and bright, poor, or both in nineteenth-century America.

For the women who lived there, Brook Farm was an empowering center; it shaped their visions and nurtured their creativity. This essay points out unique features of Brook Farm and details the achievements of its most significant writers—Georgiana Bruce Kirby, Marianne Dwight, and Abby Morton Díaz.

The creative impulse that inspired and sustained Brook Farm emerged from the meetings of Boston's Transcendental Club. The words of Ralph Waldo Emerson, especially, moved George and Sophia Ripley to purchase the West Roxbury property, where the community formed in 1841. Surprisingly few club members—only George, Sophia, and George's sister Marianne, John Sullivan Dwight, and Nathaniel Hawthorne—were among the fifteen original Brook Farmers.

The Brook Farm goals formulated by Ripley epitomized Transcendental ideals, "to combine the thinker and the worker, as far as possible, in the same individual; to guarantee the highest mental freedom, by providing all with labor, adapted to their tastes and talents . . . to do away [with] the necessity of menial services, by opening the benefits of education and the profits of labor to all" (Frothingham 1882, 307–8). Yet even Emerson declined membership, although, as he wrote, "almost . . . penitentially" (Rusk, 1939, 369).

Margaret Fuller, also a Transcendental Club member, visited the farm frequently, gave a series of her "Conversations" there, and later sent her brother to the school, but she thought Ripley "too sanguine," accusing him of not taking time "to let things ripen in his mind" (Hudspeth 1983, 174). She found her first day or two at the farm "desolate," but soon "the freedom of the place" seemed "delightful." A year later, she thought "the tone of the society . . . much sweeter," and the community "a fine studio for the soul-sculptor." Nevertheless, she firmly resisted Brook Farm membership (Fuller 1852, 73–74, 78, 75).

Even without these prominent figures, Brook Farm quickly attracted members and drew students to its school. Many of its features appealed to women and nourished their sense of autonomy. Payment to members for their labor was at an "equal rate, both for men and women"; at admissions and other business meetings, "women cast their votes without criticism"; and the 1844 *Articles of Agreement* mandated that a majority of the Council of Arbiters be women[1] (Codman [1894] 1971, 13, 135, 110–11).

The adoption, in 1844, of the principles of the French philosopher Charles Fourier ultimately led to the farm's demise in 1847. Designed for a phalanx of 1,600 members, Fourier's system was impractical for a community that never exceeded 120 at any given time (L. Swift 1900, 118). Even in the Fourier phase, women held on to equality with men.

Although women's work was heavy at Brook Farm, as at similar communities, simple food preparation, shared housekeeping, and provisions for child care lightened the burden. At harvesttime some women helped in the fields and joined in the evening cornhuskings. In cold weather the young men hung out the wash. Because such menial tasks were community activities completed in a spirit of play, gender stereotyping of work declined. Seeing this effect, some women students later became members. Other women, young and single, chose to join the community outright (Kolmerten 1990, 172).

Perhaps the most significant condition favorable to women was that no religious test could be required (Codman [1894] 1971, 12). This stipulation, which prevented any one religious sect from imposing its beliefs on the community, safeguarded women from traditional pressures of patriarchy—relegation to secondary status as sharers of Eve's guilt and subjection, particularly as childbearers, to her curse.

Another important advantage Brook Farm afforded women was education. In *Years of Experience,* Georgiana Bruce Kirby describes the excitement of entering George Ripley's moral philosophy class and Charles A. Dana's German class. "All the studies pursued at the Farm were made preeminently living," she writes. "What was acquired was assimilated and became part of ourselves for all time" (Kirby [1887] 1971, 97, 98).

Cultural opportunities also enhanced the women's lives. Visitors, besides Fuller, included musicians, writers, and reformers. Among the singers were Mary Bullard, Frances (or Eliza) Ostinelli, better known as Signora Biscaccianti, and Mary Hutchinson, who with her family worked for abolition.[2] Lydia Maria Child, writer and editor of the *National Anti-Slavery Standard,* and Elizabeth Peabody, the reformer whose shop in Boston served Transcendentalists as a center, brought news of developing controversies.

Although Brook Farm women drew inspiration from visitors, the creativity of their own members enriched their lives daily. Sophia Dana Ripley (1803–61) exemplified the new woman among them. Highly educated in history and foreign languages, she taught these subjects at the farm, read Dante in the original on special evenings, and wrote essays for the Transcendentalist literary magazine, *The Dial.* Her hours in the ironing room completed her image as thinker-worker. In her essay "Woman," she challenges images of women created by men and delineates an autonomous, intellectual path for women of the future.[3]

Caroline Sturgis [Tappan] (1819–88), another early *Dial* contributor, apparently found life at the farm congenial to literary work. Her poems reveal Transcendental personae in various relations to nature.[4] When Sturgis left the farm and the occasional solace of her friends there, she apparently ceased to write (Myerson 1980, 208).

Amelia Russell (1798–1880) brought to Brook Farm the dancing skills she acquired in Paris. She taught the children and, as Mistress of Revels and chief of the Amusement Group, arranged charades, masquerades, tableaux, and dances for the whole community (Kirby [1887] 1971, 149). After leaving the farm, Russell contributed to its recorded history two essays entitled "Home Life of the Brook Farm Association" that extoll its abundant ingenuity and imagination.

Not until the turn of the century did Ora Gannett Sedgwick describe her one and one-half years at the farm. In "A Girl of Sixteen at Brook Farm," she recalls the flirting among the young people and, in a more serious vein, the benefit of living among scholars such as the Ripleys, Dana, and Hawthorne; enjoying visits from "philosophic minds" such as Fuller, Theodore

4. *Above, left:* Georgiana Bruce Kirby (1818–1887); *above, right:* Abby Morton Díaz (1821–1904). *Each courtesy of General Research Division, The New York Public Library, Astor, Lenox, and Tilden Foundations. Center:* Marianne Dwight Orvis (1816–1901). *Courtesy of Vassar College.*

Parker, and William Henry Channing; and associating daily with women such as Kirby, Russell, Sarah Stearns, and Díaz.

In such a milieu, Georgiana Bruce Kirby, Marianne Dwight, and Abby Morton Díaz developed their respective gifts. Born in Bristol, England, three months after her father's death, Georgiana Bruce Kirby (1818–87) spent a varied childhood, which included "one golden year" on a farm (Kirby [1887] 1971, 2), two years of formal education, and a number of years of privation in a small English seaport town. At fourteen, as a governess for an English family, Kirby visited France and Canada. In 1837, she returned to London to work for the family of the Reverend E. S. Gannett, before the Gannetts brought her to Boston.

At the age of twenty-three, Kirby joined the Brook Farm community, where two of the Gannett nieces also lived. She sought to pay for her younger brother's education and to learn enough mathematics to obtain a teaching certificate. She worked eight hours a day for those privileges and when, a year later, she became a member of the association, she added two more (Kirby [1887] 1971, 132). Kirby's first work assignment included ironing, preparing vegetables, and helping wash the cups and plates after supper (Kirby [1887] 1971, 100). She also taught with Marianne Ripley in the Infant School, called The Nest, and soon took over its operation (Curtis 1961, 69). Kirby's writing about the farm, though it alludes to her "scholars" (L. Swift 1900, 80), emphasizes her own social and educational development.

Membership in the association pleased Kirby. She recalls her "first delightful experience of 'Woman's Rights'" noting that "no distinction was made on account of sex." "A proposition could be put, discussed, and voted on, with entire freedom, by women and men alike," she reports and adds that "this new sense of power and responsibility widened my horizon, and included all the benefits I was prepared to take advantage of" (Kirby 1871, 4:349).

Twenty-five years after she left Brook Farm, the *Overland Monthly* published Kirby's "My First Visit to Brook Farm" (1870), and at intervals over the next two years, *Old and New* published "Before I Went to Brook Farm" and three installments of "Reminiscences of Brook Farm." In "My First Visit to Brook Farm" Kirby dramatizes her experience by casting the Brook Farmers in classical roles: Hero [Ora Gannett Sedgwick], "she of the speaking eyes . . . graceful in her gracelessness . . . whose every mood, be it grave or gay, mischievous or compassionate, made her equally attractive"; Leander, "the youth who arrived at the Farm with such a bad reputation, and in one year had proved himself pure gold"; and Sybil [Caroline Sturgis?], "the ubiquitous–full of resource," who "had worked for Anti-Slavery Fairs, and stood by [William Lloyd] Garrison in the late mob" (Kirby [1870] 1965, 9–10).

The first of the "Reminiscences of Brook Farm" details Salome's/Kirby's arrival as a member of the community. The lighthearted opening does not obscure the seriousness of the issues Kirby treats—occupational and educational opportunities and the availability of scholarly guides, abolition, women's rights, animal rights, religious orthodoxy, the temperance movement, opposition to war, and the gain or loss attached to social visiting. She recalls the evening entertainments, where singer and audience were *en rapport* and "really profound effects were produced," thus securing "the most valuable part of the education, that which kept the soul awake and plastic to all heavenly influences" (Kirby 1871, 430).

Kirby's autobiography, *Years of Experience* (1887), contains adaptations of her essays augmented by accounts of her early life, her last years at Brook Farm, work at Sing Sing, and teaching in the Midwest. Although the autobiography lacks some of the spontaneity of the essays, it identifies people and includes significant information the essays omit.

One of the most far-reaching impressions of Brook Farm recorded in *Years of Experience* is the visit of the English reformer Charles Lane, who came to America after making the acquaintance of Emerson and Alcott. From Lane, Kirby writes, the Brook Farmers "first heard of the superior power of the mother over the character and mind of her unborn child." Greatly moved, Kirby wrote: "Never, in my most miserable moments, had I wished I were a man, and now the natural sentiment which was my 'ruling love' sprang forward with pride to account for this" (Kirby [1887] 1971, 153, 154). This was not a passing emotion. In 1852, married to Richard C. Kirby of Santa Cruz, and pregnant with their first child, Kirby wrote in her journal: "Since I was a girl of eighteen I have been ever conscious of the most intense desire to become a mother. . . . It is not that I am especially fond of little babies, for I am not, . . . but I do earnestly love to watch the unfolding of character and intellect" (C. Swift and Steen 1987, 61–62).

After hearing Lane, Kirby kept records to test his theory. In 1877, her *Transmission: or, Variation of Character through the Mother* appeared. In the introduction to the revised and expanded 1879 edition, Kirby states the desire to impress on women that "with the mother, rests the greater power to mold for good or ill, for power or weakness, for beauty or deformity, the characters of her unborn children, and that with power comes the responsibility for its use." Kirby hopes thereby to counteract past practice that held women responsible for children's dullness and traced brilliance or beauty "back to some great-grandfather or grand-aunt of the father's" (Kirby 1879, 8).

Kirby points out the rights and wrongs of sexual practice once conception has occurred, listing the conditions under which intercourse endangers the potential child. Kirby describes marriage as "a partnership for the higher development of each party, and the continuance of the race" and blames "the past *regime*" for all but annihilating, in "the highly organized and more individualized American woman," the "capacity for conjugal emotion," causing her to transmit "to her son the abnormal passions of his father, and to her daughter her own feeble, outraged conjugal capacity." Kirby looks forward to the day when parents will instruct their children in temperate use of the conjugal act (Kirby 1879, 18–19).

Kirby illustrates each section of *Transmissions* with women's narratives. Some tell of women who, enduring poverty or economic uncertainty, excessive hard work, exhaustion, jealousy, or some combination of these during gestation, passed on to their children very undesirable character traits. Others describe women who, enjoying pleasant experiences during pregnancy, gave birth to children possessed of outstanding gifts.

When Brook Farm became seriously interested in Fourierism and admitted artisans to membership, Kirby found the newcomers' lack of manners and education unbearable. Aided by Margaret Fuller, she obtained the position of assistant matron to Eliza Farnham at Sing Sing, later taught in the Midwest, and eventually found her way to California.

Although the new Brook Farm disturbed Kirby, it delighted Marianne Dwight (1816–1901), who joined the community in 1844, the year Kirby left. A joyful, sensitive, yet realistic Bostonian, Dwight had acquired a reputation as a gifted artist and teacher. In vain had James Russell Lowell recommended her to Dr. Asa Grey for employment at Harvard (Cooke 1898, 106), but at Brook Farm she used her gifts well in teaching Latin and drawing. When Marianne and her parents, John and Mary Corey Dwight, joined her brother John at Brook Farm, the association was entering its final phase, in the closing days of which she married John Orvis.

Nowhere are the day-to-day activities of the farm's last three years recorded more thoroughly or delightfully than in Dwight's letters to her brother Frank and her friend Anna Q. T. Parsons. Dwight's letters, edited by Amy L. Reed and published in 1928 under the title *Letters from Brook Farm, 1844–1847,* combine the directness and excitement of current events with candid observations about the internal politics of the association. Although she writes with fierce loyalty to the association, Dwight attempts to treat both sides of controversies, and some letters allow the reader to observe her in the process of deciding where she stands. Whether writing of the importance of work, of her concern that women succeed in creative efforts, of the pleasures of friendship, social interchange, and entertainment, of her awareness of beauty in physical and human nature, or of the necessity of overcoming the tyranny of competition, Dwight faithfully looks for evidence that the Fourier system is working.

To learn how the system works, Dwight chooses to spend time in each department. In her first letter (Spring 1844), she reports to Parsons that she finds herself in the barn, caring for three eighteen-month-old babies. Later the same day, she tells of receiving an invitation from Mrs. Ripley to join the refectory group at teatime (Dwight 1928, 1, 5).

In April Dwight enumerates her domestic assignments: waiting on breakfast table and clearing things away, working in the dormitory, sewing until dinnertime (12:30 P.M.), teaching drawing, sewing, setting the tea table, and washing teacups. She speculates that she will soon become attached to the place, for she has "felt perfectly at home from the first"; nevertheless, she, like Kirby, complains that there are not enough women to do the work (Dwight 1928, 7–8).

Shortly after her arrival, she writes to Parsons (Apr. 27, 1844) about the relaxed social atmosphere in which she and her roommate entertained two young men "(up in our room) . . . and were drawn into playing whist and talking till *eleven o'clock.*" On another evening, she walked with a similar group in the Pine Woods about sunset. Moved by this experience, she writes, "How sacred and solemn were those deep shades, and the sombre light! We threw ourselves upon our backs . . . and talked till about nine o'clock. . . . Our earnest talk strengthened my faith in Association and in Brook Farm" (Dwight 1928, 12–13). By September 19, 1844, Dwight could write to her brother that she would not exchange life at the farm for any she had ever led: "I could not feel contented again with the life of isolated houses, and the conventions of civilization. . . . Life is so full and rich here, that I feel as if . . . I were *growing* somewhat faster than when I lived in Boston" (Dwight 1928, 41).

Gradually, Dwight's role changes. In addition to her teaching, she helps Amelia Russell. A July letter to Parsons describes their amusement at having become "milliners and makers of cap-tabs," their products to be retailed in Boston. Dwight boasts of the high quality of their work and expresses hope that the community will credit their achievements. To Frank, she gives a less detailed account and, lapsing into Fourierite language, reveals her hope of finding an outlet for her "passional attraction for painting" (Dwight 1928, 25–26).

Writing to Parsons in August, Dwight declaims her expectations for her artistic group, "nothing less than the elevation of woman to independence, and an acknowledged equality with man." Dwight would have women become "producers of marketable articles," earning their sustenance "independently of man." In a week's time, she says, she has turned twenty-five or thirty dollars' worth of materials into about forty-five dollars' worth of salable items. She looks forward to starting other projects and to applying the proceeds to "the elevation of woman forever." Turning theoretical, Dwight bids Parsons to "take a spiritual view of the matter. Raise woman to be the equal of man, and what intellectual developments may we not expect?" Dwight envisions the result as total social change—the attainment of "the great work" of association (Dwight 1928, 32–33).

Dwight's talent, unfortunately, isolated her. On February 27, 1845, she writes to Parsons that she is kept busy at work six or seven hours a day, having more demands for "lampshades and other painted fancy things" than she can supply. "I seem to have gotten myself into business," she boasts; then, wishing that Parsons were there to read to her while she works, she adds, "How lonely I am lately" (Dwight 1928, 81).

This uncharacteristic loneliness does not last. Many of Dwight's letters reveal the joy she receives from communing with nature and people. Often she writes of walks in the Pine Woods, and her springtime letters relate the beauties of nature to the joys of association. On May 14, 1845, she writes: "The flowers come faster than I can paint them. . . . Every day adds so much beauty to nature! And this bright youth of the year harmonizes so well with the dawn, the youth of humanity. . . . The great doctrines of Association fire my soul every day more and more. I am awed at the vastness of the schemes it unfolds, I am filled with wonder and ecstasy." On May 16, 1845, she writes of a trip to Cow Island where she found wild geranium, lady's slipper, dogwood, trientalis, "a yellow violet, streaked with purple . . . [and] another wonder—a white predate violet." Reed describes Dwight's paintings of wild flowers as both accurate and beautiful (Dwight 1928, 97, 99, 94n).

As times passes, Dwight appears more and more caught up in the business affairs of the Farm. Her involvement suggests the community's ongoing recognition of women's abilities. She attends readings, discussions, and business meetings of the council of science, though she wonders how she will be of use there (Dwight 1928, 101). Mention of her own work all but disappears in later correspondence, for the association's new constitution (introduced in May 1845) focuses the Brook Farmers' attention on the new organization of labor. Dwight regularly alludes to an increased religious emphasis among some Brook Farmers and resentment of that emphasis among others—a tension, Reed notes, not adequately treated by the farm's "official" historians (Dwight 1928, 120n).

In a letter to Parsons (Oct. 5, 1845), Dwight acknowledges that although the whole of life should be worship, she sees for the first time the need for a specific "form of worship" adapted to "the religious sentiment." She suggests developing a worshiping series that would provide assorted services for praying, singing, silence, and preaching. These groups would meet in "various apartments, or temples, or *sanctums*" but have access also to "a large central hall where all may gather when inspired with a universal sentiment,— the hall of unity" (Dwight 1928, 121). Although Dwight's vision did not materialize, her wedding to John Orvis was one of the select times the community formed the symbol of universal unity, joining hands while standing in a circle (L. Swift 1900, 66).

When Brook Farm came to an end, Dwight did what she had said she could never do again—she went back to living in an isolated house, bringing up two children and supporting her husband in his work with the farmers' unions. Despite her epistolary skills, she did not regard herself as a professional writer.

Abby Morton Díaz (1821–1904), on the contrary, having lived at Brook Farm from 1842 to 1847, spent most of her remaining years spreading its philosophy through children's and adults' books and public lectures. Her program for teaching trades and skills to women and girls (reminiscent of Dwight's theory), begun in the East, reached even the far West.

The daughter of Massachusetts reformers Patty Weston and Ichabod Morton, Díaz became involved in social issues early in life as secretary of the Juvenile Anti-Slavery Society. Educated in Plymouth public schools, she taught with Kirby in the Infant School at Brook Farm and eventually replaced her in that post. Díaz married a Cuban she met at the farm (Manuel A. Díaz), but after the community dissolved, she supported her children alone, teaching voice and dance at her father's home in Plymouth, doing practical nursing, and organizing public entertainments. A story, "Pink and Blue," published in the *Atlantic Monthly* (1861) launched her writing career.

In his autobiography, Theodore Roosevelt places Díaz's most famous young adult book, *The William Henry Letters* (1870), among his boyhood favorites, "first-class, good healthy stories, interesting in the first place, and in the next place teaching manliness, decency, and good conduct" (Roosevelt 1913, 20). The narrative exemplifies the Transcendental belief that education should build upon children's initial closeness to nature.

Díaz's bildungsroman, *Lucy Maria* (1874), belongs to the tradition popularized by Susan Warner's *Wide, Wide World* (1850). Partially autobiographical, the novel recounts the story of Lucy Maria Carver, William Henry's twenty-two-year-old cousin, who chooses education over marriage. In order to prepare herself most suitably to teach young children, Lucy Maria willingly assumes whatever employment will advance her knowledge and lead to wisdom.

Cast in epistolary form, *Lucy Maria* addresses issues that interested the Brook Farmers: establishing a social structure devoid of unethical competition; integrating education, work, and cultural enjoyment; and developing sexual equality. Through Lucy Maria, Díaz criticizes social conditions and upper-middle-class and middle-class values and practices and encourages "*right*-forming" children rather than "*re*-forming" them (Díaz 1874a, 174). One character remarks: "'The folly of it!—leaving little children to the care of teachers who will work *cheap*, and then paying ministers *dear* to undo and do over!'" (Díaz 1874a, 169).

Díaz's works from the 1860s onward grew adamantly feminist in criticizing the patriarchal structure. The fictions included in *The Schoolmaster's Trunk, Containing Papers on Home-Life in Tweenit* (1874) take a humorous but realistic look at the problems that beset women in middle-class, rural America. Through the Tweenit schoolmaster, Mr. McKimber, for example, Díaz dramatizes the grave injustice of expecting the unaided housewife to serve her husband, sons, and hired hands not simple fare but "Pies again! Always pies!" (Díaz 1874b, 5). For the making of pies and cake, McKimber says, women neglect their intellectual development, put aside their children, who need their attention, and endanger their own physical health.

Two books, published eighteen years apart—*A Domestic Problem: Work and Culture in the Household* (1875) and *Only a Flock of Women* (1893)—illustrate Díaz's growth in feminist conviction. In *A Domestic Problem*, Díaz formulates the paramount question simply: "How may woman enjoy the delights of culture, and at the same time fulfill her duties to family and household?" (Díaz 1875, 7). She responds by asking further questions—Why do women study cookbooks but not child-rearing manuals? Why do they spend hours sewing fancy shirts and ruffled dresses to make their children *look* good but do not read with them to induce them to *be* good? Why do women spend hours dusting, cleaning, and arranging for possible visitors but do not spend time reading to their children or discussing with them ideas that build character?

Woman herself, Díaz argues, needs the "highest, broadest, truest culture." "Give her," she pleads, "chances to draw inspiration from the beautiful in nature and in art. And, above all, insure her some respite from labor, and some tranquility." Díaz calls for "wisely educated mothers" and husbands who will bring home all the publications they can lay their hands on that treat "intelligently of mental, moral, or physical training" and will say to their wives, "Cease, I pray you, this everlasting toil. Read, study, rest" (Díaz 1875, 32, 38–39).

Díaz recognizes the scarcity of enlightened men. Citing a male writer's comment—"Every married woman should be able to cut and make her own, her husband's, and her children's clothes"—Díaz quips, only partly in jest, "Every married woman whose boys take to reading should snip such newspaper articles into shreds, burn them up, and bury the ashes" (Díaz 1875, 49–50).

As Díaz saw things, immediate change could be brought about, especially in small towns and rural areas, by means reflecting the Brook Farm code: the adoption of simple dress, the lessening of husbands' demands regarding food and clothing, and men's recognizing women as equals, not appendages. She perceived the means for effecting these changes as already in place in clubs, journals, and congresses where women were articulating these ideas.

In *Only a Flock of Women* (1893), Díaz looks more deeply into the underlying causes of social problems and offers more radical solutions. The crucial question she asks in this work is why women are held in such low esteem. Her answers are cogent. First, from earliest times men's work—hunting, fishing, defending—was considered more important than women's work—cooking, serving, bearing children (Díaz 1893, 42–43). Second, the early church fathers perpetuated degrading views of woman, one of them calling her the "Devil's gateway" (Díaz 1893, 44, 135). Third, childbearing, though creatively associated with the Divine, has come to be regarded as "low and shameworthy" (Díaz 1893, 45).

Díaz emphasizes women's need for self-determination: "As moral perception and capacity of judgment are not confined to one half of humanity," she writes, "it cannot be right that either half should decide duty for the other" (Díaz 1893, 48). Díaz sees her own job as making women dissatisfied with their lot so they will act to correct social ills. Education that enables women to see themselves in a new light, she considers essential.

Practical as well as theoretical, Díaz wrote and lectured steadily. With Dr. Harriet Clisby, she organized the Women's Educational and Industrial Union in Boston and served as its president for twelve years. Her lectures covered topics treated in her books and fostered by the union. At Díaz's death, *The Woman's Journal* of April 9, 1904, carried an extensive obituary, acknowledging her influence as writer and lecturer.[5]

The creative women of Brook Farm were, as Swift writes, "women of exceptional courage" who rose to the community's ideals (L. Swift 1900, 114). Each made her mark in the world. Díaz, who lived and worked with all of these women, absorbed and extended their diverse influences to a larger sphere.

Notes

I wish to thank Leon V. Driskell who read an earlier version of this essay and provided invaluable suggestions and criticism.

   1. *The Articles of Association of the Subscribers to the Brook Farm Institute of Agriculture and Education* gives evidence of an inequality in board and tuition: "the price of board and tuitions shall be $4.00 a week for boys, and $5.00 a week for girls over twelve years of age" (Frothingham 1882, 117).
   2. Amelia Russell writes of Mary Bullard, although not by name, of the Hutchinson family, and extensively of Biscaccianti (Russell 1878, 557, 465, 466).
   3. "Woman" is signed "W.N." See also "Painting and Sculpture" (*Dial* 2, no. 1 [July 1840]: 78–81) and letter on the Zoar, Ohio, community (122–29).
   4. Caroline Sturgis's poems appeared in the *Dial*, sometimes signed "Z" and at other times unsigned. For a list of the author's works, see Myerson (1980). For verification of authorship, see Myerson (1973).
   5. See also Jane Johnson Bernardete, "Abby Morton Díaz," in *Notable American Women* (James 1971, 471–73); in *The History of the Woman's Club Movement in America* (Croly 1898, 620–21); and in an unpublished manuscript, "The History of the Women's Educational and Industrial Union" (Donham 1955).

Works Cited

Codman, John Thomas [1894] 1971. *Brook Farm: Historic and Personal Memoirs.* Reprint. New York: AMS.

Cooke, George Willis. 1898. *John Sullivan Dwight. Brook-Farmer, Editor, and Critic of Music.* Boston: Small, Maynard.

Croly, Mrs. J. C. 1898. *The History of the Woman's Club Movement in America.* New York: Allen.

Curtis, Edith Roelker. 1961. *A Season in Utopia: The Story of Brook Farm.* New York: Nelson.

Díaz, Abby Morton. 1870. *The William Henry Letters.* Boston: Fields, Osgood.

———. 1874a. *Lucy Maria.* Boston: James R. Osgood.

———. 1874b. *The Schoolmaster's Trunk, Containing Papers on Home-Life in Tweenit.* Boston: James R. Osgood.

———. 1875. *A Domestic Problem: Work and Culture in the Household.* Boston: James R. Osgood.

———. 1893. *Only a Flock of Women.* Boston: D. Lothrop.

Donham, S. Agnes. 1955. The History of the Women's Educational and Industrial Union. WEIU: B-8. Manuscript. Schlesinger Library, Radcliffe College, Cambridge, Mass.

Dwight, Marianne. 1928. *Letters from Brook Farm, 1844–1847.* Edited by Amy L. Reed. Poughkeepsie, N.Y.: Vassar College.

Frothingham, O. B. 1882. *George Ripley.* Boston: Houghton Mifflin.

Fuller [Ossoli], Margaret. 1852. *Memoirs of Margaret Fuller Ossoli.* Edited by R. W. Emerson, W. H. Channing, and J. F. Clarke. Vol. 2. Boston: Phillips, Sampson.

Hawthorne, Nathaniel. 1907. *Love Letters of Nathaniel Hawthorne, 1841–1863.* Chicago: Society of the Defobs.

Hudspeth, Robert N., ed. 1983. *The Letters of Margaret Fuller.* Vol. 2. Ithaca, N.Y.: Cornell Univ. Press.

James, Edward T. ed. 1971. *Notable American Women, 1607–1950: A Biographical Dictionary.* Vol. 1. Boston: Belknap Press, Harvard Univ. Press.

Kirby, Georgiana Bruce. [1870] 1965. My First Visit to Brook Farm. *Overland Monthly* 5, no. 1 (July): 9–19. Reprint. New York: AMS.

———. 1871. Reminiscences of Brook Farm. *Old and New* 3, no. 4 (Apr.): 425–38; 4, no. 3 (Sept.): 347–58.

———. 1879. *Transmission: Or, Variation of Character through the Mother.* New York: S. R. Wells.

———. [1887] 1971. *Years of Experience: An Autobiographical Narrative.* Reprint. New York: AMS.

Kolmerten, Carol A. 1990. *Women in Utopia: The Ideology of Gender in the American Owenite Communities.* Bloomington: Indiana Univ. Press.

Myerson, Joel. 1973. An Annotated List of Contributions to the Boston *Dial. Studies in Bibliography* 26: 133–66.

———. 1980. *The New England Transcendentalists and the Dial.* Rutherford, N.J.: Fairleigh Dickinson Univ. Press.

Ripley, Sophia. [1840] 1961. Woman. *Dial* I:362–66. Reprint. New York: Russell & Russell.

Roosevelt, Theodore. 1913. *Theodore Roosevelt: An Autobiography.* New York: Scribner.

Rusk, Ralph L., ed. 1939. *The Letters of Ralph Waldo Emerson.* Vol. 2. New York: Columbia Univ. Press.

Russell, Amelia. 1878. Home Life of the Brook Farm Association. *Atlantic Monthly,* Oct., 458–66; Nov., 556–63.

Sedgwick, Ora Gannett. 1900. A Girl of Sixteen at Brook Farm. *Atlantic Monthly,* Mar., 394–404.

Swift, Carolyn, and Judith Steen, eds. 1987. *Georgiana, Feminist Reformer of the West: The Journal of Georgiana Bruce Kirby, 1852–1860.* Santa Cruz, Calif.: Santa Cruz Historical Trust.

Swift, Lindsay. 1900. *Brook Farm, Its Members, Scholars, and Visitors.* New York: Corinth.

5

Shaker Fancy Goods

Women's Work and Presentation of Self
in the Community Context in the Victorian Era

BEVERLY GORDON

IN TRYING TO PIECE TOGETHER the experience of the past, scholars look for primary sources of information, usually in the form of written documents, such as personal testimony, record books, and eyewitness accounts. Too often, they ignore another type of primary source, one that is rich with meaning, and frequently plentiful. I refer to extant objects, to things of a particular time and place. Objects are not just remnants of the past but living embodiments of it; they not only reflect the way that people felt and behaved in a given time but are part of those feelings and behavior. *Material culture* analysis—that is, analysis of that part of culture that takes material form—offers an additional research tool that, when combined with other forms of investigation, can stimulate new modes of perceiving and comprehending. Material culture study is based on the assumption that objects reflect the belief systems of the people who made and used them. These belief systems are encoded in the objects as cultural fingerprints that researchers can learn to read or decode through a contextual examination of physical characteristics, such as form, material, iconography, and circumstances of production (Ferguson 1977, 6; Schlereth 1982, 2–3).[1]

In this article I turn to objects of the past for information about the affective reality of the people who produced them. It examines similar items made by Shaker and non-Shaker women from approximately 1860 to 1915 and, through a comparative material culture analysis, considers differences between the culture of the women who lived and worked in a self-designated egalitarian community context and the culture of their counterparts who lived in more traditional nuclear families. I focus on fancy goods (fancy-

89

work)—decorative stitched items such as pincushions, penwipers, and sewing boxes, and I conclude that the fancywork of the two groups was significantly different, with the Shaker women projecting a more serious, confident sense of themselves and their place in the world than their non-Shaker counterparts.

The Shakers used the term *fancy goods* to describe the small items the sisters made in great numbers from about the time of the Civil War to World War I and beyond. These were largely personal and household accessories, including penwipers (blotters used to soak up excess ink from fountain pens) and sewing accoutrements; boxes to hold gloves, handkerchiefs, and other items; bureau cushions (decorative cushions used to hold hatpins); and fans. Most were made for sale to the "world's people." The fancy goods epithet was first used by the Believers (Shakers were members of The United Society of Believers in Christ's Second Appearing) to describe their own products in the 1860s, but the word *fancywork* had been in common use in the "world" for thirty to forty years (Johnson 1983).[2] A satisfactory definition of the term is not easy to find. Present-day popular dictionaries define *fancywork* simply as decorative or ornamental needlework. The *Oxford English Dictionary* defines it a little more broadly as "ornamental as opposed to plain work, especially in needlework, crochet and knitting" (1961, 4:62). Nineteenth-century usage of the term was more inclusive, incorporating not only sewn and stitched work but sculptural forms in shell, wax, molded leather, human hair, and a wealth of other materials. There was no clear point where plain work became ornamental (often, goods were expressly referred to as "useful *and* ornamental" [italics mine]), and few handwork forms by definition could not be fancywork.

As the broad scope of the term implies, *fancywork* was often an important part of the lives of worldly Victorian women. Fancywork departments appeared regularly by midcentury in women's magazines, and a plethora of instruction manuals appeared in the second half of the nineteenth century. Fancy fairs, where fancy items were sold for fundraising purposes, were ubiquitous and popular events, and women gave these items to one another as gifts or tokens of affection. Advertisements for fancywork supplies were common in newspapers throughout the country. The large number of surviving examples also poignantly indicates the former prevalence of fancywork production. Fancywork was seen as an appropriate activity for women: it was picturesque, light, and feminine (i.e., it was fancy and ornamental); but it was also productive (i.e., it was work and useful), and it resulted in objects that could add to the refinement of the home environment. Both the product and the pastime were domestic, removed from the world of commerce and industry. Fancywork embodied, in other words, the inherent limitations and contradictions of women's place in mainstream middle-class society (see Gordon 1988).

In the worldly context, fancywork production was generally a solitary activity. Women worked in their homes, alone, using odd available moments to complete their projects. They might occasionally bring projects along when they got together with other women, but the small size and precious nature of the items did not call for or encourage group cooperation. Each item was unique, and because it was made to embellish the home or to give to a friend or family member, it often carried sentimental, personal associations.

The meanings of fancy items and the circumstances of production were markedly different in a Shaker community. The sisters made some objects for themselves, and they too gave items to one another as tokens of affection, but for the most part these were goods, made as sale items for anonymous outsiders, and they functioned in a more public and anonymous context. Fancy goods production, furthermore, was from the outset largely a community or group endeavor and was conceived as an industry that was in fact a lifeline of economic support.

By the 1860s the Believers were finding it more cost effective to purchase many of the necessities they had formerly made themselves—they used outside blacksmiths and shoemakers, for example, and purchased much of their cloth and even some of their agricultural products. New money-making endeavors were called for. The effects of an increasingly industrialized society were compounded by a change in community demographics, moreover, as women were beginning to greatly outnumber men. Visitor Charles Nordhoff noted in 1875 that the ratio of women to men was roughly two to one (Nordhoff [1875] 1962, 181), and in some communities it was as high as three to one (Brewer 1986, 228–38). It was natural for the Believers to develop some of their women-identified activities into income-producing industries. Energies that had gone into more basic sewing and weaving took a new turn into fancy goods production, and the fancy goods trade became the single most important source of support for the Believers. The transition to women's industries occurred at different rates in different communities but was generally rapid. In Alfred, Maine, for example, not a single men's industry was left by the early 1870s (Johnson 1983).

The fancy goods trade emerged at the time it did, also, because of a new customer base. By the 1860s railroad lines had been extended to the vicinity of most of the northeastern Shaker villages, and there was a burgeoning tourist trade in areas such as Lebanon Springs, New York, and Poland Springs, Maine. The Believers found a ready market for their small fancy items, for worldly travelers bought them as souvenirs or reminders of their encounter with the Shakers. Fancy goods shops were established in nearly every community, and regular product lines were developed. Representative items were taken to resort areas and to events such as state fairs. Some communities followed an extensive summer resort circuit, taking the salespeople far from home. Individuals from Maine, for example, routinely took their goods to as far away as Cape May, New Jersey, and to the Massachusetts islands of Nantucket and Martha's Vineyard. Sales excursions fell into both the male and the female domains; individual predisposition rather than gender seems to have determined who did the actual selling (Johnson 1983). By the turn of the century some communities even took out patents on some of their products and published catalogues for the mail order trade.

Although some items were one of a kind, made by individual sisters, most followed standard prototypes and involved many people's labor. These were clearly perceived as women's industries, but available brethren helped out with specific tasks, usually those that fell in the general class of men's work, such as construction and woodwork. The group process and division of labor can be seen clearly in the case of poplar ware, that is, goods made with a unique fabric woven from strips of poplar wood. Poplar ware formed the backbone of the fancy goods trade in New England from 1860, when it was first developed, until well into the twentieth century. A series of eighteen steps was involved in its production. Brethren cut the trees from moist land on community property during the winter and brought the logs to the Shaker sawmill, where they cut and split the frozen wood. Sisters then shaved the pieces into paper-thin sheets, dried and straightened them, and slit them into strips. These were individually positioned in a fine cotton warp and woven in a variety of patterns on a narrow loom (Gordon 1980, 45–48, 216–23; McCool 1962). Considerable effort was involved in this process, and production demands were great. In the early years of the twentieth century in Sabbathday Lake, for example, each sister was expected to weave a yard of poplar cloth a day (Johnson 1983). Sisters worked together on many of the production tasks, and there were sometimes work bees to get specific jobs finished.

When the poplar cloth was removed from the loom it was used to cover boxes and containers of well over a hundred different types. These were invariably edged with white kid and were usually lined with satin. The final detailing of an object was usually the work of a single sister, and some individuals had distinctive finishing styles. It is unusual to find multiple examples that are identical in every respect. The objects combined the advantages of mass production, in other words, with the personal stamp of the individual.

5. Detail of poplar cloth woven ca. 1920 in Sabbathday Lake, Maine. The darker stripes are strips of sweetgrass and dyed straw, added as pattern accents. Patterns of this type were common to the Sabbathday Lake community and were particularly associated with an individual sister, Ada Cummings. Approximately fifteen strips of poplar are woven in each inch. *Courtesy of Beverly Gordon.*

On the surface they were similar to items made in the world–they took the form of the same types of pin trays, sewing cases, pincushions, and such that were illustrated in women's magazines and made in individual homes– but at the same time they were unique and represented an elaborate cooperative production process that could never have been accomplished in anything other than a community context.

In addition to clues about the diversity within uniformity possible in the group production process, there are other kinds of cultural information

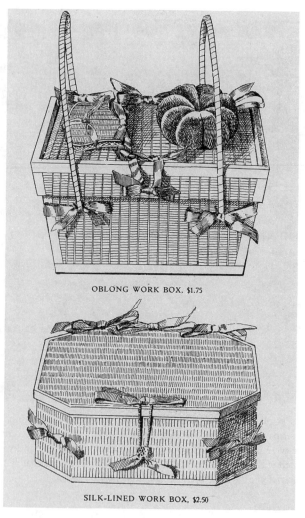

OBLONG WORK BOX, $1.75

SILK-LINED WORK BOX, $2.50

6. Illustration of two finished poplar boxes from "Products of Diligence and Intelligence," a catalog of fancy goods published in the New Lebanon Shaker Community in 1908. Poplar cloth was glued to the sides of precut cardboard boxes and edged with white kid. Workboxes were usually outfitted with other sewing accessories, such as the needle book and pincushion attached to the oblong example illustrated here. The ribbons on the surface of the box are not only decorative but functional; each serves as a clasp or hinge or attaches miscellaneous accoutrements to the inside. *Courtesy of Beverly Gordon.*

embedded in extant fancywork objects. A comparative examination of the body of Shaker and non-Shaker fancywork indicates differences in many dimensions.

It is instructive, for example, to compare the objects that were and were not made in each context. Because both Shaker and non-Shaker fancy items were domestic objects, we can rightly surmise that both Shaker and non-Shaker women were involved with domestic tasks. However, some popular mainstream fancy items were not made in the Shaker communities. Most notably, there were no purely ornamental or functionless items in the Shaker repertoire. Worldly women spent long hours fashioning bouquets or wreaths of wax or colored wool, for example, which they later mounted in picture frames or under glass domes. Such items were not made by the Shakers.[3] Although they were among the most popular mainstream fancy items, tidies, doilies, antimacassars, or other furniture covers, which were more decorative than functional and would have cluttered rather than streamlined the environment, were also generally eschewed by the sisters. (A tidy was a small decorative furniture cover usually placed on the arm of an upholstered chair. A doily might look similar but was made to go on a table. An antimacassar was placed on the back of an upholstered chair or sofa to absorb oily substances like the popular Macassar hair pomade.) "Wall pockets," common in the "world" as receptacles for everything from newspapers to hair clippings, were not standard Shaker goods, although some examples appear in photographs. Wall pockets were also largely decorative, but they could keep things tidy and thus did make sense in a Shaker context.

The sisters avoided other items that were an anathema to their way of life. Calling cards, which middle-class Victorian women carried and presented when they went visiting, were well represented in mainstream fancywork: there were hundreds of designs in women's magazines and manuals for calling card cases and receivers, and plentiful extant examples can be found in a variety of materials and patterns. Shaker women did not go visiting in the same manner, of course, and it would have been against their philosophical and religious framework to represent themselves with such personal or individual markers. Although they might have made them for their customers, no Shaker calling card cases have been found. Similarly, embroidered smoking caps and slippers, made for men's relaxation and popular in the "world" in the 1860s and 1870s, were too self-indulgent and showy to conform to the Shaker ideal and were never produced.

We also see materials that were common in worldly fancywork but nonexistent in Shaker fancy goods. Novel and ephemeral materials such as fish and pinecone scales stirred the Victorian imagination, and there were long features in the women's magazines with instructions for "skeletonizing"

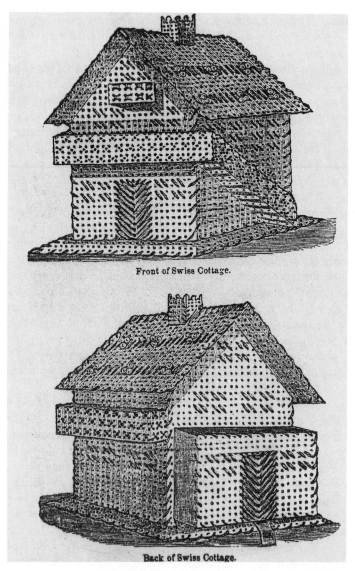

Front of Swiss Cottage.

Back of Swiss Cottage.

7. Illustration from the "Work" section of *Godey's Lady's Book,* May 1867, showing a design for a miniature Swiss cottage. The object was to be made of perforated cardboard and decorated with beads, ribbon, and silk thread. Ostensibly, it was designed to "hold pins, pens or wafers," but it would have been too small and fragile to function in this manner. Extant fancywork items of this kind indicate no signs of use. *Courtesy of Beverly Gordon.*

leaves and making jewelry or sculpted forms out of human hair. Perforated paperboard, a thin material with holes punched at regular intervals, was also popular for different kinds of fancies, as were eggshell and dried flowers, grasses and mosses. The Believers were exposed to these materials and patterns, and as their creative use of poplar wood makes clear, they were inventive with what they fabricated, but they did not incorporate ephemeral, short-lived and essentially faddish materials into their work. When they used a fragile material like poplar cloth, they were certain to mount or secure it so it would wear well.

Both Shaker and non-Shaker fancy goods were often made with rich fabrics, including silk and velvet. In both cases the objects were "well dressed"–they were honored with a kind of finery that indicated they were treasured and enjoyed. Such materials were common to the wardrobes of both groups of women; although the Shakers did not wear silk or velvet dresses, they did wear silk kerchiefs and other silk accessories in the Victorian period and applied a limited amount of velvet trim to their bonnets and bodice coverings. In the Shaker pieces, then, the rich fabrics were not foreign or external but were part of the contextual environment. Worldly fancywork was often further embellished with lace and elaborate ruching, but this was not part of the Shaker fancy goods vocabulary. A small amount of lace trim was incorporated in the sisters' clothing in the late nineteenth century, but it was minimal. Even in terms of technique, lacework applications (including crochet) were not significant in Shaker fancywork until the turn of the century, when they remained the idiosyncratic work of individual sisters rather than standard products that formed the group identity of any given community.

The argument that the sisters' fancy goods were in some senses an extension or reflection of their clothing and their sense of themselves is supported by other characteristics. The color palette of Shaker goods was somewhat unique. Bright, rich colors were evident on some items, such as paper-covered boxes made in the 1870s (Johnson 1986, 1).(which are especially well represented in the Sabbathday Lake collection), but the most consistently used colors were gentle but cheerful hues such as pink, mauve, and light blue. (Poplar ware was always a light beige, trimmed with white and colored cloth accents.) Worldly fancywork colors were trendy. During the 1880s, for example, black silk and velvet, seen on both mainstream garments and on the popular "crazy quilts" of the day, were also prevalent on small fancy items such as needle cases and penwipers. By the late 1890s, on the other hand, fancy items were made from the same kind of white gauzy fabrics seen on the latest dresses. Shaker fancywork rarely incorporated either black colors or white or sheer materials; restrained but upbeat colors were used repeatedly, despite the vicissitudes of outside fashion.

Fancy objects made in the Shaker community and the worldly household also communicated a different sense of self through contrasting form and iconography. Shaker fancywork was straightforward; items were what they appeared to be in every instance. Much mainstream fancywork, on the other hand, was a tour de force; it consisted of one item masquerading or pretending to be another, or one material appearing to be another. A tape measure dispenser came in the form of a coffeemill; a pincushion appeared as a bellows or a shoe or a fish; penwipers were made to look like sheafs of wheat, pond lilies, or animals. Feathers were worked to look like fur; bulrush pith was worked to look like ivory; wool was made to look like moss (the masquerade was taken so far that the ends were singed slightly to emulate the brown tips of the natural variety); coral was simulated by cotton cord set in tinted wax (see for example Roche 1861; Urbino 1860; Work Section 1868, 1870). The blotting function of Shaker penwipers was always apparent. No Shaker fancy goods appeared in the form of household tools or manufactured products such as bellows or coffeemills, and none came in disguise, seeming to be made of a more grandiose or curious material.

One of the ways of understanding the distinction between Shaker and non-Shaker products is to say that worldly fancywork was self-consciously cute; it appealed to the sentimental and had a childish quality. Many items looked like toys. Some penwipers appeared to be stuffed animals (a toy mouse was mounted on a bed of cloth leaves), and others looked like doll accessories, such as miniature caps or parasols. Actual dolls or doll parts were even incorporated into some items; instructions for making "little companions" (sewing cases) called for breaking off the legs or heads of dolls and incorporating the pieces into the finished product (Weaver 1865a, b). Like the bellows mentioned earlier, objects were miniaturized, and in the process tamed and trivialized. A four-inch-high cottage, made of perforated paper and suggested in *Godey's Lady's Book* in April 1867 as a receptacle for wafers or pins, is a case in point (see Gordon 1988, 55–58). It was decorated with steel beads to create the effect of "little stones," and it had a "little balcony." A house was in fact reduced to a "little box." The cottage and many other items like it were referred to in the women's press as "trifles," "frivolities," and even "airy nothings." They were, literally, made light of. Worldly women could have made fancywork with different forms and materials and different iconographic imagery. They could have referred to their own work in different terms. Because they chose what they did, we can state that they presented themselves as frivolous, nonserious, almost childlike people.

A different image emerges from Shaker fancy goods. Miniaturization was not operative in Shaker work in the nineteenth century, and no little

8. Many suggestions or designs for fancy objects printed in women's magazines bore Mrs. Jane Weaver's name. "Little Companions" like this one from *Peterson's Magazine,* January 1865, were to be made of dolls (or doll parts) and were dressed and accessorized. The Shaker sisters dressed dolls also, but they outfitted them as fellow sisters rather than as diminutive friends. They did not make them more amusing by adding details like the pincushion hat worn by the illustrated figure. *Courtesy of Beverly Gordon.*

cottages or companions were produced. One standard penwiper form of a later era incorporated a doll, but this was not a broken toy. A small porcelain figure was procured especially for the product, and its ink-absorbing surface, the skirt, was not hidden or disguised. Some toys were made by the Shakers, but not on a production basis, and they were intended to be given to children, not to adults.

Without the self-conscious miniaturization and masquerade, Shaker fancy goods gave the impression of seriousness and maturity. The Believers spoke about their work, moreover, in different terms. Far from being airy trifles, these objects were called "products of diligence and intelligence"– the actual name of a fancywork catalogue published in New Lebanon in 1908. The only childish fancy items seen in the Shaker repertoire were made later in the twentieth century and were unique items made according to individual whim. The standard items, the ones the sisters used to present themselves most publicly, were always confidently "intelligent" and serene.

The sisters also proclaimed their sense of self-worth in their fancy goods through iconographic references to themselves. Female dolls dressed in Shaker outfits were sold in Shaker shops and were accurate in all details–the construction of their dresses and bonnets and the arrangement of their undergarments were true to life, and they wore garments made from the same fabric as the sisters' own. The dolls were themselves of high quality, made of the best china, and typically imported. Customers who could not afford or did not want completely dressed dolls could also purchase individual, meticulously constructed bonnets that could help transform any doll into a Shaker for an afternoon. An analysis of the sales records of the fancy goods shop in the Enfield, Connecticut, community in 1910 indicates that doll bonnets were the single most popular handmade item with worldly customers (Braisted 1908–11).

The sisters used their own names to advertise their community products. Dorothy cloaks, which were sold through the fancy goods stores and mail order catalogues, were named after a particular sister, Eldress Dorothy Durgin of Canterbury, New Hampshire, who patented the design. A range of goods was marketed under the Hart and Shepard label in the same community. The corporate marker was taken from the names of two sisters, Emeline Hart and Lucy Ann Shepard. The fact that the sisters made and sold items that represented them and even carried their names reflects a strong sense of self and a great communal pride. The objects were sent out as representatives or ambassadors into the world at large; they were not just items made by the sisters but were symbols of them. They stood for and reinforced Shaker separateness or distinctness and were markers of the Believers' unique outsider-group status in the larger society.

In sum, a different picture of Shaker and mainstream Victorian women emerges through a material culture study–an analysis of the fancy work produced in their different cultural contexts. Both groups of women were identified with domestic tasks and the domestic sphere, and both spent time producing similar small objects that could be used within that sphere. The

9. Sister Martha Burger is shown tending the fancy goods store in New Lebanon, New York, ca. 1900. Both standard and more idiosyncratic items are visible in this photograph. Standard products include the wool dusters that are suspended from the ceiling; cushion/spool holders *(center front);* miniature fancy baskets *(on the table);* balls of wax *(behind spools, center front);* and a dressed doll *(rear of table).* Crocheted items are tacked to the rear wall. *Courtesy of New York State Museum, Albany, New York.*

production process might be rewarding in both cases, but it differed, and the meanings of the objects differed as well.

Worldly women did fancywork on a haphazard basis, more or less according to personal whim. Such activity was culturally approved, as it filled idle moments and resulted in objects that helped make the house a tasteful and thus ennobling environment but never challenged the assumption that serious (as opposed to fancy) work took place in the outside or public sphere. The objects were decorative accessories rather than functional necessities and reflected women's roles as accessories to, rather than perpetrators of, life's major dramas. The objects were personally meaningful to the women who made them and were charged with sentiment, but they were on the whole fashioned to appear cloying and sweet, childish, frivolous, and even escapist.

Shaker women, in contrast, did not do fancywork at all; rather, they made fancy goods. The goods were made on a regular basis; indeed, the sisters were expected to make them, and the bulk of their time was often involved in their production. The goods were understood to be the product of serious labor—the Shakers did not make a distinction between the public and private sphere so much as they made a distinction between the Believers' and non-Believers' spheres, and by definition, all Believers worked. Consequently, Shaker fancy items were perceived as products of labor, as serious objects. They were fashioned to be functional, straightforward, and attractive, but they were always well—even lovingly—made. They did not appear cute or childish, but cheerful and pleasing. They were valued not just for their role in the economic well-being of the group but for themselves, not sentimentally or individually so much as collectively, as products of the group of women who made them. They were simultaneously like the objects of the broader society and different from them, and they reflected the sisters' position as people who were part of the broader society and yet unique within it.

The image that emerges is one of strength and pride. The Shaker women turned what was in another context a peripheral activity into a profitable industry and supported themselves and their brethren through their communal effort. They had removed themselves from the "world" in order to form a more perfect society, built on a community of faith where men and women were equal partners, and they believed in what they were doing and in the rightness of their vision. They sent their fancy goods, their products, out to the "world" as symbolic ambassadors or markers of themselves and their lifestyle. These were products of a confident group of women, we must conclude, a group with diligence, intelligence, and integrity.

Notes

I am grateful to the National Endowment for the Humanities for a 1988 Travel to Collections Grant which enabled me to revisit major Shaker museums.

1. The term *material culture* refers both to the subject matter of the study, material, and to its purpose, the understanding of culture (Schlereth 1982, 3). Material culture methodology is evolving, but the now almost classic formulation was posited by Fleming (1974).

2. Shaker scholars may be familiar with the discussion of "fancy articles" in the Millennial Laws of 1821; see Gordon (1980, 204). However, the *fancy goods* term was used in a somewhat different context by the Civil War period, more as a descriptor for a class of goods than as a judgment about the degree of ornamentation of particular objects.

3. One exception is in the Shaker Museum in Old Chatham, New York. A framed memorial to Eldress Lizzie Downing (d. 1903) of South Union, Kentucky, consists of a wreath of artificial flowers mounted around her photograph. This is an anomaly, but the two Kentucky communities retained their agricultural character long after those in the northeast and never had the same kind of fancy goods industry.

Works Cited

Braisted, Alice. 1908–11. *Record Book.* Edward Deming Andrews Memorial Shaker Collection, Henry Francis duPont Winterthur Museum, Winterthur, Del., 885, 248.

Brewer, Priscilla J. 1986. *Shaker Communities, Shaker Lives.* Hanover, N.H.: Univ. Press of New England.

Ferguson, Leland. 1977. *Historical Archeology and the Importance of Material Things.* Columbia, S.C.: Society for Historical Archeology.

Fleming, E. McClung. 1974. Artifact Study: A Proposed Model. *Winterthur Portfolio* 9, no. 1: 153–61.

Gordon, Beverly. 1980. *Shaker Textile Arts.* Hanover, N.H.: Univ. Press of New England.

———. 1988. Victorian Fancywork in the American Home: Fantasy and Accommodation. In *Making the American Home: Women and Domestic Material Culture, 1840–1940,* ed. M. F. Motz and P. Browne, 48–68. Bowling Green, Ohio: Bowling Green State Univ. Popular Press.

Johnson, Theodore E. 1983, July. Tasty and Ornamental: The Shaker Fancy Goods Trade. Lecture at Shaker Collecting Seminar offered by Shakertown, Pleasant Hill, Ky. Audiotape in possession of author.

———. 1986. *Ingenious and Useful: Shaker Sisters' Communal Industries, 1860–1900.* Poland Spring, Maine.: Shakers, Sabbathday Lake.

McCool, Sister Elsie. 1962. Shaker Woven Poplar Work. *Shaker Quarterly* 2, no. 2 (Summer): 3–5.

Nordhoff, Charles. [1875] 1962. *The Communistic Societies of the United States.* Reprint. New York: Hillary House.

Products of Diligence and Intelligence. 1908. Catalogue. New Lebanon, N.Y.

Records Kept by Order of the Church. 1856–71. Church Family, Mount Lebanon, N.Y. Emma King Library, Shaker Museum, Old Chatham, N.Y., 10, 342.

Roche, Mlle. 1861. Coral Case for Flowers. *Peterson's Magazine* 39, no. 6 (June): 498.

Schlereth, Thomas J., ed. 1982. *Material Culture Studies in America.* Nashville, Tenn.: American Association of State and Local History.

Urbino, Levina. 1860. *Art Recreations.* Boston: J. E. Tiltson.

Weaver, Jane. 1865a. Doll Pincushion. *Peterson's Magazine* 48, no. 3 (Sept.): 209.

———. 1865b. The Little Companion. *Peterson's Magazine* 47, no. 1 (Jan.): 79.

Work Section. 1860a *Godey's Lady's Book* 59 (Feb.).

———. 1860b. *Godey's Lady's Book* 60 (July).

———. 1867. *Godey's Lady's Book* 74 (Apr.).

———. 1868. *Godey's Lady's Book* 77 (Dec.).

———. 1870. *Godey's Lady's Book* 80 (Jan.).

6

"In the Bonds of True Love and Friendship"

Some Meanings of "Gospel Affection" and
"Gospel Union" in Shaker Sisters' Letters and Poems

ROSEMARY D. GOODEN

WHEN I BEGAN RESEARCHING the Shaker manuscript collection in the Western Reserve Historical Society, I was struck by the repetition and use of two phrases, "gospel affection" and "gospel union," in Shaker journals, diaries, and letters. Other words and phrases—"little," "union," "bonds of love and union," "one of Mother's little children," and various couplings of "gospel"—also appeared frequently. I concluded from my preliminary examination of Shaker sisters' writings in particular that both the experience and the written expression of religious devotion conveyed in the terms "gospel affection" and "gospel union" were central to Believers' lives (Shakers is the familiar name given members of the United Society of Believers in Christ's Second Appearing). For Shaker writers, gospel affection and gospel union denote the expression of spiritual love for Mother Ann Lee, the sect's founder, affection and love for other Believers, and loyalty to the Shaker way, which leads to union with other Believers and Mother Ann.

In this essay I focus on friendship and sisterhood among sisters in the Society of Believers by examining sisters' letters and acrostic poems to show how sisters expressed gospel affection to one another, how they maintained gospel union, and how affection and union were institutionalized in writing and sometimes in the exchange of gifts or "tokens of love and union."

The social experiences of eighteenth and nineteenth-century American women have been extensively documented in studies of female bonding (Cott 1977), the feminization of American culture (Douglas 1977), and female friendship (Smith-Rosenberg 1975). In analyzing women's private writings as historical evidence, especially their letters, diaries, and journals, scholars

104

10. "A Special Visit," ca. 1915, from a photo postcard. *Seated:* Laura Bailey (Sabbathday Lake, Maine); *standing, left to right:* Jessie Evans (Canterbury, New Hampshire), Myra Green (Canterbury, New Hampshire), and Alice Smith (Hancock, Massachusetts). The four Shaker sisters were enjoying a visit together at the Sabbathday Lake community. *Courtesy of Richard Brooker Collection.*

have made us aware of both the prevalence and the significance of friendship and love between women and the importance of correspondence in nurturing and sustaining such friendships. Moreover, sisterhood, both in theory
and practice, was and continues to be shared by most women in America,
although the expression of sisterhood and its attendant rituals have varied
over time.

Sisterhood was a vital aspect of Shaker women's lives, from youth through
old age. Sisters formed intimate, affectionate relationships with one another
despite the society's warning against the formation of "special" friendships.
Such friendships did exist, not just among eldresses where close friendships
were expected and accepted but also among the rank-and-file sisters, and
these relationships endured throughout life. Neither physical separation nor,
ultimately, death diminished sisterhood in the Society of Believers. The symbolic presence of Mother Ann unified sisters and was essential to maintaining the bonds of affection and union.

Among sisters there existed a "female world of love and ritual" that excluded brethren.[1] Although this was a result in part of the structure of Shaker
society and its tenets, especially separation of the sexes and celibacy, this
female world of love and ritual among sisters was also a continuation and
expansion of the social experiences of women who joined the Society of
Believers; such relationships were the norm in American culture in the nineteenth century. A primary component of the Shaker female world of love
and ritual was the exchanging of symbolic and tangible gifts, especially in
letters and poems. Often in sisters' letters, gospel affection is expressed in
poems sent as tokens of love and accompanied, sometimes, by a gift of a
silk kerchief, a bottle of wintergreen oil, or something to be shared with
others—a new song or a pattern for making a hat or a dress.

The written expression of affection and union is illustrated most vividly
in letters exchanged among sisters. The strength of bonds is indicated by
the sheer number of letters sisters wrote to one another. When one reads
their letters, one is impressed by the sense of sorority and community between female Shakers. Shaker sisterhood, however, was unique, informed
by particular values, beliefs, and most importantly, a distinctive theology:
Ann Lee claimed to be the female parent or spiritual mother of the godhead, and also the fulfillment of the Second Advent of Christ in spirit form.

Like New England women who wrote diaries between 1780 and 1830,
the impetus for Shaker women's writing letters was religious and reflected
the Calvinist tradition of self-examination and exposure of one's entire being to God. As Robley Whitson has noted, during the eighteenth century
travel and *travail* were used interchangeably in American culture. Believers
also used these words, along with *labor,* to express spiritual growth and prog-

11. Catharine Van Houten (1817–1896) and Phebe Van Houten (1817–1895), members of the North family, Mount Lebanon, New York. This photograph of the Van Houten twins, taken when they were seventy years old, was clearly meant to illustrate their special relationship, linked by a shared birth as well as by Shaker sisterhood. The twins were brought to the Shakers when they were young. *Courtesy of Richard Brooker Collection.*

ress toward perfection. Whitson summarizes the meaning of "travel in the gospel":

> To travel in the Gospel, thus embraced three levels of meaning: movement from one locus to another, arduous and sometimes painful labor, and the labor of childbirth. Going to the "new place" and bringing forth "new Life" meant a commitment to hard work. . . . Travel implies both the individual person and the community of persons. Each one labors to progress into the fullness of the gifts of life in Christ, and so all together are committed to progression. (Whitson 1983, 86–87)

Salutations and closings, basic components of any letter, assume special significance in sisters' letters. The salutation in most letters written by Shakers, both male and female, indicates devotion and affection for the person or group addressed. Such greetings as "Beloved and respected Elder Benjamin & Company," "Much Respected and well beloved," "Beloved Eldress Lydia," "Dearly Beloved brethren and sisters," and "Respected Mother" are common. The language of these salutations not only indicates that Believers' relationships were deeply affectionate and loving but also confirms the presence of a hierarchy and reflects Believers' fidelity to specific Shaker tenets, such as gospel union and gospel affection. This devotion is usually affirmed in the first paragraph of a letter.

The language of these salutations and greetings of the first paragraph, therefore, renews the covenant or union between members while evoking the symbolic presence of Mother Ann, the source of gospel affection and gospel union.

The closing in Shaker correspondence likewise expresses feelings of devotion and affection. The desire to preserve community or union is expressed, for example, in such closings as, "So farewell from the pen of your little sister Molly" and "Accept this as a token of my love." Although the recipient of her letter is not a Shaker but a relative of a Shaker, Eldress Nancy Moore closes her letter to Jane Thatcher with a closing found in many letters by Shaker sisters to other women: "In the bonds of love and true friendship I close" (Moore 1875).

Eunice Bathrick's purpose for writing "Letters to My Gospel Companions in Zion's Domain" is to express "gospel affections" to old friends and to renew her bond with sisters in the Society of Believers she had met fifty years earlier. In an 1870 letter to Harriet Hastings, for example, Bathrick writes: "Having so good an opportunity to scribble a few lines to you, I feel to embrace it to renew the convenant of love which subsists between Mother's dear children individually and collectively" (Bathrick 1870–1871).

Bathrick wrote during a time of crisis at her home community, Harvard, Massachusetts. She sought not only to cement bonds with other Believers but also to encourage the sisters, especially the younger sisters, who might read these letters to persevere in their travel in the gospel. Bathrick uses familiar Shaker expressions and images to convey her love for her sisters and to reaffirm her belief in Shakerism. While the central theme of her letters is the expression of feelings of love and devotion among sisters, a secondary yet closely related theme concerns the power of a particular Shaker vocabulary to provide for the Believer a sense of continuity with the past and an escape from the trying circumstances of the present.

Although letters were effective substitutes for personal visits, Eunice Bathrick hoped to see her family of cherished sisters. Sometimes, however, her letters conveyed a sense of isolation. For example, in a letter to Sister Adah in February 1871, Bathrick writes: "I feel quite lonesome, and to suppress this feeling I resort to my pen, knowing that by writing to some one of your blessed number I shall bring you all near, even as I saw your lovely faces when blessed with the privilege of visiting you in your sacred home." Bathrick reaffirms her relationship not only with the group of Believers in Sister Adah's home but also with Sister Adah personally. Her letter assumes a tone of deep affection: "Time nor space cannot diminish this treasure of love you have won. The love of Believers never can grow cold, because they are cemented together in bonds of gospel union which cannot be severed."

Although sisters' letters reveal unequivocally the presence and persistence of intimate, loving relationships, one has to consider the question of hidden conflict. What is concealed in these writings is as important as what is revealed. The expression of interpersonal conflict and its resolution, for example, is patently omitted from the sources consulted. The written expression of negative feelings was evidently frowned upon, but it is reasonable to assume that sisters did experience anger, fear, loneliness, indeed the whole range of human emotions, in addition to the love and sense of serenity that give the basic tone to their letters. Moreover, since Believers were aware of the didactic purpose of their writings, it is quite possible that the darker side of communal living was purposely omitted.

Like other American women, sisters wrote not only letters but poems to and about one another for many occasions, including birthdays, holidays, and memorial services. Poems were written, for example, as tributes to particular sisters and presented as birthday gifts. Most importantly, sisters wrote poems to express devotion to Mother Ann and affection to each other. Poems as gifts of love and affection were included in letters sisters wrote to one another.

The beginning of a tradition among Shaker sisters for writing acrostic poems is difficult to document. The acrostic poem, however, appears to have been a popular form among nineteenth-century American women and was apparently suitable for women of varying skills, whether rudimentary versifiers or more sophisticated poets. The acrostics in this discussion are part of a collection of fifty-two poems, forty-seven of which are acrostics, presumably written and compiled by Maria Lyman, whose name appears on the frontispiece (Lyman n.d.). Of the forty-seven acrostics, only four are about brethren. The rest are about sisters, with one acrostic to Mother Ann Lee. It appears that all the subjects belonged to the same Shaker family, and the four brethren who are the subjects of the poems comprise the family's ministry–two elders and two deacons. Additional poems in the collection include "Composed on the Death of Eldress Agnes Munsell," "A Christmas Hymn," and short verses.

These poems express affection and honor not only for the ministry and Mother Ann, but for the common sisters as well. The expression of gospel affection in these poems is as varied as the individual sisters of whom they speak.

Although these poems are idiosyncratic and highly personal, a central purpose unifies their content: to express gospel love or affection to the subject of the poem. The enumeration of the sisters' virtues or exemplary characteristics is important for future Believers who may read the poems, which might also be described as testimonials. Affirmation of union with other Believers who display these virtues and whose lives demonstrate fidelity to the Shaker way is also expressed.

The acrostics also are significant for what they reveal about the piety of common sisters and eldresses in a particular family and their relationships with one another. The poems idealize sisters as happy, obedient (in an almost childlike way), virtuous women whose relationships with each other were basically peaceful, harmonious and, most importantly, loving. The sisters in these poems are regarded as model sisters who deserve praise and honor for their exemplary lives. They possess the personal and spiritual attributes valued most by the Society of Believers: faithfulness, zeal, service, diligence, obedience, patience, joy, peace, and love in both temporal and spiritual matters. The possession and cultivation of such qualities make a sister a model of piety and, therefore, the recipient of what appear to be effusive displays of affection and esteem from other sisters. These outstanding sisters, then, have union (or unity) with other Believers who demonstrate these qualities. Such exemplary piety, which indicates fidelity to the Shaker way and, consequently, visible progress toward perfection, also pleases "Mother." "Mother" refers not only to Mother Ann but also to Mother Lucy Wright, her immediate successor. The term is also used as a title of address for eldresses who were regarded as spiritual mothers. For example, Eldresses Hannah Kendall and Anna White were also called "Mother." Sometimes spiritual motherhood is indicated by the phrase "Mother of Israel."[2]

Lyman's "Acrostic on Esther Markham" demonstrates the basic vocabulary, structure, tone, and diction characteristic of the acrostics in this collection and is representative in its expression of gospel affection:

E sther is certainly sure of salvation
S ince she always keeps in a low humble station
T rials nor crosses don't turn her aside
H ere she remains adorned like a bride
E very such soul to Heaven will go
R ight to their Mother when they leave here below. (Lyman n.d.a.)

Esther Markham, described as a faithful Believer since youth, has demonstrated exemplary mercy, truth, hard work, and faithfulness, qualities highly valued by the Society:

M ercy and truth hath here met together
A nd righteousness too, we behold in our sister, who
R uns at the call of the young and the old
K eeps jogging along through hot and through cold
H alf of her talents I can't here display
A dapted they are to the work of the day.
M any do know this nought but the truth
S ince she has proved faithful in age and in youth. (Lyman n.d.a.)

The centrality of Mother Ann as a symbol of devotion among Believers is indicated in this collection by Lyman's inclusion of a poem in her honor, "Acrostic on Mother Ann Lee." This poem epitomizes the expression of gospel affection in its use of particular Shaker imagery, symbols, and vocabulary to express love and adoration as well as the pledge of faithfulness to the Shaker way. An important Shaker symbol, the golden chain, is also mentioned: "And since I am encircled round by this pure gold chain / No evil can my peace destroy while steadfast I remain." A chain was symbolic of union and strength; a golden chain expressed the "heavenly sphere." The poem additionally reflects how Believers, particularly the sisters in this family, perceived themselves in relation to Mother Ann, their spiritual mother. Sisters apparently felt toward Mother Ann as one would toward one's natural or birth mother; they looked to her for guidance, love, and a close, nurturing, emotional relationship in a mystical union. They also viewed themselves as one of "Mother's little children" because they were steadfast in obeying "her gospel." "Mother's love," moreover, was vital to their existence as Shakers:

M y blessed Mother I do love, her gospel I adore,
O may I meet with her above when time with me is o'er
T o me it is of great worth, her blessing here to feel.
H ow can I but my thanks express, my joy I can't reveal
E ach day I will obedient be, her name I'll ever praise,
R ejoice that I am in the ark, yea here I'll spend my days.
A nd since I am encircled round by this pure golden chain
N o evil can my peace destroy while steadfast I remain.
N or do I fear to risk my all, with Mother for my guide,
L eading me on to perfect bliss, in her I can confide
E ternal ages may roll round, by faith I'll firmly stand
E ach soul will yet acknowledge this to be the gospel plan. (Lyman n.d.b.)

The written expression of gospel affection and gospel union, especially in sisters' letters and poetry, and the exchanging of gifts, both symbolic and tangible, to express such devotion were of paramount importance in sisters' lives. Shaker Sisters developed a particular vocabulary, distinctive genres, and adapted conventional literary forms, such as the acrostic poem, for their particular use. Along with exemplifying meanings of affection and union, sisters' writings shed some light on their literary output as well as on the literary sisterhood that nurtured and sustained such creativity. Also, sisters' writings, especially their poems, provide some insights into their inner lives and feelings. Cheryl Walker has suggested that "poems are one great untapped source of American women's history. They are cultural documents rich with information about women's psyches and women's lives" (Walker 1982, 2). Shaker sisters' poems reveal a great deal about their temporal and spiritual concerns, their sense of self, and their bonds of affection and union with other women.

Their writings, especially poems, essays, and more public writings, provided a creative outlet for Shaker sisters and apparently were considered to be as vital to the community as other creative and economic enterprises such as making palm-leaf bonnets or manufacturing and producing silk. Finally, I would suggest that Shaker women's writings ought to be viewed as part of a larger body of writing concerned with delineating women's history and women's responses to a variety of religious and social experiences. Our understanding of American women's history will be more complete if we look at the writings of women both within and outside the mainstream of American culture.

Notes

1. I am using Carroll Smith-Rosenberg's term in the broadest sense to describe relationships among sisters. I am not suggesting that sisters' relationships were identical to those of the women Smith-Rosenberg has studied.

2. The phrase derives from the Old Testament Book of Judges. "The peasantry ceased in Israel, they ceased until you arose, Deborah, arose as a mother in Israel" (Judg. 5:7).

Works Cited

Abbreviation

WRHS Wallace Cathcart Shaker Manuscript Collection. Western Reserve Historical Society, Cleveland, Ohio.

Bathrick, Eunice. 1870. Letter to Harriet Hastings. September WRHS IV: B 19.
———. 1870–71. Letters to My Gospel Companions in Zion's Domain, WRHS IV:B 2.
———. 1871. Letter to Sister Adah. Feb. WRHS IV:B 2.
Bauman, Richard. 1983. *Let Your Words Be Few.* Cambridge: Cambridge Univ. Press.
Cott, Nancy F. 1977. *The Bonds of Womanhood: "Woman's Sphere" in New England, 1780–1835.* New Haven: Yale Univ. Press.
Douglas, Ann. 1977. *The Feminization of American Culture.* New York: Knopf.
Gooden, Rosemary D. 1987. The Language of Devotion: Gospel Affection and Gospel Union in the Writings of Shaker Sisters. Ph.D. diss., Univ. of Michigan.
Lyman, Maria. n.d.a. Acrostic on Esther Markham. WRHS X:A 1.
———. n.d.b. Acrostic on Mother Ann Lee. WRHS X:A 1.
Moore, Nancy E. 1875. Letter to Jane Thatcher. Jan. 31. WRHS IV:B 21.
Smith-Rosenberg, Carroll. 1975. The Female World of Love and Ritual: Relations Between Women in the Nineteenth Century. *Signs: A Journal of Women in Culture and Society* 1 (Autumn): 1–29.
Walker, Cheryl. 1982. *The Nightingale's Burden: Women Poets and American Culture Before 1900.* Bloomington: Indiana Univ. Press.
Whitson, Robley Edward, ed. 1983. *The Shakers: Two Centuries of Spiritual Reflection.* New York: Paulist.

PART THREE

Women and Structures
of Leadership in Community

Introduction

THREE ARTICLES IN THIS SECTION examine patterns of female leadership and authority in community. The first two articles discuss the Shakers and the degree of gender equality they practiced during their long history. The focus of evidence presented, however, differs in the two treatments. Nickless and Nickless emphasize the influence on the Shakers of nineteenth-century communitarian thinking, especially after radical reformers (for example, Owenites) joined the Society of Believers and began publishing their views on gender equality in the society's periodical, *The Shaker*. Nickless and Nickless also take a critical look at the business and accounting practices of the Shaker communities, illustrating the unequal valuation of men's and women's work and the disparate business responsibilities of male and female officeholders. Brewer, on the other hand, places her analysis within the context of the overall decline in Shaker membership and the consequent increase in gender imbalances, which she believes led to internal struggles within the society and motivated female members to try to augment their spiritual and temporal authority. Her account also provides a spicier and less saintly version of Shakers' behaviors—both male and female—than do many scholarly accounts. Nevertheless, both articles conclude that gender equality was never realized or perhaps even desired among the Shakers.

Basic information about the Shakers can be found in the introduction to part 2. Additional recommended sources are Jean Humez, ed., *Gifts of Power: The Writings of Rebecca Jackson, Black Visionary, Shaker Eldress* (1981), and Marjorie Procter-Smith, *Women in Shaker Community and Worship: A Feminist Analysis of the Uses of Religious Symbolism* (1985).

The third article in this section explores the role of female authority in Catholic sisterhoods in the United States. Mary J. Oates delineates the struggle of the female heads of convents to retain their authority. The male hierarchy of the Catholic church frequently attempted to diffuse female leadership of convents, thus circumventing traditional female power within the church. The two Catholic sisterhoods mentioned most often in this ar-

117

ticle are typical of hundreds of communities in their growth and the challenges they faced to their female leadership. Sisters of St. Joseph originated in France in 1650, making their first U.S. establishment in St. Louis in 1836. Sisters of Notre Dame de Namur, founded in France in 1804, sent pioneer sisters to Cincinnati in 1840. In 1965 membership in all U.S. sisterhoods reached a peak of 179,954 and then declined dramatically to 103,269 in 1990. A recommended general source on Catholic sisterhoods in the United States is Mary Ewens, O.P., *The Role of the Nun in Nineteenth-Century America* (New York: Arno, 1978).

7

Sexual Equality and Economic Authority

The Shaker Experience, 1784–1900

KAREN K. NICKLESS and PAMELA J. NICKLESS

THE UNITED SOCIETY OF BELIEVERS IN CHRIST'S SECOND APPEARING (the Shakers) was, many believe, the first utopian religious community with a feminist theology and a commitment to woman's equality. Shaker communities were established in the late eighteenth century; thus the Shakers would number among the first advocates of sexual equality. Scholars have presented the Shakers as not only advocating full equality between the sexes but putting that doctrine into practice. Edward Deming Andrews in 1933 argued that "from the first women were coequal with men in all the privileges and responsibility of leadership" (Andrews 1933, 180). Only recently have scholars begun to examine critically the role of the Shaker sisters in community decisions (Brewer 1986; Kern 1981; Nickless 1982).

We argue that the Shaker commitment to sexual equality was not an early feature of Shaker life. Shakers acquired a woman's rights ideology only when converts from other utopian movements began to influence Shaker practice in the last decades of the nineteenth century. The first section of this paper reexamines the origins of the Shaker commitment to woman's rights and argues that such a commitment does not predate 1869. The second section examines the economic institutions of Shakerism. We find that for most of the history of the church, economic authority in Shaker business affairs rested with the male minority.

The founder of the Shakers, Mother Ann Lee, emigrated to the colonies with eight disciples in 1774. The Shakers believed that Mother Ann embodied the female principle of the godhead, that she was God's second representative on earth. Historians have interpreted the dual godhead as the cornerstone of the church's doctrine of sexual equality. Since God had now forgiven both sexes for the fall from grace, men and women had to be treated as equals in the sight of God. In this view, the Shaker dual system of government confirms the Shaker commitment to sexual equality (Andrews 1953; Desroche 1971; Melcher 1941).

The dual system of government was characteristic of Shaker communities. Within each community, individuals organized into families, sometimes numbering over a hundred people. Each family consisted of female and male members living together in one building. Shaker brothers and sisters inhabited separate sides of the house. Each family had two sets of offices: elders and eldresses governed spiritual affairs, while deacons and deaconesses watched over temporal affairs. A board of trustees managed community finances. According to historians, each sex held half the offices at each level, creating a separate government for each sex.

The division of labor within the communities into man's work and woman's work was complete and strict. Because the Shakers practiced celibacy and did not believe in unnecessary mixing of the sexes, men and women did not work together. Because most historians believe that the Shakers valued man's work and woman's work equally, they find this sexual division of labor compatible with economic equality (Campbell 1978).

For more than a century, scholars and Shakers alike have believed in the early Shaker commitment to sexual equality. That the twentieth-century Shaker professes a belief in sexual equality is without doubt. To be questioned is the extent of gender equality in the communities of the past or in early Shaker theology. Were Mother Ann Lee and her followers eighteenth-century "pioneer[s] in equality of the sexes, insisting on recognition of women's rights and abilities?" (Melcher 1941, 43). Can we trace the doctrine and practice of Shaker female equality in an unbroken chain from the 1770s?

Ann Lee left no written work of her views on woman's role, but we can attempt to infer her views from the recollections of her converts. Bishop and Wells's recollections in *Testimonies of the Life, Character, Revelations and Doctrines of Mother Ann Lee and the Elders with Her,* first published in 1816, and Green and Wells's *Testimonies Concerning the Character and Ministry of Mother Ann Lee and the First Witnesses of the Gospel of Christ's Second Appearing; Given by Some of the Aged Brethren and Sisters of the United Society, Including a Few Sketches of Their Own Religious Experience,* published in 1827, recalled Mother Ann's life and words. These testimonies do not portray a woman concerned with woman's rights. Although Ann Lee was the undisputed leader of the Shakers, it is clear she considered herself an exception to the rule of female subjugation.

Mother Ann's remarks to Joseph Meacham on the role of woman support this contention. Meacham questioned whether it was proper for a

12. A Shaker schoolmistress and her pupils at Canterbury Shaker Village, early twentieth century. The Shakers carefully schooled the children they raised in both academic subjects and vocational training. Today, visitors to Canterbury Shaker Village can still see a teacher's handwriting left on the blackboard from the last classes held there. *Courtesy of The Winterthur Library: The Edward Deming Andrews Memorial Shaker Collection.*

13. Shaker Sister Sarah Collins weaving a chair seat. *Courtesy of The Winterthur Library: The Edward Deming Andrews Memorial Shaker Collection.*

woman to head a church. Mother Ann replied by comparing the church to a family. "Where they . . . stand in their proper order, the man is first, and the woman second in government of the family . . . but when the man is gone, the right of government belongs to the woman" (Bishop and Wells 1888, 17).

Ann Lee saw her role as the leader of the church in the absence of Jesus Christ. She acknowledged Jesus Christ as her "Lord and Head; for no other man is my head but Jesus Christ." This did not mean all women should obey only Christ. Mother Ann gave clear advice to wives. She admonished them to be "subject, and obey your husband in the Lord" (Green and Wells 1827, 137).

After Ann Lee's death, a dual hierarchy was established under the leadership of Joseph Meacham (1787–96). Meacham appointed Lucy Wright to head the female side of the church. Under Meacham's rule, the Shakers gathered into communities. None of the few surviving documents from this period suggests a concern with sexual equality. Instead, the development of a dual government appears to have been necessary to the smooth functioning of a celibate community.

Although the quarter-century of Wright's leadership (1796–1821) is used repeatedly to make a case for sexual equality among the Shakers, an examination of the documentary evidence provides no support for this thesis. During Wright's tenure, the Shakers published two important books, *The Testimony of Christ's Second Appearing Containing a General Statement of All Things Pertaining to the Faith and Practice of the Church of God in This Latter-Day* (Youngs 1808) and *The Manifesto, or a Declaration of the Doctrine and Practice of the Church of Christ* (Dunlavy 1818). These books presented Shaker theology to the world for the first time. They can be searched in vain for a trace of Shaker belief in the equality of the sexes.

The first of these books, *Testimony,* described the basic tenets of Shaker faith, among which were the duality of the deity and a dual messiah. However, the position of the female in godhead and society was not equal to that of the male. "The Father is first . . . , and the Mother is the second" in the godhead. In society as well woman held a secondary position (Youngs 1808, 501).

Ten years after *Testimony* the Shaker church published John Dunlavy's *Manifesto,* the definitive work on Shaker theology. This work does not support the theory of a Shaker belief in sexual equality. In Dunlavy's discussion of Christ, he consistently called Christ *Jesus* Christ, not the Christ spirit, a term that would include Ann Lee. A discussion of God's attributes did not divide them into paternal and maternal, as would later become common. Christ in the second appearing was called "he" throughout *Manifesto,* with no mention of Ann Lee. The first and only reference to a female in the godhead occurred on page 515 out of 520 pages. Even then, Dunlavy did not mention Ann Lee by name, and the female role was subordinate.

Thus, although *Testimony* and *Manifesto*, two landmark Shaker treatises, present a dual deity and messiah, the female role in the godhead was secondary to the male. The dual nature of God was stressed less than other beliefs, notably celibacy and community of goods. The dual hierarchy of Shaker communities, when described, had woman working in her "proper lot and order." While Lucy Wright did not author any significant Shaker publications, she enthusiastically endorsed *Testimony* and *Manifesto,* and thus we infer shared their view of woman's sphere. After Wright's death in 1821, the publication of a third major Shaker book, Green and Wells's *Summary View of the Millennial Church or United Society of Believers, Commonly Called Shakers* (1823), did not reverse the pattern.

Beginning in 1837 the Shakers launched a decade of intense revival and spiritualism known as Mother Ann's Work. Women played a dominant role in the revival, and it might be imagined that the pattern would now change. Paulina Bates wrote one of the two published "inspired" books. This was the first Shaker book written by a woman. Tellingly, Bates was only a vessel; *The Divine Book of Holy and Eternal Wisdom, Revealing the Word of God, out of Whose Mouth Goeth a Sharp Sword* was the work of a spirit, an "Angel of God" (Bates 1849, iii–iv).

The Divine Book provides evidence on the Shaker view of woman's role in society. The ministry had final authority over the authenticity of revelations; the views expressed in *The Divine Book* must have been acceptable to them. Bates reiterated the duality of the messiah, but both Ann Lee and woman were to be subservient, "the woman in subjection to the man, as her head and Lord." The "Angel of God" also gave "particular instructions to females," including non-Shaker females: "Honor thy husband that he may honor thee; yield and subject unto him." *The Divine Book* urged wives to rise early, be clean and thrifty and beware of "the clamorous tongue" (Bates 1849, 67–68, 516–17).

With one exception, Shaker tracts exhibited no interest in woman's rights before 1869, but Shaker publications did show a change in emphasis. This change was evident in the preface added to the 1848 edition of *Summary View* (Green and Wells). In the preface the Shakers set themselves apart as an example to other utopian-socialists (Bestor 1950, 40–41). The Shakers, by the mere fact of their communism and long existence, became a part of the utopian-socialist movement. Shaker communities gained members through contacts with reformers. Although the numbers gained from failed utopian communities were small, these men and women brought secular reform ideas, including a belief in woman's rights, to the Shakers.

Before 1869 the only trace of a Shaker commitment to sexual equality is found in the writings of Frederick Evans, an Owenite who had participated in other less successful utopian experiments. In all likelihood, he brought ideas about woman's rights with him to the Shaker church when he joined the New Lebanon (later called Mount Lebanon) community in 1830 (Evans [1888] 1972). Frederick Evans was the most important convert from the outside world's utopian movement. He exerted immense influence on both Shakerism and the popular image of Shakers. In 1843 he became elder of the North family at New Lebanon, remaining there until his death in 1893. By 1870, the world, and most Shakers, considered him the chief spokesperson for the sect. His many works dominated the society's publications. Frederick Evans's credentials and interests read like a roster of nineteenth-century radical views. As a Shaker he continued to work for such radical plans as woman's rights and dietary reform.

If Evans and other radicals had been the only speakers for the late nineteenth-century Shaker church it would be simple to prove the church advocated sexual equality. However, some Shakers voiced concern with this newfound infatuation with worldly reform (Andrews 1953, 232–35; Whitworth 1975, 56–63). Unaware that different opinions existed in the Shaker hierarchy, observers considered Elder Evans the chief elder and spokesperson for the entire Shaker church. This annoyed some Shakers, but the conservatives made no known attempt to remove Evans from the ministry. Whether through the apathy or sympathy of the ministry, Evans remained prominent and spoke for the Shaker church (Whitworth 1975, 62–64).

As early as 1859, Frederick Evans proclaimed the Shaker communities a bastion of woman's rights. Women were treated equally, according to Evans, but in their own sphere (Evans 1859, 55). By 1875 Evans had modified his rationale of the sexual division of labor from one of "natural spheres" to a practical justification. Charles Nordhoff described Evans's philosophy: "In fact, while they call men and women equally to the rulership, they . . . hold that in general the woman's work is in the house, the man's out of doors" (Nordhoff [1875] 1962, 166).

Elder Evans's feminism continued to change through the years, perhaps because of the strong women at Mount Lebanon's North family. These included his co-leader Eldress Mary Antoinette Doolittle, and Sisters Catherine Allen, Jane Knight, and Martha Anderson, all contributors of articles on woman's rights and sexual equality to the Shaker periodical, *The Manifesto*.[1] In 1869, in a passage typical of the times, Frederick Evans described male and female attributes. He called the male part of the godhead "the Source of all power," the female "love and tenderness." He considered women intuitive and spiritual, men originators and inventors. By 1888, at the age of eighty, his stereotyped view had changed and he credited women not with faculties different from men's but "with all the faculties that men have and a great many more that men do not possess" (Evans [1888] 1972, 105–6; A Remarkable Old Man, 1888 reprint, 4).

The influence of the secular utopian-socialist movement was direct. Many Shaker radicals who called for worldly reform and church reform in the pages of *The Manifesto* had either been Owenites or were the children of Owenite parents. Calls for reform came most often from the Mount Lebanon community. The most prolific writers at Mount Lebanon were Frederick Evans, Mary Antoinette Doolittle, Catherine Allen, Jane Knight, Martha Anderson, Lucy Bowers, Alonzo Hollister, and Daniel Fraser. Evans and Fraser were Owenites who were originally attracted by Shaker communism. Knight joined the Shakers at age twenty-two with her father, who was an Owenite. Only Doolittle was reared in the Shaker church; further research may discover radical backgrounds for the remaining authors (Allen 1890; Doolittle 1880; Knight 1880).

That the Shaker commitment to woman's rights and sexual equality developed first at Mount Lebanon and that much of it was imported does not diminish the importance of that commitment. It *was* a reality, an idea put forth by the community that held the status of mother church, the intellectual center of Shakerism. Many of the leaders of the church at this time believed in equality of the sexes; how much this belief influenced the beliefs of ordinary members is difficult to know (Whitworth 1975, 59–60).

In sum, the Shakers did not advocate equality of the sexes before 1869. Earlier references to woman's rights were the work of a known radical. Although Shaker institutions lent themselves to feminist interpretation, the Shakers did not proclaim a belief in woman's rights until radicals from the utopian-socialist movement joined the church. The contemporary view of the Shakers as advocates of woman's rights has its roots in the Evans era of Shaker history. The Shakers were not harbingers of the woman's movement; they were in concert with the contemporary woman's movement.

If the Shakers' commitment to sexual equality changed over the decades, were these changes reflected in their economic institutions? Does the sexual division of labor represent a confinement of woman to menial tasks and the traditional role of woman, or was woman's labor valued as highly as man's labor? Direct evidence on the value placed on woman's work is scarce. Under Joseph Meacham's leadership a man's contribution to the traditional family was apparently valued more highly than a woman's. When a division of family property was necessary, as when some family members joined the Shakers and others did not, the covenant signed by converts provided guidelines for that division: "it was felt right for the Father to have twice as much as the Mother, the Mother twice as much as the Son, the Son twice as much as the Daughter" (Andrews 1953, 67). Woman's contribution to the traditional family was clearly valued at half that of man's.

The Shakers endeavored to be self-sufficient in their communities and produced a variety of products. Andrews in *The Community Industries of the Shakers* lists the following as "Occupations for Shaker sisters": weaving and the manufacture of cloth; the work of the sisters' sewing shops; palm-leaf hats and straw bonnets; kitchen and dairy industries; boxes and baskets, knitted wear, and miscellaneous products; and dyeing. In addition the sisters "were occupied with . . . domestic tasks." The processing of the herbs in the Shaker herb industry was also sisters' work. The Shaker brethren handled the basic work of farming, the garden seed industry, the medicinal herb industry, blacksmithing, milling, carpentry, brickmaking, coopering, broom manufacture, tanning, and a host of other miscellaneous manufactures (1933, 179–218). Because of the celibate nature of Shakers' lives, the sexual division of labor was strict.

The Shaker occupational segregation mimics the division of labor found in early nineteenth-century America. Shaker sisters were even more likely than other agricultural women to work indoors. Relieved of heavy labor, they were not relieved of the responsibility for looking after the personal needs of the menfolk. Every morning while the men were in the fields or engaged in other activities, the sisters would enter the male side of the house and "tidy-up" for the brethren, including making the beds and straightening personal belongings. Each sister would be assigned a brother to look after, to mend his clothing and to see to his general needs (Andrews 1953, 123, 181).

By the Evans years, some discussion of the sexual division of labor was occurring in *The Manifesto*. Evans argued that while the sisters were equally called to leadership, their proper sphere was in their own occupations. Other Shaker advocates of sexual equality concurred with the sexual division of labor as necessary to a celibate order. All supported the continued division of labor by sex in Shaker homes. In spite of the restricted sphere of Shaker sisters, the radical Shakers repeatedly lambasted the idea of a female sphere in the outside world. Shaker Sister Ruth Webster wrote in 1876: "Her sphere is wherever she can do the *most* good. . . . Her *right* is to occupy the position in which she can best help her fellows" (Webster 1876, 41–42).

The radical Shakers of the late nineteenth century were committed to perfect equality of the sexes and argued that their sexual division of labor

did not imply inequality. Evans and other Shakers pointed to the dual government of the Shaker church as an example of the Shaker commitment to
equality. If the sexual division of labor merely reflected the traditional alloca-
tion of jobs in an agricultural community and the reality of maintaining
a celibate order, the question of who wielded power in the communities
becomes critical. Our examination of the records indicates that the Shaker
communities were not ruled equally. Women ran their own departments,
but men oversaw the entire community (Nickless and Nickless 1987).

It is true that Shaker sisters ran their own industries, and their own
side of the house. This was a continuation of a traditional rural division
of labor into proper male and female spheres. The sisters kept their own
books, much as a farm wife might have kept track of household expenses.
Responsibility for the community as a whole remained with the brethren,
specifically the trustees who transacted the business affairs and held the deeds
and other financial documents for the community. This is apparent in Seth
Wells's "Importance of Keeping Correct Book Accounts," written in 1836.
Wells described the way the family books should be kept. He stated, "Tho'
the Sisters have but little to do in the business of commerce; . . . they are
allowed to keep a Book account of the incomes of their own separate earn-
ings and the expense of purchases made for their particular use." The sisters
kept any money earned by their own labor and disposed of it as they saw
fit. The deaconesses kept the sisters' account and entered it on the books
of the family as a whole. The Church and Second families at New Lebanon
used this procedure, and Wells recommended its churchwide adoption (Andrews 1933, 180). Because so much of the sisters' domestic labor was not
income producing, their economic contribution would have been under-
stated in the family account books.

An examination of the financial records at New Lebanon substantiates
the impression that the sisters' work was considered less important than
the brothers'. The records include an inventory of the stock and value of
the whole community by family. The reports were made by the trustees
and deacons for 1839–64 ("Inventory of Money and Stock"). While these
records purport to show the value and holdings of the church, in only
one year (1850) is an inventory of the sisters' work listed, and even then
it is listed for only one family (the Second family) without a monetary
evaluation.

These records also show a distinction being made between sisters' money
and family money. The Second family lists money that "We have on hand"
and then lists separately "Money belonging to the Sisters." The record continues to list money in the bank, seeds on commission, and brothers' industries and then debts due from the various New Lebanon families and

other communities. Produce and livestock are also listed. Only the Second family routinely listed sisters' money. Other families listed it sporadically or not at all ("Inventory of Money and Stock" 1839–1864).

There may, of course, be several explanations for this method of book-keeping, but the simplest is that the sisters did not play an important role in the financial management of the community. There are very few extant records that record any information about the financial transactions of the sisters. Records of the Mount Lebanon community in the Western Reserve collection contain no records kept by a deaconess. Andrews lists only one journal kept by a deaconess at Mount Lebanon in his sources for *Community Industries of the Shakers*.

This lack of extant records suggests either that few sisters kept accounts, or that their accounts and enterprises were considered less important than brothers'. This is the impression given by the annual stock and value records of the New Lebanon community. Supposed to be records for the family and community, they are almost exclusively records of the brothers' enterprises. It is hard to escape the conclusion that at least until 1864 the brothers' work was considered the church's work.

Contrary to the previously held views of historians, the office of trustee was not held by both men and women. Trustee's responsibilities included keeping the books and handling all transactions with the outside world. The trustees' office often contained rooms for overnight guests, a restaurant for guests, and a store selling goods of Shaker manufacture. The sisters who worked in the office were office deaconesses and aided the trustees, presumably as secretaries and clerks.

Not until 1880 did trustee become a job held by Shaker sisters. This happened first at North Union, Ohio, and was reported to other communities via *The Manifesto*. The North Union Shakers dissolved their board of four male trustees and replaced it with two sisters and two brothers. A letter to *The Manifesto* justified this action: "This might seem a new departure. But is it not in keeping with the leading principles of our church organization from the beginning, which have advocated equality of the sexes?" (Reynolds 1880, 139).

From around 1880 into the twentieth century the sisters took an increasingly active role in community business. This happened because of an increase in the ratio of women to men in the communities, and because of the increased prominence of sisters' industries. With the decline of male-dominated enterprises such as herb manufacture and furniture, the sisters' fancywork, a post–Civil War development, became the most important industry. This fancywork consisted of small items made by the sisters, including penwipers, fans, pincushions, and dusters. Even furniture manufacture became an interest of the sisters (Andrews and Andrews 1975, 84; Gordon 1980, 206).

This transition to sisters' industries created tension in the communities. The financial records of the Mount Lebanon community include a document titled "Covenantal Principles: Relative to financial business arrangements between Brethren and Sisters among Believers." This 1870 document was an attempt to clarify the financial relationship between brothers and sisters in the same family. It shows that by the 1870s some friction had developed between them. The document stated clearly that there was to be no division of property made between brethren and sisters. The type of bookkeeping advocated by Seth Wells and followed by the Second family at Mount Lebanon until at least 1864 was no longer useful ("Principles" 1870).

The testimony of one apostate suggests that the increasing role of the sisters in church government bothered the brethren. Nicholas Briggs, a Shaker for forty years, reported that the brethren controlled the community in spite of the dual government. He explained, "Although the Shakers . . . recognized the . . . equality of the sexes, yet . . . both cannot lead, and . . . the initiative was . . . conceded to the brethren. As there was no divided financial interest, the brethren only were Trustees." Briggs recalled the sisters taking charge of their own industries, something he considered an innovation. "Little by little they acquired the larger portion of the authority and deciding voice. It proved to be a mistaken policy. It caused dissension and was a fruitful cause of the loss of some of their best men" (Briggs 1920, 61–62). Clearly, perfect equality of the sexes did not exist in Shaker communities. Although financial practices may have differed among communities as well as throughout the century of active Shakerism, the available evidence does not support the view that Shaker sisters were equal partners in Shaker business decisions.

The Shakers were not eighteenth-century advocates of either woman's rights or sexual equality. Notions about sexual equality came to the Shaker church from the secular reform movements of the nineteenth century. In Shaker institutions, the doctrine of sexual equality found fertile ground, and many Shakers came to believe that the church had always advocated perfect equality of the sexes. Economic authority within the Shaker communities was held by the male minority until the late nineteenth century. Because the increasing participation of women in the decision-making process coincides with the demographic and economic decline of many Shaker communities, it is difficult to know whether the increasing role for women demonstrates the Shakers' new commitment to sexual equality or a pragmatic approach to the failure to recruit or retain male members. It seems likely that the prominence of the sisters' industries after the Civil War and the increased influence of the sisters was the result of the overall decline of the Shaker church.

Note

1. From 1871 to 1899 the Shaker church published a monthly periodical to serve both as a house organ and to inform the world of Shaker ideas. Known collectively as *The Manifesto*, it was published as *The Shaker, Shaker and Shakeress, The Shaker Manifesto,* and *The Manifesto.*

Works Cited

Research support for this article was provided by a University of North Carolina at Asheville Faculty Intramural Research Grant.

Abbreviation

WRHS   Wallace Cathcart Shaker Manuscript Collection, Western Reserve Historical Society, Cleveland, Ohio.

Allen, Catherine. 1890. *Biographical Sketch of Daniel Fraser.* Albany, N.Y.: Weed, Parsons.

Andrews, Edward Deming. 1933. *The Community Industries of the Shakers.* Albany, N.Y.: Univ. of the State of New York.

———. 1953. *People Called Shakers: A Search for the Perfect Society.* New York: Oxford Univ. Press.

Andrews, Edward Deming, and Faith Andrews. 1975. *Fruits of the Shaker Tree.* Stockbridge, Mass.: Berkshire Traveler.

[Bates, Paulina.] 1849. *The Divine Book of Holy and Eternal Wisdom Revealing the Word of God, out of Whose Mouth Goeth a Sharp Sword.* Canterbury, N.H.: Shakers.

Bestor, Arthur Eugene. 1950. *Backwoods Utopias: The Sectarian and Owenite Phases of Communitarian Socialism in America: 1663–1829.* Philadelphia: Univ. of Pennsylvania Press.

Bishop, Rufus, and Seth Y. Wells, eds. 1888. *Testimonies of the Life, Character, Revelations and Doctrines of Mother Ann Lee and the Elders with Her.* Albany, N.Y.: Weed, Parsons.

Brewer, Priscilla J. 1986. *Shaker Communities, Shaker Lives.* Hanover, N.H.: Univ. Press of New England.

Briggs, Nicholas A. 1920. Forty Years a Shaker. *Granite Monthly* 52 (Feb.): 60–64.

Campbell, D'Ann. 1978. Women's Life in Utopia: The Shaker Experiment in Sexual Equality Reappraised, 1810 to 1860. *New England Quarterly* 51 (Mar.): 23–28.

Desroche, Henri. 1971. *The American Shakers: From Neo-Christianity to Pre-Socialism.* Amherst: Univ. of Massachusetts Press.

Doolittle, Mary Antoinette. 1880. *Autobiography of Mary Antoinette Doolittle*. Mt. Lebanon, N.Y.: Shakers.

Dunlavy, John. 1818. *The Manifesto, or A Declaration of the Doctrine and Practice of the Church of Christ*. Pleasant Hill, Ky.: P. Bertrand.

Evans, Frederick W. 1859. *Compendium of the Origin, Principles, Rules and Regulations, Government, and Doctrines of the United Society of Believers in Christ's Second Appearing*. New York: Appleton.

———. [1888] 1972. *Autobiography of a Shaker and Revelation of the Apocalypse*. Reprint. Philadelphia: Porcupine.

Gordon, Beverly. 1980. *Shaker Textile Arts*. Hanover, N.H.: Univ. Press of New England.

[Green, Calvin, and Seth Y. Wells]. 1823. *A Summary View of the Millennial Church or United Society of Believers, Commonly Called Shakers*. Albany, N.Y.: Packard & Van Benthuysen.

Green, Calvin, and Seth Y. Wells, eds. 1827. *Testimonies Concerning the Character and Ministry of Mother Ann Lee and the First Witnesses of the Gospel of Christ's Second Appearing; Given by Some of the Aged Brethren and Sisters of the United Society, Including a Few Sketches of their Own Religious Experience*. Albany, N.Y.: Packard & Van Benthuysen.

Inventory of Money and Stock Held at the Beginning of Each Year. 1839–64. WRHS II:B 38.

Kern, Louis J. 1981. *An Ordered Love: Sex Roles and Sexuality in Victorian Utopias: The Shakers, the Mormons, and the Oneida Community*. Chapel Hill: Univ. of North Carolina Press.

Knight, Jane D. 1880. *Brief Narrative of Events Touching Various Reforms*. Albany, N.Y.: Weed, Parsons.

Melcher, Marguerite. 1941. *The Shaker Adventure*. Princeton: Princeton Univ. Press.

Nickless, Karen K. 1982. Origins of Shaker Feminism. Master's thesis, Univ. of South Carolina.

Nickless, Karen K., and Pamela J. Nickless. 1987. Trustees, Deacons and Deaconesses: The Temporal Role of the Shaker Sisters, 1820–1890. *Communal Studies* 7:16–24.

Nordhoff, Charles. [1875] 1962. *The Communistic Societies of the United States*. Reprint. New York: Hillary House.

Principles Concerning Financial Business Arrangements among Shakers. 1870. WRHS I:A 11.

Remarkable Old Man, A. 1888. Reprint. WRHS.

Reynolds, W. 1880. Letter to the Editor. *Shaker Manifesto* 10 (June): 139.

Webster, Ruth. 1876. Let Woman Choose Her Sphere. *Shaker* 6 (June):41–42.

Whitworth, John M. 1975. *God's Blueprints: A Sociological Study of Three Utopian Sects*. London: Routledge & Kegan Paul.

[Youngs, Benjamin S.]. 1808. *The Testimony of Christ's Second Appearing Containing a General Statement of All Things Pertaining to the Faith and Practice of the Church of God in This Latter-Day*. Lebanon, Ohio: John M'Clean.

8

"Tho' of the Weaker Sex"

A Reassessment of Gender Equality among the Shakers

PRISCILLA J. BREWER

IT IS WIDELY ACCEPTED that the United Society of Believers in Christ's Second Appearing (commonly called Shakers) practiced gender equality. Founded in the eighteenth century by an English mystic named Ann Lee, the sect permitted women to participate in spiritual and temporal leadership. Shaker organization has been hailed as progressive, even feminist (Andrews 1963, 56; Campbell 1978, 24; Foster 1981, 36; Kitch 1989, 125; Ruether 1981, 51). A few scholars, however, have disagreed (Kern 1981, 124; Procter-Smith 1985, 229).

The Shaker experience is open to interpretation. The spiritual equality of brethren and sisters stemmed from the sect's commitment to celibacy; the Shakers did not intend to create a social system in which men and women were politically or economically equal. Although they allowed women wider participation in government than most other contemporary American Protestant groups, authority within the sect was gender specific. Shaker attitudes about gender traits were traditional. Only late in Shaker history did women share in the management of legal and financial affairs.

Evidence suggests, in fact, that the position of Shaker women deteriorated after Lee's death in 1784. The effusion of largely female-produced, spiritual "gifts" in the 1837–54 period can be interpreted, at least in part, as a response to this trend. Only when the adult male/female ratio began to plummet after 1860 did Sisters approach economic and political equality. As women gradually assumed authority over the sect's future, they reasserted its fundamental female spirit.

In the sect's early history, feminine spirituality and authority were linked in Ann Lee. As a child, she was "favored with . . . visions." As she grew

133

older, she struggled to come to terms with human depravity and became convinced that sexuality and sin were related. After experiencing a crisis conversion, she joined a group of dissident Quakers. These seekers, Lee felt, "were favored with a greater degree of divine light, and a more clear and pointed testimony against . . . sin than had hitherto been made manifest" but remained open to further revelation (Green and Wells 1848, 13–14).

In 1770, Lee conveyed important "new light." Christ had appeared to her and explained that the root of human sin and misery was "the very act of transgression, committed by the first man and woman in the garden of Eden." Salvation, therefore, hinged on celibacy. After hearing this revelation, group members recognized Lee "as their spiritual Mother" (Green and Wells 1848, 14–16). Her authority stemmed from her identification as the second living embodiment of the Christ spirit. Her vision and power over sin could be shared by anyone; in spiritual terms, gender was insignificant.

Only after Lee and eight followers came to America in 1774 and attracted numerous converts did they apply spiritual principles to the organization of communal life. As long as Lee was alive, her blend of spiritual and temporal talents directed converts' lives (Bathrick 1869, 65; Bishop and Wells 1888, 171). She knew the risk of excessive reliance on spiritual guidance. Converts fired by the power of her message still had to survive in the everyday world; obedience to the "leading gift" was crucial (Bathrick 1869, 80–81). Individual spiritual development could occur only in the context of community. Members of both sexes had to subordinate their concerns to the sect's larger goals.

But Mother Ann, as she was called, did not intend to do away with patriarchy entirely. In justifying her leadership to potential converts, Lee used the analogy of family government. "As . . . nature requires a man and a woman," she explained, "so, where both stand in their proper order, the man is first, and the woman . . . second." Only when no men were present could the "right of government" fall to a woman (Bishop and Wells 1888, 16–17). Thus, in the absence of a visible male Christ, Lee could lead the "family of Christ."

Lee's death led to a restructuring of the sect's government. At first, authority passed solely to men, first to James Whittaker and then to Joseph Meacham. In 1788, however, Meacham decided to make Lucy Wright his partner in the lead ministry, arguing that "man and . . . woman have equal rights . . . in the . . . government of the Church" (Bishop 1850, 91).

This move proved controversial, suggesting how entrenched male authority had become. Brother Calvin Green remembered that Wright "had great prejudice to overcome" (Green 1861, 16–17). Reuben Rathbun recalled: "It was . . . without any difficulty they acknowledged Elder Joseph

[as] father . . . but as to a mother, it was . . . so unexpected that there was . . . a labor before the matter was finished" (Rathbun 1800, 9). This "labor" involved the apostasy of a large number of members, mostly men, who objected to being governed, as apostate Angell Matthewson put it, "by women or elders ruled by women" (Garrett 1987, 237).[1]

Other practices confirm that early Shakers did not have a well-defined concept of gender equality. When a male convert's estate was divided, his wife was allowed half of his portion and any daughters half the amount granted to sons (*Book of Records* 1791–1869, 8). And, as converts were organized into administrative units called "families," men emerged as leaders (*Book of Records* 1791–1869, 3).

The division of labor and authority within these "families" followed traditional patterns. Men farmed, pursued trades, and handled business with the "World." Male "trustees" legally owned church property, served as guardians of minors placed in the sect's care, and witnessed the signatures of adults signing Family covenants (*Book of Records* 1791–1869, 58). Women managed domestic affairs. Even "office sisters" (the counterparts of male "trustees") were reminded that they were merely "counselors to [the trustees] in outward things" (*Book of Records* 1791–1869, 13).

The Shakers carefully separated male and female "spheres." Elders governed men; eldresses governed women. But this parallel structure did not mean that men and women exercised equal authority. In fact, the role of female leaders was similar to that of women in the outside world, despite their titles. Brother Calvin Green explained: "The female ought to have a correspondent & equal power in her sphere, with the male in his sphere" (Green 1861, 18–19).

Meacham's poor health complicated matters. He resigned in 1796, informing Wright shortly before his death that "thou, tho' of the weaker sex, . . . will be the Elder . . . after my departure" (Bishop 1850, 91). Some members were uncertain about the appointment, however, making it difficult for Wright to exercise total authority. The language of an 1815 family covenant is revealing:

> Since the decease of . . . Joseph Meacham, the . . . Ministration of . . . gifts and the . . . protection of souls have rested with . . . Lucy Wright, whom we still acknowledge . . . as our spiritual Mother . . . and we consider her together with the Ministry and Elders who act in union with her as a spiritual Ministry invested with . . . authority by the revelation of God. . . . To the said Ministry . . . appertains the Power to . . . appoint to office . . . such [members] as they shall judge to be qualified. (*Book of Records* 1791–1869, 33)

Note that Wright was "still" acknowledged as "spiritual Mother" but that her temporal power was limited. In 1814, for example, she "felt a gift" to have a house at the New Lebanon, New York, community moved but could not command the brethren's obedience. Pleading the press of business, they postponed the work "for a more convenient season." Only by beginning to dismantle the house herself could Wright shame them into undertaking the job (*History of Lower Family* n.d., n.p.). The difficulty she encountered in this case illustrates two important trends. First, leaders' power, even that of the first eldress, had become gender specific. Second, some members no longer felt it necessary to obey divinely inspired instructions. The risk to Shaker union and order was substantial.

Members' behavior was, in fact, deteriorating. In 1813, an elder at New Lebanon reported: "We sometimes discover . . . some little tory that would wish to betray our souls. . . . There are three or four scoundrels of this grade. . . . Mr. Slug, Mrs. Lounge-about, Great I and Old Fret!" (White and Taylor 1904, 134). The Shakers' spiritual quest was becoming lost in a morass of petty detail. How were they to make enough money, plant enough crops, and build enough buildings to handle the influx of converts? How would they educate the increasing numbers of children in the communities?[2] How were members to relate to outsiders? What would they eat and wear? How should they worship and behave?

The focus of Shakerism shifted from the life of the spirit to the everyday world, making the spiritual equality of men and women less important. As the sect grew, economic expansion became critical. Wright worried about this trend, complaining in 1815: "The sense seems . . . so drowned in temporal things that there can be but little . . . desire for the gifts of God. . . . I . . . would be thankful . . . if the sense . . . could be satisfied with less . . . of this world's treasures" (Green 1861, 88). The New Hampshire ministry noticed the same problem, reporting: "We are . . . satisfied that this craving earthly sense is . . . too prevalent among us" (Ministry Canterbury 1819).

The pressure to make money increased sisters' temporal responsibilities. Men continued to dominate the sect's leadership, but the sisters' role expanded. They assisted in the herb and garden seed industries and manufactured a wide variety of sales items (*Journal of Domestic Events* 1843–1864, Dec. 1853; Clark 1831–1836, Dec. 1835). The financial success of many Families increasingly hinged on such work.

Sisters recognized their growing economic importance and some resented the fact that they exercised little control over decision making (Brewer 1986, 98–99). This feeling grew as increasing numbers of male members proved unreliable. At least two elders refused to acknowledge the authority of superiors (Green 1860, 55–58; Ministry Alfred 1816). Several prominent brethren left the sect, taking with them large amounts of church property (*History of Lower Family* n.d., n.p.; Clark 1831–1836, October 1, 1835; Ministry Hancock 1839). Rank-and-file brethren also demonstrated weakened commitment. At the New Lebanon Church Family, for example, the adult apostasy rate climbed from 2.5 percent between 1801 and 1810 to 14.8 percent in the 1840s. Men accounted for three-quarters of these departures (Brewer 1986, 210).

These trends threatened the sect's future. Although the sisters were not immune (Brewer 1986, 94–95, 210), the rash of problems involving brethren led to a reassessment of gender traits. Mother Lucy felt that women were less likely than men to break rules, reminding the sisters: "You have a greater privilege than the brethren do; you are more gathered in and . . . ought to . . . labor to keep a good substance so that [they] can feel . . . you have been faithful" (Green 1861, 131). The sisters, sheltered from the corrupting influences of the world, were more responsible than the brethren for the sect's spiritual purity.

Titles did not change, and the separation of gender spheres survived, but some sisters took their implied duties seriously. When Brother William Evans caused trouble in the Canaan, New York, Lower Family in the 1830s, for example, sisters took matters into their own hands. Evans "would not work," one recalled, "but was very willing to . . . give orders to those who would. . . . He would take the manners book and bolt into the sisters rooms and give instruction." When Evans offered advice about cooking, the sisters rebelled. Because "the brethren had not the power or lacked the disposition to get rid of him," Sisters Hannah Bryant and Harriet Sellick "took him by the collar and put him into the street and threw his clothes after him" (*History of Lower Family* n.d., n.p.).

Bryant and Sellick were justified in taking decisive steps only because Evans threatened to invade their "sphere," and even under these circumstances, they had first appealed to male leaders for help. Shaker women who wished to stem the tide of moral and spiritual decay remained in a disadvantageous position. The leadership structure did not allow them sufficient authority to effect the changes many considered necessary. A new approach was required.

Between 1837 and the mid-1850s, during a revival called Mother's Work, Mother Ann (in spirit form) again exercised combined spiritual and temporal authority (for a fuller discussion of Mother's Work, see Brewer [1986, 116–35]). Her most able assistant was Holy Mother Wisdom, the female element of the deity. Although a few men figured prominently as both spirit messengers and as their human voices, the revival was overwhelmingly female in character (Youngs 1856–60, 121). Physical evidence of the revival supports this conclusion. One hundred seventeen of the 121 signed or attributed "gift drawings" that survive from this period were produced by sisters (Patterson 1983, 45–99). Prevented from exercising truly equal authority, a small but influential group of sisters found an alternative. Their response to decades of increasing tension was that "of a peripheral group within a stratified society which, while recognizing the importance of women's contributions, nevertheless assigned [them] . . . secondary status" (Procter-Smith 1985, 207).

At first, inspired messages emphasized sisters' misdeeds. In 1837, for example, Sister Ann Maria Goff dreamed that she had died and returned as a spirit to her earthly home "to see if order was being kept." She was horrified to see sisters gossiping and laughing when they should have been meditating in preparation for meeting (Bathrick 1874, 250–51). Lucy Wright's spirit was equally shocked to see sisters preparing for meeting by "standing a long time before their looking-glasses prinking their caps and the handkerchiefs with lust in their hearts saying such a one or such a one will notice me and think I look very handsome" (Orders Given by Mother Lucy 1839–1842, Feb. 12, 1839).

The sisters had evidently become slovenly as well as vain. Mother Lucy's spirit berated the Hancock sisters, saying they were "not to comb their heads, wash their feet, smoke, or take snuff, or lay down in any part of the kitchen" (Mother's Pure Teaching 1841–1845, n.p.). Holy Mother Wisdom displayed similar concern when she visited a Shaker dwelling in 1841, "looking into the cupboards and turning up the corner of the carpets &c." (*Church Order Journal* 1841–1846, Dec. 29, 1841). The emphasis on spiritual housecleaning was plain (Procter-Smith 1985, 200–202).

Gradually, female instruments and spirits extended the focus of their efforts outside the sisters' sphere (*Account of the Meetings* 1845, 3), but reform was minimal and transitory. As a result, inspired messages became increasingly apocalyptical ([Bates] 1849, 101–3). Finally, it became clear that the revival had failed. After the mid-1840s, female instruments focused on the creation of "gift drawings," colorful records of visions that were intended to comfort elderly Believers or encourage promising young members. Devout Shakers were reminded that Mother Ann had neither forgotten nor forsaken them. But these drawings were highly individual expressions of Shaker faith. They suggest that the feminizing, spiritualizing effects of the revival had not substantially altered the direction of the society.

Mother's Work failed to effect a total revitalization of the sect because many members came to doubt its legitimacy. Leaders tried to maintain control of the revival by requiring that all "gifts" be approved before being announced, but this precaution did not prevent problems. Elder Giles Avery noted that some instruments controlled by "lower class" spirits enunciated "conflicting and contradictory statements" (Procter-Smith 1985, 12–13). Some apostatized, undermining whatever faith their colleagues had in the truth of their communications (Youngs 1837–1857, Oct. 30, 1839; Patterson 1983, 86).

Even a few leaders questioned the authenticity of "gifts." "I once swallowed . . . every thing that came . . . from the heavens," Elder Freegift Wells noted, "but after . . . I got confounded by receiving a Message . . . which I knew was a . . . lie . . . I found it necessary to be . . . on my guard" (F. Wells 1850, 16–17). Wells was not the only doubter. In 1845, the New Hampshire Ministry informed the Lead Ministry about conditions in Maine: "Unbelief in the present manifestation is too prevalent. Even their former Elder Brother James Pote seems to have little if any faith in the present work . . . and . . . some of the young have gathered weakness from him" (Ministry Canterbury 1845).

The Believers who recorded doubts about the revival were men. Elder Frederick Evans recalled later that the instruments "had given much trouble because they imagined themselves reformers, whereas they were only the mouthpieces of spirits, and . . . themselves of a low order of mind. They had to teach the mediums much," he remembered, "after the spirits ceased to use them" (Nordhoff [1875] 1966, 158). Although Evans did not single out female instruments, he considered women to be less balanced and more flighty than men. When William Hepworth Dixon visited New Lebanon in the 1860s, he observed: "All the ladies have looking-glasses in their rooms, though they are . . . told . . . to guard their hearts against the abuse to which these vanities might lead. 'Females,' says Frederick . . . , 'need to be steadied some'" (Dixon 1867, 311).

Other brethren agreed that women possessed undesirable character traits. In a guide for young Shakers, Luther Wells implied that sisters sometimes spoke harshly. "One of the most important female qualities is sweetness of temper," he noted. "Heaven did not give to woman insinuations and persuasions for her to be imperious [or] . . . a sweet voice to be employed in *scolding*" (L. Wells 1858, n.p.).

Hervey Elkins, who was a member of the Enfield, New Hampshire, church family for fifteen years, was also convinced that Shaker life made women unwomanly. Having decided that traditional domesticity was woman's lot, he criticized the behavior of some sisters toward one of their younger colleagues. "Ellina," as Elkins called her, had fallen in love with a young Brother, "Urbino."[3] Both were tempted to leave the sect but decided to confess their plight to the elders and struggle to overcome temptation. Elkins, a close friend of "Urbino's," was shocked to see how some of the middle-aged sisters in the family treated "Ellina." "Enmity and jealousy were wrought to so high a pitch, that . . . there was no peace for her. . . . Envious women, belching fury upon the recipient of an attention which they coveted; hypocritical women, pretendingly hating that tie which they had once strove to fasten, but which fell asunder . . . from the lack of those graces which strengthen it . . . reproached her in look and gesture" (Elkins 1853, 112).

Although Elkins, an apostate, was not a typical Shaker, his perspective is intriguing. When combined with the views of Evans and Wells, a very negative image of Shaker women emerges. Their portrayal as unreliable, vain, domineering, envious, and even hateful is certainly extreme, but its formulation in the years just after the failed revival may be significant. Did Shaker men resent the largely female-led effort to circumvent their authority? The evidence is far from conclusive but the coincidence of timing is suggestive.

In the same period, a new inspired voice appeared—one that Shaker leaders found difficult to accept. Although Rebecca Jackson's experience was complicated by Shaker racial attitudes, gender was also important. After Mother's Work, Shaker leaders decided that female spirituality was not the route they wished to pursue in their efforts to revitalize the society.

Jackson, a free black seamstress from Philadelphia, was a mystic. To "keep her spirit eye clear," she controlled her body through prayer, fasting, sleep deprivation, and celibacy (Humez 1981, 17). Jackson accepted Shakerism in 1843 and moved to the Watervliet, New York, community in 1847. "Always led by an invisible lead," she believed that God wanted her to evangelize urban blacks (Humez 1981, 250). Shaker leaders, however, were unenthusiastic. Jackson thought them hypocritical, recalling: "After I came . . . and saw how Believers seemed to be gathered to themselves, . . . I wondered how the earth was to be saved, if Shakers were the only people of God on earth, and they seemed to be busy in their own concerns, which were mostly temporal" (Humez 1981, 220).

Jackson's assessment was perceptive. By the 1850s, temporal worries had indeed come to dominate the Shaker world. Although racism may have affected their decision, Shaker leaders considered Jackson's individualized female spirituality risky.[4] Not since Lucy Wright's day had a woman exercised the kind of authority she sought. Permission to establish a Shaker "out-family" among Philadelphia blacks was grudgingly given. A handful of converts joined, several of whom moved to Watervliet after Jackson's death in 1871. The time had not yet arrived for Shakers of either sex to participate in outer-directed reform.

Ironically, the sect's internal politics took an activist turn the year Jackson died with the establishment of *The Shaker,* a monthly newspaper. Its first editor, Elder Frederick Evans, had always denied the existence of a spiritual world (Evans 1830), valuing instead practical communism. He called the Society "the seed-bed of radical truths; the fountain of progressive ideas" (Evans [1888] 1972, x). This philosophy permeated *The Shaker* from the beginning.

Feminism was one of these "radical truths." In the first issue, Brother Chauncy Sears discussed the gender equality implicit in the Shaker belief in a male/female deity. "Woman," he concluded, "has inalienable rights as natural and sacred as those [of] man." But much had to be done if these "inalienable rights" were to be acknowledged. "We are aware," Sears observed, "that a just conception of woman's true sphere has increased . . . but we must not conclude . . . that perfection has been attained" (Sears 1871).

Coincidentally, the Shakers were facing the necessity of enlarging "woman's true sphere." Between 1860 and 1880, membership dropped from 3,489 to 1,849 (Bainbridge 1982, 355). Gender imbalance became increasingly marked. Early Shaker communities included roughly equal numbers of men and women (Brewer 1986, 68, 256n. 31), but the situation changed markedly after 1850. In 1860, the sect was 59.1 percent female, a proportion that reached 72.2 percent in 1900 (Bainbridge 1982, 360).[5] Finding qualified male members to fill positions of responsibility grew difficult (Ministry Canterbury 1848). If the sect was to survive, the sisters would have to be called upon.

Elder Thomas Damon of Hancock, Massachusetts, proposed that the sect's covenant be revised to redress the imbalance between economic and spiritual authority. He estimated that the Society had lost more than $200,000 since 1820 as a result of the mismanagement and apostasy of trustees and recommended that ministry and rank-and-file members be given official control of financial decisions. Because the majority of members were female, Damon advocated amending the covenant to permit "females in the Order of Trustees to hold . . . money in their own names" (Damon ca. 1870, n.p.).

Implementation was gradual. North Union, Ohio, was the first community to have a female trustee (Reynolds 1880). The Canterbury, New Hampshire, Shakers took similar steps in the 1890s (Durgin 1896). In 1903, the New Lebanon north family went even further; several members were appointed to a finance committee chaired by a sister (White and Taylor 1904, 214–15).

Members wondered if other changes would follow. Should eldresses truly share power with elders? Would women take over entirely as older male leaders died? Eldress Anna White considered this possibility, asking: "When the few worthy brethren pass off the stage, will the sisters be able to hold the fort?" She answered yes, pointing to their increased economic authority as evidence of their executive ability. "Women are making rapid and successful strides in every department that has . . . been under man's control," she noted, "and I am sure, when we look at the history of Believers, it has been the man and not the woman . . . who has taken advantage of the trust reposed in him" (Taylor 1912, 75). Sisters, she implied, would be more faithful.

Anna White was the Shaker equivalent of the New Woman. Born in 1831, she came from a long line of religious seekers; she converted to Shakerism in 1849. Unlike many new members in this period, White's faith had a strong foundation (Taylor 1912, 13). She also proved to be a capable leader. Appointed junior eldress of the New Lebanon north family in 1865, she became coeditor of the renamed *Shaker and Shakeress* in 1873 and was made senior eldress in 1886. Until her death in 1910, she was the foremost female advocate of progressive Shakerism. She was also one of few Shakers to form close ties to the worldly reform community. A member of the National American Woman Suffrage Association (an irony, considering that Shakers traditionally did not vote), she also served as vice-president of the National Council of Women. In addition, she was vice-president of the New York chapter of the Woman's International League of Peace and Arbitration and helped organize a peace conference at New Lebanon in 1906 (Taylor 1912, 68, 76).

White transformed Shakerism into an agent of national and global political and social reform. In justifying her public activities, she argued that gender equality had always been part of Shaker ideology. "Ann Lee first declared . . . Woman's Freedom and Equality," she asserted, "[and] embodied it in spirit and letter in the organization that is founded upon her teachings" (White and Taylor 1904, 386).

Much of the confusion over Shaker gender roles stems from such testimony. Scholars who have relied heavily on published statements have highlighted only a portion of Shaker ideology.[6] Although public records accurately reflect the progressive beliefs held by some Believers at the turn of the century, they misrepresent both the ideology and reality of gender relations throughout Shaker history. They even contradict Mother Ann's own views of male and female roles.

In the late nineteenth and early twentieth centuries, progressives like White did not speak for all Shakers. Many conservative members believed not only that men and women were different but that men were naturally dominant. Eldress Harriet Bullard, for example, described her relationship to Shaker Brethren in this way: "As a sister in the spiritual family of Christ,

14. Shaker sisters and girls in the laundry, North family, Mount Lebanon, New York. *Courtesy of The Shaker Museum and Library, Old Chatham, New York.*

I . . . have the association of brethren upon whom I can depend for my spiritual and physical protection. . . . We, as their sisters, are enabled to be their ministers of comfort and love" (White and Taylor 1904, 391). Even Sister Antoinette Doolittle, whom Kitch called "liberal" on the issue of women's rights (Kitch 1989, 16), emphasized traditional patriarchal power relationships when she argued that "man is the lawful head . . . and will always have the supremacy." "Woman," she concluded, "must act her part as co-worker, filling her sphere" (Doolittle 1871, 21–22).

Successful female leaders possessed traditional feminine traits. An anonymous Believer argued in 1905 that a Family Eldress should serve as a "ministering agent . . . alive to the needs of the . . . people." She should possess "forgiveness," "tact," "sensitiveness," and "sympathy." If "disintegrating forces" threatened her family, she should "reveal, warn, [and] encourage." Her mission was to "sweeten and straighten, and bring all into the loving union. . . . She is the family mother. . . . Her smile is the sunshine of the home" (*The Motherhood of God* ca. 1905, 22–23).

The Shakers did not agree on the issue of gender equality. Some, like Anna White, argued that spiritual equality had gradually and naturally led to an equal division of economic and political authority. But most Believers

15. Eldress Emma Neale *(seated)* and Sister Sadie Neale. *Courtesy of The Winterthur Library: The Edward Deming Andrews Memorial Shaker Collection.*

16. Three Shaker sisters making pastries, in an attitude reminiscent of a Dutch painting. *Courtesy of The Winterthur Library: The Edward Deming Andrews Memorial Shaker Collection.*

appear to have felt that men and women should exercise unequal authority because of their distinctive characteristics. Men were more rational and had greater executive ability, while women were more sensitive and intuitive. Women's interpersonal skills were superior to those of men; they used power indirectly, through spiritual and emotional influence.

Shaker sisters were forced into roles of economic decision making and, ultimately, primary governmental authority only because of the worsening gender imbalance. But as women assumed control of the sect, they reasserted its traditional spiritual and maternal focus. Eldress Dorothy Durgin of Canterbury, New Hampshire, summed up this attitudinal change in 1894, noting: "We are as we hope to be, strongly and warmly attached, hand and soul, to the great, pure, noble Mother-heart above" (Durgin 1894).

Notes

1. For an account of apostasies in this period, see Brewer (1986, 28, 210).

2. Between 1800 and 1830, the population of the eleven Shaker communities in the eastern United States increased from 1,373 to 2,316 (68.7 percent); many of these additions were children. At the New Lebanon Church Family, for example, children under age sixteen comprised 62.6 percent of new members in this period (Brewer 1986, 209–15).

3. Although evidence is inconclusive, Elkins' reliability on other points suggests that the un-Shaker names Ellina and Urbino mask the identity of real members.

4. Historian Jean Humez (1981, 269) argued that Jackson subconsciously regarded at least some white Shakers as racists. Although the Believers claimed to identify with all oppressed peoples throughout history, regardless of color, few blacks joined the sect. In 1840, for example, census enumerators found only thirty-four blacks (some still slaves) living in Shaker villages (Bainbridge 1982, 355–56).

5. Bainbridge's figures include children. Gender imbalance was even worse among adult members. In 1860, the population of the eastern villages was 62.2 percent female; the proportion reached 76.3 percent by 1900 (Brewer 1986, 219).

6. Kitch argued that because the views of members like Sears and White were published, they "can be assumed to be at least representative of those of other believers" (Kitch 1989, 4). Her contention is not supported by manuscript evidence.

Works Cited

Abbreviations

HSV   Hancock Shaker Village, Pittsfield, Mass.
WM   Edward Deming Andrews Memorial Shaker Collection, Henry Francis du Pont Winterthur Museum, Winterthur, Del.
WRHS   Wallace Cathcart Shaker Manuscript Collection, Western Reserve Historical Society, Cleveland, Ohio.

An Account of the Meetings Held in the City of Peace, City of Union and City of Love on the 25th of Dec. 1845. 1845. Hancock, Mass. Williams College Library, Williamstown, Mass.

Andrews, Edward D. 1963. A People Called Shakers. New York: Dover.

Bainbridge, William Sims. 1982. Shaker Demographics 1840–1900: An Example of the Use of U.S. Census Enumeration Schedules. *Journal for the Scientific Study of Religion* 21:352–65.

[Bates, Paulina]. 1849. *The Divine Book of Holy and Eternal Wisdom, Revealing the Word of God, out of Whose Mouth Goeth a Sharp Sword*. Canterbury, N.H.: Shakers.

Bathrick, Eunice, comp. 1869. *Testimonies and Wise Sayings, Counsel and Instruction of Mother Ann and the Elders*. Harvard, Mass. WRHS VI:B 10–13.

———. 1874. *A Second Book Copied from Br. Alonzo Hollister's Manuscripts. Copied for Elder John Cloutman*. Harvard, Mass. WM 805.

Bishop, Rufus, comp. 1850. *A Collection of Writings of Father Joseph Meacham Respecting Church Order and Government*. New Lebanon, N.Y. WRHS VII:B 59.

Bishop, Rufus, and Seth Y. Wells, eds. 1888. *Testimonies of the Life, Character, Revelations and Doctrines of Mother Ann Lee and the Elders with Her.* Albany, N.Y.: Weed, Parsons.

A Book of Records Kept by Order of the Deacons, or Trustees of the Second Family . . . 1791–1869. New Lebanon, N.Y. HSV.

Brewer, Priscilla J. 1986. *Shaker Communities, Shaker Lives*. Hanover, N.H.: Univ. Press of New England.

Campbell, D'Ann. 1978. Women's Life in Utopia: The Shaker Experiment in Sexual Equality Reappraised, 1810–1860. *New England Quarterly* 51:23–38.

Clark, Asenath. 1831–1836. *Ministerial Journal*. New Lebanon and Watervliet, N.Y. Copy at HSV.

Church Order Journal. 1841–46. New Lebanon, N.Y. WRHS V:B 135.

Damon, Thomas. ca. 1870. "Considerations Illustrating the necessity of some Revisions in the Direction and Management of Temporal Concerns." Hancock, Mass. WM 766.

Dixon, William Hepworth. 1867. *New America*. Philadelphia: Lippincott.

Doolittle, Antoinette. 1871. God's Spiritual House. *Shaker* (Mar.): 21–22.

Durgin, Dorothy. 1894. Letter to Eliza Ann Taylor. Mar 3. WRHS IV:A 8.

———. 1896. Letter to Alonzo G. Hollister. Oct. 28. WRHS IV:A 8.

Elkins, Hervey. 1853. *Fifteen Years in the Senior Order of Shakers*. Hanover, N.H.: Dartmouth Press.

Evans, Frederick W. 1830. Letter to George H. Evans. June 11. WRHS IV:A 36.

———. [1888] 1972. *Autobiography of a Shaker and Revelation of the Apocalypse*. Reprint. Philadelphia: Porcupine.

Foster, Lawrence. 1981. *Religion and Sexuality: Three American Communal Experiments of the Nineteenth Century*. New York: Oxford Univ. Press.

Garrett, Clarke. 1987. *Spirit Possession and Popular Religion: From the Camisards to the Shakers*. Baltimore: Johns Hopkins Univ. Press.

Green, Calvin. 1860. Biography of Elder Henry Clough. New Lebanon, N.Y. WRHS VI:B 24.

———. 1861. Biographic Memoir of the Life, Character and Important Events in the Ministration of Mother Lucy Wright. New Lebanon, N.Y. WRHS VI:B 27.

Green, Calvin, and Seth Y. Wells. 1848. *A Summary View of the Millennial Church or United Society of Believers, Commonly Called Shakers.* 2d ed. Albany, N.Y.: Packard & Van Benthuysen.

History of the Lower Family. n.d. Canaan, N.Y. WRHS V:B 84.

Humez, Jean McMahon. 1981. *Gifts of Power: The Writings of Rebecca Jackson, Black Visionary, Shaker Eldress.* Amherst: Univ. of Massachusetts Press.

Journal of Domestic Events and Transactions. 1843–1864. New Lebanon, N.Y. HSV.

Kern, Louis J. 1981. *An Ordered Love: Sex Roles and Sexuality in Victorian Utopias—the Shakers, the Mormons, and the Oneida Community.* Chapel Hill: Univ. of North Carolina Press.

Kitch, Sally L. 1989. *Chaste Liberation: Celibacy and Female Cultural Status.* Urbana: Univ. of Illinois Press.

Ministry Alfred, Maine. 1816. Letters to Ministry New Lebanon, N.Y. May 4 and Sept. 7. WRHS IV:A 1.

Ministry Canterbury, N.H. 1819. Letter to Ministry New Lebanon, N.Y. Feb. 19. WRHS IV:A 3.

———. 1845. Letter to Ministry New Lebanon, N.Y. Jan. 1. WRHS IV:A 5.

———. 1848. Letter to Ministry New Lebanon, N.Y. Nov. 4. WRHS IV:A 5.

Ministry Hancock, Mass. 1839. Letter to Ministry Harvard, Mass. Mar. 19. WRHS IV:A 19.

Mother's Pure Teaching. 1841–1845. Hancock, Mass. WRHS I:B 82.

The Motherhood of God. Ca. 1905. N.p.: Shakers.

Nordhoff, Charles. [1875] 1966. *The Communistic Societies of the United States.* Reprint. New York: Dover.

Orders Given by Mother Lucy. 1839–1842. Hancock, Mass. WM 748.

Patterson, Daniel W. 1983. *Gift Drawing and Gift Song.* Sabbathday Lake, Maine: Shakers.

Procter-Smith, Marjorie. 1985. *Women in Shaker Community and Worship: A Feminist Analysis of the Uses of Religious Symbolism.* Lewiston, N.Y.: Edwin Mellen.

Rathbun, Reuben. 1800. *Reasons Offered for Leaving the Shakers.* Pittsfield, Mass.: Chester Smith.

Reynolds, W. 1880. Letter to Editor. *Shaker* 10 (June): 139.

Ruether, Rosemary. 1981. Women in Utopian Movements. In *Women and Religion in America: The Nineteenth Century,* edited by Rosemary Ruether and Rosemary Keller, 46–53. New York: Harper & Row.

Sears, Chauncy. 1871. Duality of the Deity. *Shaker* 1 (Jan.): 6–7.

Taylor, Leila S. 1912. *A Memorial to Eldress Anna White and Elder Daniel Offord.* Mt. Lebanon, N.Y.: Shakers.

Wells, Freegift. 1850. A Series of Remarks Showing the power of the Adversary in leading honest souls astray through the influence of inspired Messages. Or a Lamentation because the beauty of Zion hath faded, and Her Light become dim. Watervliet, N.Y. WRHS VII:B 266.

Wells, Luther. 1858. Juvenile Guide Book. Watervliet, N.Y. WRHS VII:B 273.

White, Anna, and Leila S. Taylor. 1904. *Shakerism: Its Meaning and Message.* Columbus, Ohio: Heer.

Youngs, Isaac N. 1837–1857. *Personal Journal*. New Lebanon, N.Y. Emma King Library, Shaker Museum, Old Chatham, N.Y., 10, 509.

———. 1856–1860. *Concise View of the Church of God and of Christ on Earth Having its Foundation In the faith of Christ's first and Second Appearing*. New Lebanon, N.Y. WM 760.

9

Organizing for Service

Challenges to Community Life and Work Decisions in Catholic Sisterhoods, 1850–1940

MARY J. OATES

CATHOLIC SISTERHOODS, like other voluntary organizations, were situated in a culture that affected their public acceptability and effectiveness. This essay examines aspects of the religious and social environments in which sisters lived and worked in the century of rapid community growth after 1850. Disharmonies between internal community structures and external corporate works that developed in these years presented more serious implications for the welfare of female than male religious communities. In assessing these problems, records of sisterhoods with members in Massachusetts are frequently used to exemplify national trends, a legitimate course because most of these groups had motherhouses and convents located in other states, and decisions made with regard to a problem arising in one diocese generally became communitywide policy on the matter.

Organized service to society was an obligatory tenet of most of the numerous women's communities that evolved in this period. While the women's efforts were channeled into traditionally female work, the orientation to service outside their own communities, embodying a religious calling to a common and celibate life, became an increasingly positive feature attracting new members. In the diocese of Boston, for example, sisters were approximately equal in number to churchmen, including priests, brothers, and seminarians, in 1870. By 1940, however, the more than four thousand sisters outnumbered the men by two to one (Oates 1980, 144). These proportions were similar in other dioceses across the country. The religious motive is especially significant, for if teaching or providing social services were the only goal of a group of women, they would have little reason for organizing under the aegis of the church.

In choosing a decidedly unconventional life-style, sisters had always been at variance with social norms governing female behavior. By the late nineteenth century, however, they faced additional hurdles in two environments. They had become the most numerous and visible symbols of Catholicism in a heavily Protestant culture, and they were endeavoring to progress as professionals in a religious milieu traditionally governed by men. Popular stereotypes about women's capabilities and professional status characteristic of the period were held by bishops and clergy at least as strongly as by their lay counterparts.

Constitutions of sisterhoods established as a basic tenet the spiritual equality of members, and all shared in community resources. Great esteem was accorded superiors and senior sisters. It was demonstrated outwardly in the title of "mother" for higher superiors and in the ordering of sisters by rank, determined usually by date of entrance into the community. Community constitutions expressed not only the group's aims and corporate work but also precise rules according to which sisters promised to live. To a shared religious heritage could be added, within most communities, considerable homogeneity in ethnic, educational, and social class backgrounds of members. A common life and work, limited opportunity for contact with persons outside the community, the adoption of religious names and uniform garb all helped to nurture enduring bonds of friendship, loyalty, and mutual support. The ceremony of religious profession of vows gave formal and public expression to the lifetime commitment of members to their chosen community.

Professed sisters participated in choosing a superior general and several councillors, who held final authority in all matters affecting the community. The term of office of the superior general was limited in duration, so that, in principle at least, a group's welfare could not become indefinitely dependent upon a single individual. Elected leaders appointed superiors for all local convents. These were women distinguished by strong community spirit and faithful observance of regulations. Their role in preserving group cohesiveness was basic because individual convents were often geographically remote from each other and from the motherhouse. A characteristic admonition of one superior general to her local superiors reveals the high priority placed upon uniformity of observance: "Remarks have been made regarding the difference in practice in some houses. The customs and regulations are the same for all and nobody should be able to say such a Superior is too strict, etc., etc. In some minds the lack of uniformity appears to indicate a want of harmony" (Julia 1891, n.p.).

Ideally, within sisterhoods, women were not isolated, men were not in charge, and women did not have to be concerned with pleasing them. In reality, however, female groups met far greater challenges to their auton-

omy than did religious communities of men because the canon law governing religious was not uniform for men and women. The most critical difference was that the privilege of exemption from episcopal interference in
community affairs and government was reserved to male religious orders.
When in 1752 Rome ceased approving new orders, permitting only the establishment of congregations that by definition did not enjoy the exemption privilege, clerics increasingly preferred to organize as "pious societies"
rather than as congregations. Because members of a pious society took no
special vows, the group could not be classified as a true religious institute,
although its constitutions had to have church approval. Thus, absence of
the exemption privilege posed little risk to the autonomy of the pious society.

Women, on the other hand, were not permitted to establish pious societies. The only structure for which they could obtain church approval was
the nonexempt congregation. Every female congregation was either diocesan
(that is, approved by the local bishop) or pontifical (approved by authorities
in Rome). Bishops were given much wider jurisdiction over diocesan communities than over pontifical groups. In the vital matter of the election of
superiors, for example, while they presided over elections in pontifical communities, they could veto election results in diocesan groups (Bachofen 1929,
101). Many American bishops concluded that it was also their prerogative
to intervene at will in the direction of female communities. As a result, in
the interpretation of constitutions, in the determination of appropriate works
to be undertaken by members, and in the establishment of social customs
to be observed, notable distinctions developed between male and female
communities.

Over time, as their charitable works expanded, sisters found regulations
requiring them, but not male religious, to observe a cloistered life-style increasingly burdensome. In addition to the strict rules spelled out in constitutions, clerics frequently imposed new customs that inhibited further
the mobility and social activities of women religious. At the turn of the
century, for example, an episcopal agent unilaterally countermanded current practice in one large teaching community by writing to the mother
superior: "At the Christmas and Easter recess, it is my wish that the Sisters
stay at home. Should it be necessary to make a rule to that effect I shall
do so" (Magennis 1903). Strict limitation on contact with the world not
only placed sisters in a position of greater dependence on men in conduct-
ing their community affairs, but it also adversely affected their professional
work. Because changes in the official text of community constitutions could
be introduced only with difficulty, sisterhoods tried to resolve conflicts between work obligations and cloistral rules by adhering to what they defined
as the spirit rather than the letter of the law. This course prompted wide-

spread objections from churchmen who insisted that they honor the restrictive precepts of cloister and continue to practice the stereotypically female virtues of silence and humility.

Episcopal supervision of female communities extended to apparently minor matters as well. For example, during the 1870s Bishop James Healy of Portland, Maine, reserved to himself the right to approve or disapprove religious names given to novices of the Sisters of Mercy. Outlawing the custom of handshaking by sisters, he required them to "bow courteously" instead. Although sisters had long attended school events such as plays and graduations, this practice, too, was forbidden (Healy 1973, 399–400). Bishops even took it upon themselves to modify the religious habits distinguishing the various communities, a recurring intrusion that sisters found extremely objectionable.

Ecclesiastics justified such conduct by asserting that women needed male direction. All women were properly subordinate to men, the wife to her husband and the nun to ecclesiastical authorities. Rationale for this belief, widely proclaimed in pulpit and Catholic press, was summarized by an 1896 writer: "Woman is not, and in the eternal fitness of things never can be, unqualifiedly man's coequal or superior. Woman being after and from man, does not represent humanity in the full and complete sense that man does" (MacCorrie 1896, 614). In fact, however, episcopal motives were far more pragmatic. The sisterhoods collectively provided at extremely low cost nearly the entire labor force for thousands of church schools, hospitals, and charitable agencies across the country, and churchmen intended to control its deployment. Intervention in details of daily life within the communities, more the rule than the exception before 1950, effectively buttressed episcopal influence over community work, income, and property.

A bishop's interest in the work of sisters tended to focus mainly on how it related to shifting needs within his diocese. Theoretically, with the establishment throughout the country of numerous congregations of women, each highly specialized by work, he could simply invite an appropriate group to enter the diocese to meet the latest challenge. Practically, however, growing demand for the services of sisters after 1880 often meant that communities engaged in the desired activity could not be induced to take on added responsibilities in another diocese. The tendency was therefore to prevail upon groups already working within the diocese to redefine their chosen field of endeavor to encompass the need of the hour.

Communities struggled to augment their legal prerogatives and collective authority by initiating cross-diocesan ties among societies of the same rule (Savage 1923, 117) and, more often, by applying for Roman approval. The application of an Iowa sisterhood for pontifical status echoed general sentiment: "Approbation is a guarantee for unity. Rules thus protected will be the same everywhere; no local authority can prevail against them. A Congregation so approved . . . becomes a unified, immutable, independent and universal Society" (Doran 1912, 292–93). Diocesan officials countered these maneuvers wherever possible. A sister-annalist described an 1850 event that was soon repeated across the nation: the bishop of Nashville persuaded some sisters in her community to break away from their motherhouse and to form a new diocesan group under his control. She concluded sadly that "his priests were entirely in sympathy with his plans" (A Member 1898, 22). In 1890, a sisterhood seeking pontifical approbation was informed that Cardinal Gibbons of Baltimore disapproved: "The great objection of the Cardinal was that you would be entirely outside of his jurisdiction and that you would do what you please against his will" (Sabetti 1890).

If a pontifical congregation's constitutions stated its goals narrowly and unambiguously it was better able to resist pressures to undertake extraneous works than if the language was expansive. Careful phrasing of constitutions did not protect the numerous diocesan sisterhoods, however. Like many of his colleagues, Cardinal William O'Connell simply denied that a Boston diocesan teaching community, the Sisters of St. Joseph, possessed any authority in the matter of work determination. Throughout his long tenure from 1908 until 1944, he insisted that they assume numerous projects unrelated to their corporate work, and this in a period when there was a shortage of teachers for their many schools: "I want the Sisters to do all kinds of work. Some of them don't want to do anything but teach" (Aloysius 1921).

Among "all kinds of work" churchmen included domestic service, a subject of special sensitivity for American sisters. In local convents, necessary daily housework was simplified, divided among all the members, and done expeditiously in order to devote as much time and energy as possible to the group's charitable enterprises. Requests that sisters be assigned to toil as servants in seminaries, rectories, and retreat houses, or to clean the parish church, offended the conviction of sisters. Many lay Catholics, however, felt that such attitudes on the part of sisters were deviant, and they did not share sisters' beliefs that they, like priests and brothers, should do only significant work in the service of the church.

But this painful battle, which focused so immediately on the definition of "woman's sphere of labor," was not won for decades. Proposals that sisters assume domestic duties multiplied after 1850 as the number of diocesan seminaries expanded. In 1856 Bishop James Roosevelt Bayley of Newark wrote to a sister superior that he planned to open a seminary and was "very anxious to obtain some Religious to take charge of the Infirmary and domestic arrangements, as is the custom in France" (Logue 1950, 148).

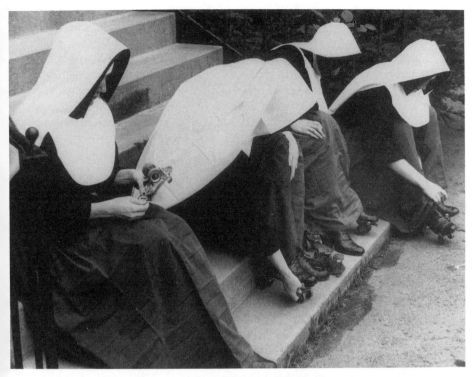

17. Novice Sisters of Notre Dame going roller skating, ca. 1940. *Courtesy of Archives, Sisters of Notre Dame de Namur, Ipswich, Massachusetts.*

A Benedictine superior in Minnesota resigned rather than acquiesce to continuing such work in 1877. "The final break was . . . caused by Mother Antonia's attempt to get the convent released from the onerous task of doing the monastery laundry" (McDonald 1957, 73). At the turn of the century, Rochester's Bishop McQuaid was advising his fellow New Yorker, Archbishop Corrigan, to get nuns for domestic work in his seminary; not only should women do women's work, but "men cannot keep a clean house" (McQuaid 1896). By this date, however, pontifical communities were making progress in the struggle to free sisters from domestic work, a breakthrough reflected in a superior general's terse instruction to local superiors in 1911: "Where the Sisters make the Altar Bread for the Parish Church, they ought to try to discontinue this work as soon as possible. We have no time for it" (Julia 1911).

A preponderance of American sisters by 1890 were employed in parochial schools in working-class neighborhoods. These schools and their convents were parish owned, with sisters receiving from the parish their housing and a small annual stipend. By this date, formal professional training was becoming an essential credential for public school teachers in most states. The tension betweeen the subordinate position of sisters in the ecclesiastical organization and their work as professionals was nowhere clearer than in the matter of the education of parochial school teachers. On the one hand, strict rules of life required that they remain secluded from society and work under the supervision of pastors, the legal principals of the schools. These men tended to be more concerned with having a full complement of teachers than with their qualifications, especially as the supply of new teachers never met the demand for their services. On the other hand, the communities were well aware of their shortcomings in training young sisters to standards acceptable in public schools (Oates 1984, 63). Annals of sisterhoods during the years of rapid school expansion after 1880 are filled with statements of regret about the persisting dilemma. A provincial superior commented on her community's new normal program: "The Normal School opened with a class of twenty-two, but alas! for its hopes, scarcely a day has passed since, but demands from some quarter or other threaten the career of its pupils; and so they have gone" (Annals 1889–1896, 127–28). Not until the Sister Formation Movement of the 1950s were communities generally victorious in the struggle to keep young sisters out of the schools until they had bachelor's degrees.

The financial health and stability of the congregations, of course, affected their ability to educate novices and to care for sick and aged members. Remunerations made to teachers in parochial schools during these years appear to have been fairly uniform across dioceses. The experience of Boston Sisters of Saint Joseph reflected general practice. In 1910 full-time teachers received housing without board and an annual salary of $200, a figure that had not changed in urban teaching communities since the 1860s. By 1921 the stipend had risen to about $250, reaching $300 in 1937.

Because this diocesan community was required to report periodically to the local bishop on its financial condition, it is possible to evaluate the adequacy of these stipends for the needs of a growing community. While per capita expenses in reporting convents rose by 43.7 percent between 1909 and 1921, teachers' salaries rose by only 24.9 percent.[1] In recognition of this fact, the corporation of the congregation, composed of the superior general and her council, held the central tax levied on each teaching sister to meet communitywide expenses to approximately fifty dollars a year, although central costs were also rising. These corporation receipts were used

to finance the construction and maintenance of a residence for sick and re-
tired sisters and another for postulants and novices, as well as to cover medical and educational costs of the entire membership.

The corporation was forced to rely more and more on supplementary
sources of income to compensate for insufficient contributions from stipends.
All communities staffing parochial schools placed great emphasis on the need
for sisters to earn more income after school hours, especially by giving music
lessons, because one music teacher could account for a disproportionate share
of current revenue in a local convent. No effort was made to camouflage
the reason for introducing these special lessons. A description by a midwest-
ern chronicler of the circumstances in her community about 1910 was representative of most teaching sisterhoods throughout the period: "If at all
possible, Mother Seraphine sent a Sister to teach music in every convent
with a school, as the salary paid Sisters was insufficient for the simple necessities of life" (Graham 1950, 51). In addition to their full-time work in
the schools, sisters also taught religion to children enrolled in public schools
during after-school hours and on Sunday mornings. Such work was compensated only when it was carried on in parishes that had no schools. Then
pastors paid fifty dollars annually per sister for the lessons.

Most pontifical congregations with heavy commitments to parochial
schools endeavored to open at least one tuition-charging academy, and more
if possible, in order to earn additional income. In Boston the diocesan community maintained its motherhouse and supported sisters engaged in community administration and other nonsalaried work entirely from surplus
revenues of a single academy for girls. Without these additional funds and
some charitable donations, this sisterhood would have been unable to support itself.

In contrast to congregations specializing in parochial school teaching,
those managing social institutions appear at first glance to have held greater
direct authority over their work and hence, like male communities, might
be expected to earn better salaries. Carney Hospital in Boston and Saint
John's Hospital in nearby Lowell, for example, were incorporated (in 1865
and 1867, respectively) by the Sisters of Charity, "their associates and suc-
cessors" (Sullivan 1895, 348). Article one of the by-laws of Saint Elizabeth's
Hospital for Women, another local institution established in 1872, stated
that "the Treasurer shall always be the Superior of the [Franciscan] community in charge of the Hospital" (Saint Elizabeth's 1880). The original corporation of this hospital was composed of two laymen and five Franciscan
sisters.

But the authority of sisters in establishments they founded had begun
to erode significantly even before 1900. For example, by 1882 the provision

that a sister be treasurer had been removed by amendment of the Saint Eliza-beth's Hospital charter, and in 1900 the board of directors included only one woman, a sister. After 1900, as diocesan-owned charitable agencies be-came more numerous, sisterhoods staffing them enjoyed, for the most part, only nominal representation on their boards.

Salaries paid sisters working in these diocesan hospitals, homes, and or-phanages exhibited less uniformity than those received by parochial school teachers. On average, sisters received in 1909 fifty dollars per year in addi-tion to both room and board (Filiatrault 1909: Saint Theodore 1917). Be-cause they had little leverage on governing boards, their stipend levels were occasionally modified without prior consultation. For example, an orphan-age in Lowell, Massachusetts, provided an annual stipend of $150 by 1924. But in 1932 the executive committee instructed its secretary to apprise the superior general of the Sisters of Charity "that it was necessary to reduce the salary of each of the sisters at the Orphanage [by] $25.00 per year" (L'Orphelinat 1925, 1932).

Throughout the nineteenth century many bishops contended that property purchased by women's religious communities within diocesan bor-ders became thereby a diocesan asset. Sisterhoods never conceded in this matter, and their bitter disputes with local bishops occasionally reached the secular press. The *Toledo Journal* (Mar. 27, 1889) provides a vivid account of a typical controversy over property between the Grey Nuns of Montreal and Bishop Gilmour of Cleveland. The latter insisted that the sisters trans-fer the property of Saint Vincent's Hospital, Orphan Asylum, and Home for the Aged to him as trustee. They refused, arguing that they had founded the institution and had donated some $40,000 "as a nest egg," with the rest of the money needed to furnish it "contributed by the citizens of To-ledo irrespective of creed." When he pressed his claim, the women appealed to the highest-ranking American churchman, Archbishop Gibbons of Balti-more, and ultimately to the Propaganda in Rome. They won their case, but Bishop Gilmour retaliated in a particularly painful way by giving "strict or-ders forbidding priests to say Mass at the Hospital. . . . He also forbade the Sisters from soliciting alms for the support of their institutions."

Over time the communities worked hard to devise strategies that would ensure appropriate compensation for the labor of sisters and that would pro-tect their assets from being redirected to other uses. The most important change was that the rather casual oral agreements of the nineteenth century between sisterhoods and churchmen became more formal. Written contracts were drawn up specifying in detail sisters' work responsibilities and reim-bursement. In 1912, a superior general sympathized with a local superior about some unpleasant encounters with "the powers that be," in this case the diocesan chancellor: "The only thing I see is that it has all been kept up *too cheap* for them all these years. . . . I think we should have all our contracts in writing, so that in case of changes or deaths the writing would stand. I am getting *written contracts* ready for all the parochial schools" (Meagher 1912). Pontifical communities assiduously guarded internal financial data from the purview of nonmembers. Superior generals warned local superiors not to answer questions posed by local churchmen. Said one: "According to our Rules and Customs: 1) No Bishop or Pastor is to exercise any supervision over our accounts . . . and 2) what we buy with our own money belongs to us" (Julia n.d.).

While property disputes became less common over time, the salary issue remained a matter of grave concern for most sisterhoods throughout the period. Inadequate financial support was adversely affecting the quality of community life and work. Drawn away from their areas of primary service to raise funds to support the establishments in which they labored and to supplement their low salaries, sisters continued to find social and professional integration an elusive goal before 1940.

Like most Catholic women in the century following 1850, sisters appeared to honor the social prescription that "woman's place is in the home" because they lived in communities apart from the world. There was, however, a critical difference. While model Catholic mothers of the era worked only in the confines of their homes in domestic labor and child care, sisterhoods minimized the time spent by members in domestic work in order to provide philanthropic services in an extensive network of schools and social agencies.

With the professionalization of the fields of nursing, teaching, and social work in the late nineteenth and early twentieth centuries, the communities became increasingly aware not only of the concern for social progress that they shared with the Protestant mainstream but also of the confining aspects of the structures within which, as women religious, they were expected to function in the church. Although they encountered severe challenges before 1940 to their rights to conduct their own internal affairs and to determine their corporate works, American sisters responded to them resolutely, firm in their conviction that their communities had enduring significance not only for their members but also for the church and the wider society.

Note

1. Compiled from data in Institution Files. Archives, Archdiocese of Boston. 4:14–19.

Works Cited

Abbreviations

AABO   Archives, Archdiocese of Boston
ASND   Archives, Sisters of Notre Dame de Namur
ASSJ   Archives, Sisters of Saint Joseph
AUND   Archives, University of Notre Dame

Aloysius, Sister M. 1921. Diary. Oct. 15. ASSJ, Brighton, Mass.

Annals, Sisters of Notre Dame de Namur, Waltham, Mass. 1889–1896. ASND, Ipswich, Mass.

Bachhofen, Charles Augustine. 1929. *A Commentary on the New Code of Canon Law.* Vol. 3. *Religious and Laymen.* St. Louis: B. Herder.

Doran, Sister M. Lambertina. 1912. *In the Early Days: Pages from the Annals of the Sisters of Charity of the Blessed Virgin Mary.* St. Louis: B. Herder.

Filiatrault, Sister M. P. 1909. Letter to Cardinal William O'Connell. Nov. 9. Institution Files. AABO 2:15.

Graham, Sister Clara. 1950. *Works to the King: Reminiscences of Mother Seraphine Ireland.* St. Paul: North Central.

Healy, Kathleen. 1973. *Frances Warde: American Foundress of the Sisters of Mercy.* New York: Seabury.

Julia, Sister Superior, n.d. [early 1890s]. Letter to Sister Superiors, Cincinnati. ASND, Ipswich, Mass.

———. 1891. Letter to Sister Superiors, Cincinnati. Dec. 10. ASND, Ipswich, Mass.

———. 1911. "Recommendations." No. 18, Apr. ASND, Ipswich, Mass.

Logue, Sister Maria Kostka. 1950. *The Sisters of Saint Joseph of Philadelphia.* Westminster, Md.: Newman.

L'Orphelinat Franco-Amèricain, Lowell, Mass. 1925. Financial Report. Oct. 1, 1924–Oct. 1, 1925. Institution Files. AABO 11:23.

———. 1932. Minutes of meeting of executive committee. Nov. 10. Institution Files. AABO 11:23.

MacCorrie, John Paul. 1896. The War of the Sexes. *Catholic World* 63:605–18.

McDonald, Sister M. Grace. 1957. *With Lamps Burning.* Saint Joseph, Minn.: Saint Benedict's Priory.

McQuaid, Bishop Bernard. 1896. Letter to Archbishop Michael Corrigan, Rochester. July 25. AUND.

Magennis, Rev. Thomas. 1903. Letter to Mother Mary Genevieve, Jamaica Plain. Apr. 18. ASSJ. Brighton, Mass.

Meagher, Mother Rose. 1912. Letter to Sister Stanislaus Tully, Nazareth. Dec. 3. Sisters of Charity of Nazareth, Kentucky Collection. AUND.

Member of the Community, A. 1898. *History of the Sisters of Charity of Leavenworth, Kansas.* Kansas City: Hudson-Kimberley.

Oates, Mary J. 1980. Organized Voluntarism: The Catholic Sisters in Massachusetts, 1870–1940. In *Women in American Religion,* edited by Janet Wilson James,
141–69. Philadelphia: Univ. of Pennsylvania Press.

———. 1984. Professional Preparation of Parochial School Teachers, 1870–1940.
Historical Journal of Massachusetts 12:60–72.

———. 1985. "The Good Sisters": The Work and Position of Catholic Churchwomen in Boston, 1870–1940. In *Catholic Boston: Studies in Religion and Community, 1870–1970,* edited by Robert E. Sullivan and James M. O'Toole, 171–
200. Boston: Archdiocese of Boston.

Sabetti, S.J., Father. 1890. Letter to Mother Clement, Woodstock. Sept. 14. ASSJ,
Philadelphia.

Saint Elizabeth's Hospital for Women. 1880. Minutes of the Annual Meeting. Feb. 2.
Corporation Records. AABO.

Saint Theodore, Sister. 1917. Letter to Sister S. Honoré, Sept. 1. Institution Files.
AABO 11:22.

Savage, Sister Mary Lucida. 1923. *The Congregation of St. Joseph of Carondelet.* St. Louis:
B. Herder.

Sullivan, James J., ed. 1895. *One Hundred Years of Progress: A Graphical, Historical
and Pictorial Account of the Catholic Church of New England, Archdiocese of Boston.*
Boston: Illustrated.

PART FOUR

Women's Status and
Male Power in Community

Introduction

THIS SECTION EXAMINES four communities either strongly patriarchal in structure, or led by powerful male spiritual figures, or both. The Mormonism, officially called The Church of Jesus Christ of Latter-Day Saints (LDS), was established by Joseph Smith (1805–44) in 1830. It was a patriarchal faith that believed its members were descendants of the lost tribes of Israel and were destined through apostolic succession to establish a theocratic kingdom of God. Mormons settled first in Kirtland, Ohio, but in 1839 founded Nauvoo, Illinois (population 11,000 in 1844). Radically sectarian, Mormons believed in a plurality of worlds and gods, in man's ability to obtain divinity through obedience, and in "celestial marriage," or polygyny. Reaction against them led to persecution: Joseph Smith and his brother Hyrum were murdered by a mob in 1844. Under the leadership of a new prophet and patriarch, Brigham Young (1801–77), Mormons moved west and settled in the valley of the Great Salt Lake in 1847. In 1852 their practice of polygyny (legitimized in a revelation to Smith in 1832 and secretly put into practice in Nauvoo before 1844) was publicly acknowledged. Approximately 25 percent of the Mormon population "lived the faith" or practiced polygyny. The church discountenanced plural marriage in the Woodruff Manifesto (1890), which also established the end of the political kingdom of Mormondom and of their early communitarian lifestyle. This was the price the Mormons paid for the statehood of Utah (1896). Religious and public authority resided in the priesthood of the LDS church, which until 1978 excluded African-American males, and still excludes women. From the first, the denomination has remained vigorously evangelical. In 1988 it had 4.3 million members in 9,500 congregations in the United States. Worldwide membership was 7 million in 1989. It is one of the most powerful Christian denominations in the world. Best sources on this group are James V. Allen and Glen M. Leonard, *The Story of the Latter Day Saints* (Salt Lake City: Deseret Books: 1976), and Leonard J. Arrington and Davis Bitton, *The Mormon Experience: A History of the Latter Day Saints* (New York: Knopf: 1979).

The Oneida Community (1848–80), Madison County, New York, was founded by the charismatic John Humphrey Noyes (1811–86) as a continuation of his abortive Putney Community (1843–48) in Windham County, Vermont. It was grounded in Bible Communism and Perfectionist theology (a postmillennial belief that each individual had the potential to conquer sin). Its social life was characterized by four institutions: "complex marriage" or pantagamy (all community adults are married to each other); "male continence," a form of *coitus reservatus* as a contraceptive practice; "stirpiculture" (1868–1878), or eugenic reproduction; and "mutual criticism," a form of community guidance and shaping of individual personality to meet communal ideology. The community economy relied on the manufacture of silk thread, animal traps, and silver flatware. The population ranged from 51 in 1848 to 306 in 1878. At dissolution the community reorganized into a joint-stock company, Oneida Company, Ltd. Sources on the community are Maren Lockwood Carden, *Oneida: Utopian Community to Modern Corporation* (1969), and Richard DeMaria, *Communal Love at Oneida: A Perfectionist Vision of Authority, Property, and Sexual Order* (New York: E. Morrow, 1978).

The Farm was a multigenerational, largely self-sufficient agricultural commune (based on sorghum) founded in 1971 near Summertown, Tennessee, by Stephen Gaskin and a small group of followers, refugees from the hippie scene of the Haight-Ashbury. The spiritual basis of the community combined Eastern Zen and the sacramental use of marijuana. Until 1979 Gaskin was the undisputed patriarch of the community; he relinquished power as the community began to lose population, and the polity of The Farm became more democratic. Initially, plural marriage was practiced, but by 1973 monogamy predominated. It was a naturalist community, allowing no use of artificial drugs (including for contraception) and practicing natural childbirth ("spiritual midwifery") and strict vegetarianism. A form of community criticism of individuals reinforced social and ideological precepts. The Farm was strongly pronatalist and took in unwed mothers for childbirth, adopted unwanted children, encouraged the elderly to settle in the community, and took in some handicapped adults. In 1983 the community abandoned its communitarian organization and became a joint-stock company. In that form, it continues to exist with a population of about 280 (its peak population was about 1,200 in the late 1970s). The Farm maintains an active international social service organization called Plenty, which is involved with ecological projects and Third World problems. There are no extended scholarly examinations of The Farm. Best sources of information are those published by the community itself: Stephen Gaskin, *Hey Beatnik! This Is*

The Farm Book (1974), and Ina May and The Farm Midwives, *Spiritual Midwifery* (1975).

The Lubavitchers (Habad Hasidim) are a rational-mystic sect of Hasidism founded by the patriarch Shne'ur Zalman of Lyady (1745–1813), and led by his lineal descendants, the Schneersohn family, down to the present. Originally from Russia and Eastern Europe, the Lubavitchers began their emigration to the United States in the 1920s and 1930s. Rebbe Joseph Yitzchak Schneersohn (1880–1950) arrived in Crown Heights, Brooklyn, in 1940. Since the mid-1960s, large numbers of unaffiliated Jews have joined the sect, and today they are by far the most numerous and prominent of the Hasidim in the United States. Hasidic law strictly forbids the practice of birth control, and even in the contemporary United States, the overwhelming majority of Lubavitcher women abide by religious law. There is strong community pressure to have large families, and even extended spacings between births can cause adverse social pressure. Children are of central importance to Lubavitcher (and broader Hasidic) culture, and lack of fecundity remains among the most prominent grounds for divorce in the sect. Despite a theology that emphasizes inwardness and contemplation, coupled with strict observance of tradition and ritual, Hasidim remain open to technology, modern educational techniques, and sophisticated public relations methods. Dancing is a central part of their ritual and by Jewish law requires strict separation of the sexes. Women's roles are generally domestic and maternal, though there have been several outstanding female Lubavitcher thinkers. Their central yeshiva (Tomchi T'mimim) is located in Brooklyn, and their educational organization, Merkos L'Inyone Chinuch, has established over sixty-seven schools (overwhelmingly for males) since 1941. Lubavitchers also maintain a nationwide relief organization, with branches in fifty-six U.S. cities, called Ezrat Pleithm-Vesidurom. They publish most of the Hasidic literature produced in the United States through their publishing house, Kehot. Lubavitchers remain the most open of the Hasidim and are militantly evangelical. There are no population figures available for this group. Best sources for further information are Lis Harris, *Holy Days: The World of the Hasidic Family* (New York: Summit, 1985) and Naftali Lowenthal, *Communicating the Infinite: The Emergence of Habad School* (Chicago: Univ. of Chicago Press, 1990).

10

"Diamond Cut Diamond"

The Mormon Wife vs. the True Woman, 1840–1890

KATHY MARQUIS

"THE WOMEN OF THIS COUNTRY want to crush us, but it will be diamond cut diamond." That was the outcry in 1878 as two thousand Mormon women challenged the moral superiority of their gentile (non-Mormon) sisters (Marshall 1881, 187). They had gathered to protest the mounting antipolygamy campaign against Mormons (the Church of Jesus Christ of Latter-day Saints). The diamond metaphor was apt because each side felt it had the one true answer to the role of women in the family, the unit on which all society rested and that women created and nurtured. Each side was sure it provided the only true defense against moral decay.

In her classic 1966 article "The Cult of True Womanhood, 1820–1860," Barbara Welter has described the true woman as a person of purity, piety, submissiveness, and domesticity. All four qualities were equally valued on both sides of the polygamy battle, though to different ends. Both sets of women assumed the traditional gender role, with its implicit sexual double standard: women want and need only monogamous sex, while men desire many sexual partners. Only polygamy offered men a more expanded (and less guilty) alternative. How was it that these two groups arrived at such similar notions of the ideal wife while supporting such anthithetical forms of the basic unit of society—the family? The search for answers must begin with an inquiry into the origins of the role of Mormon wife.

Within a larger context of religious upheaval and the birth of alternative and semicollective communities, the Mormons can be seen as one of many dissatisfied groups searching for answers in new rules and beliefs. As determined pioneers, they combined their faith in divine inspiration with a solid practical sense of how most productively to organize their converts.

Though they developed a communitarian agricultural base into one of the most successful of western settlements, Mormons in the nineteenth century were more widely known for their practice of "plural marriage" or polygamy than for collectivized cultivation of an inhospitable land. Drawing an ire previously reserved for slaveholders, Mormons fought a losing battle to uphold plural marriage, their "principle." But by 1890, after military defeat at the hands of the U.S. Army (the Mormon War of 1857) and legal defeat via federal law (the Edmunds-Tucker Act, 1887) and the provisions of statehood, polygamy went underground, its adherents dwindling in number each year.

Perhaps most significant, and yet least acknowledged by either side was the class nature of the battle. Eastern middle-class critics, equating their class values with America's true Christian creed, pitted themselves against a nonconforming group that valued unladylike manual labor and encouraged a mounting birth rate.

To illustrate the roots of Mormonism and its appeal, I found it useful to keep in mind the lives of two early members. One was Fanny Stenhouse, an English convert, who married an apostle of the Mormon church. The other was Joseph Smith, the first Mormon prophet, who was also president and founder of the Church of Jesus Christ of Latter-day Saints.

Both Fanny Stenhouse and her husband, T. B. H. Stenhouse, left the church in about 1880. It was only after they left that she published her story, *An Englishwoman in Utah: The Story of a Life's Experiences in Mormonism.* But if one may doubt her sincerity and analysis of the church, her background remains significant for the many ways in which it parallels Smith's. At the same time, it represents the considerable number of early Mormons who came as immigrants, mainly from Great Britain and Scandinavia, but also from other countries (Marshall 1881, 225).

Stenhouse begins her story with her humble and pious origins in England. This was the early nineteenth century, and in the backwash of the Enlightenment many Europeans longed to regain some kind of strong faith. Stenhouse and her parents were caught up in each wave of revivalism that swept through their part of the country. When she was fourteen she and her parents converted to the Baptist faith, and soon afterward she traveled to France to teach fancy needlework in a school. As the parents of her charges objected to her Protestantism, she took several years of Catholic instruction but neither changed her mind nor gave up her religion. She even rejected marriage to a young Frenchman because she found married women in French society too "loose."

Upon returning to England, she and her parents were swept up in yet another new movement—the missionary Mormons and their call to "gather to Zion" (travel to Utah). Here, at last, was a fundamentalism that Stenhouse could accept. Though she never described the Mormon religion in detail, it clearly captured her imagination and loyalty as the previous religions had not. What then follows in her autobiographical reminiscences is a series of tragic tales, as the "horrible whisperings" of polygamy became a terrible reality. But apostasy was a mortal sin, so she traveled to Utah, sighing and muttering apprehensions all the way, lived among the Mormons for many years until finally, unable to endure it any longer, she left the church.

To turn our attention to Joseph Smith and his family in upstate New York is to come upon the American counterpart of the Stenhouse saga (see Cross 1956). The Smiths belonged to those men and women who were disillusioned by poverty but not ready to pack up and head west, and who were not imbued with any Jacksonian individualism to pull themselves up by their bootstraps. Numerous Protestant sects held temporary promise for those in search of a collective, all-affirming faith, and in 1820 the Smiths converted to Presbyterianism. Thereafter, Smith's history differs according to who is telling it, but roughly three years later he was "shown" the gold plates of Moroni upon which were inscribed the wisdom of the *Book of Mormon*. In 1830 the *Book of Mormon* was published, with Smith listed as author.

Both Smith and Stenhouse arrived at Mormonism through a process of trial and error. What gave Mormonism its special appeal (and its terror to outsiders) was the literal way in which it planned to reward its followers, the disinherited. Mormonism is a creed that puts unusual emphasis on the material. Initially, this creed included a surrender of all goods to the common fund, but as the sect grew more pragmatic this requirement was replaced by a tithing system. Mormons believed in a living God who will return with the millennium to rule the city of the saints (the chosen people) for a thousand years. All family ties were to remain intact when members entered the celestial kingdom (Mormon heaven); life in heaven was thus determined by one's latter days on earth. Like many other millennial sects of the day, Mormons assumed the Judgment Day to be imminent. But unlike other sectarians, Mormons wished to acquire land for the kingdom and set up a working political unit on earth to prepare for the end (a goal-oriented creed: you *can* take it with you). To nonbelievers, this looked suspiciously like a group of strange-thinkers bent on gaining political power and flaunting not only the law of the land but the unwritten conventions of American society.

Thus, the Mormons posed many political and social threats: their hunger for land; their eventual growth to imposing size as a colony; and their anachronistic union of church and state, which bonded them in a way that no one religious or political group could hope to undermine. As such, none of the purportedly civilized eastern areas they settled in would tolerate them for long. First in New York, then in Ohio, in Missouri, and still later in their own town of Nauvoo, Illinois, they searched for Zion. With them they carried a reputation for immorality, lawlessness, and crudity that is difficult to substantiate yet is marked in contemporary observations (Ferris [1856] 1971; Marshall 1881; Merriam 1894; Mulder and Mortensen 1958; Stenhouse 1881; Ward 1856). In 1844, Joseph Smith and his brother, Hyrum, were lynched in a jail in Carthage, Illinois, by an angry mob of anti-Mormons. In the late 1840s and early 1850s, spurred by the increasingly violent anti-Mormon sentiment and led by Brigham Young and other Mormon elders, the group made its final move west to Utah.

Most of the early Mormons were from rural or small town working-class backgrounds, while their critics and observers were largely middle-lass and urban, particularly in Utah. Only rarely did western sightseers comment on Mormon life beyond urban Salt Lake City. Hence, they told little of how Mormon agrarian life was organized. Yet it was in rural Utah, Arizona, New Mexico, and Idaho that Mormon colonizing was most innovative, compared to contemporary patterns of American farm life. For example, some Mormon settlements were planned collectively so that homes were in a central location. From these Mormons went out daily to their farm plots, returning to the settlement at dusk (Lowry 1930, 11). In this way, they avoided the lack of social and economic support and the terrible emotional isolation so common to American farm families. Theirs were only partial collectives, because each family remained a separate unit. But the religious cohesion and the spatial closeness nourished a strong group spirit that helped them survive, and many prospered. In this setting a man's many wives (and children) enabled him to better operate the farm. But the gentile observer saw only a harem, an interpretation that was crucial to gentiles' perceptions of Mormon marriage and family life.

Kimball Young, a twentieth-century Mormon sociologist, notes that "spiritual wifism," or the concept of the ideal mate, was popular during the time that Joseph Smith formulated or received his initial views on marriage and the family (K. Young 1954, 90). Together with the emphasis on materialism in Mormon religion, this idea may partly explain Smith's approach to marriage. The Mormon family was decidedly patriarchal, and marriage began with the man. He was directed to enlarge his own personal celestial kingdom by marrying and then increasing the size of his family to his own glorification. The domestic focus was crucial, of course, to a young colony, creating a stable work- and emotional-support unit. Brigham Young instructed his people, "Let every man in the land over eighteen years of age take a wife . . . fit you up a little log cabin, if it is not more than ten feet square, then get you a bird to put in your little cage . . . you will then have something to encourage you to labor" (B. Young 1925, 301). Marriage could be "for time" (on earth alone) or "for eternity" (in heaven) or both. One was permitted to marry "for time," while attaching oneself to another "for eternity," but it was assumed that a man would marry for both and thus ensure a large celestial progeny. More significant was the doctrine that no unmarried women would be accepted into heaven.

Non-Mormons were appalled at this reversal of one of their most basic assumptions: the moral superiority of women. The Mormons had simply found a different moral anchor for their society in the patriarchal husband: each man was an integral part of the church and its authority. This was quite different from the rest of American society where the woman was considered the stabilizing influence in the home, that bastion against the corrupting influence of industry and commerce. But, in each case, the figure of stability met the same sorts of needs, though neither side, of course, saw it that way. And so, for gentiles, Mormonism came to represent an inherent degradation of womanhood.

Another sore point was the constant childbearing that was asked of Mormon women. Other women were expected to bear children, too, as one of their primary functions. But they felt they got and deserved a degree of respect as moral guardians and child raisers. They stayed at home to remain pure and raised enough children to make a small but adequate testament to their husbands. These were middle-class mores, though just as valid for lower-class families, at least those who hoped to rise socially. Initially, help in building a labor/colonizing supply came from the converts migrating to Nauvoo and later to Salt Lake City. But the long-range plan was to encourage high birth rates. Mormons' unique metaphoric rationale for this obvious need was that "souls were waiting to be housed" before entering heaven.

It may be noted that what Mormons practiced was not polygamy (multiple spouses for either sex). What they called "plural marriage" is more correctly termed polygyny, or many wives for one husband. However, most sources use the term "polygamy," and so it will appear here, though it will be understood to have been an option for men only. Ironically, the original stance on plural marriage in the *Book of Mormon* is unequivocally negative: "For there shall not any man among you have save it be one wife; and concubines he shall have none" (Smith 1830, 172).

Fawn Brodie in her biography of Joseph Smith, *No Man Knows My History,* speculates on the unique options for women in Nauvoo. She suggests it was a place where unhappy women, divorced women, and women with a past to hide could gather to a new creed that would rebaptize them and welcome them (Brodie 1971, 304). One of the earliest women's societies in the nation, the Female Relief Society, was founded by Joseph Smith in 1842. Mormon women may have been sharply limited to their role as mothers of the sect but were otherwise obviously needed and encouraged to contribute to the collective welfare.

Then, in 1843, Joseph Smith announced a new revelation from God concerning marriage. This doctrine, continual revelation, again challenged Christian society by claiming that God's messages to man had not ended with Jesus Christ—an insufferable impudence in the eyes of gentiles. Smith's new doctrine on marriage proclaimed that "if any man espouse a virgin, and desire to espouse another, and the first give her consent; and if he espouse the second, and they are virgins, and have vowed to no other man, then he is justified; he cannot commit adultery, for they are given unto him; for he cannot commit adultery with that that belongeth unto him and to no one else . . . And if he have ten virgins . . . he [also] cannot commit adultery" (Smith 1891, 88–89).

Most sources, except those published by the Mormon church, agree that Smith had actually been "sealed" (married) to several women before the date given for his revelation. Brodie states that of Smith's first twenty-one wives, fourteen were already married to other men, thus creating a form of polyandry in Nauvoo. She also hints that an early dissident, J. C. Bennett, a physician, seduced many women, promising—and carrying out—abortions when necessary (Brodie 1971, 310). This trend was rather short-lived and was quickly curtailed when the revelation was made public in 1852. But it may explain why women would not have seen "the principle" as offensive—they had plural husbands themselves—why they gave it initial acceptance, and why they did not move to stop the practice before it grew. By the time women like Stenhouse learned of polygamy, it was accepted church doctrine and not to be questioned. Both then and later came other justifications of Mormon polygamy. It was argued, for example, that more wives meant less housework per person and was less costly than servants.

For many women going west, especially before "the principle" was officially announced, the prospect of marriage into a sect that had planned communities waiting for its members, all ready and established, may have been enough to quash any doubts they had about its social structure. For some women, a certain amount of independence may have resulted. Many polygamous families hoped to acquire separate dwellings for each wife and her children, and as the family income grew, this did often happen. Husbands generally spent periods of days and weeks with each wife, rather than rotating daily. Martha Hughes Cannon, Utah state senator and plural wife, said the Mormon wife was "not so much a slave as a single girl," because "if her husband has four wives, she has three weeks of freedom every single month" (Cannon 1974, 28).

With the passage of time, plural marriage was accepted by generations of Mormon children, although not quite so readily as the church would have it. In general, religious conviction played a strong part in women's decisions to join polygamous families or to accept the addition of another wife. Mormon women were often said to be the most faithful and religious members of the sect.

As the official name of the church implies, Mormonism is at base a Christian faith, and the biblical acceptance of polygamy was widely proclaimed. From the Old Testament the example most cited was Sarah offering her servant, Hagar, to Abraham as a concubine when Sarah herself could not bear children. This was taken literally by many Mormon women who found themselves infertile. As for the New Testament, it was asserted that the wedding at Cana was that of Jesus himself to both Mary and Martha, and that later he also wed Mary Magdalene. How else could one account for the undue familiarity (by Victorian standards) shown by these women to a man they considered to be fully human while on the earth? (Gallichan 1915, ix). Also implied was the importance of building up one's celestial kingdom. Here again, it was obvious that many women could bear for a man a total number of children that no one woman could hope to equal, although this did not prevent each woman from having as many children as possible. Such, then, were some of the reasons why women may have accepted plural marriage. We know that all was not smooth going, however, from Joseph Smith's threats to recalcitrant wives and from Brigham Young's admonition: "If you lift up your heels against this revelation . . . you will go to hell as surely as you are living women" (Larson 1971, 44).

In the late 1850s, intense national sentiment grew against Mormon power. Government troops marched against the Mormons, and there was nationwide Mormon vilification (Furniss 1960). In 1881, David King Udall spoke of the "waves of persecution," noting that "men were being imprisoned and women were going into exile for conscience's sake. . . . Only the deepest religious conviction on the part of all of us could have sustained us in consummating the plan" (Udall 1959, 99).

This recurrent theme of self-denial was also central to the image of American womanhood across the nation.[1] For Mormon women, however, it was stressed in ways that few gentile, middle-class women would be called upon to experience. As observers, gentiles sensed this but felt it to be merely a universal womanly quality pushed to its extreme, "a grievous sorrow and burden, only cheerfully submitted to and embraced under a religious fanaticism and self abnegation rare to behold, and possible only to women" (Bowles

1966, 114). In fact, what historian Nancy Cott has called the Cult of Domesticity[2] had asserted its influence on Mormon women just as surely as it had on the female population at large. The standards of morality and delicacy of mind, the emphasis on family and maternal duties and on submissiveness to one's husband – all were expected of Mormon women no less than of gentile. Polygamy aside, where the ideologies differed radically was over the issue of work.

Mormons were pioneers. Still largely agrarian, they feared the values of an industrializing, newly leisured culture that scorned manual labor as degrading. Their leaders worked hard to thwart the encroaching eastern emphasis on female delicacy and ornamental value. In 1869, the transcontinental railroad pushed through the West bringing gentiles in great numbers, and a threat to the Mormons' insular mores. It was no coincidence that in the same year Brigham Young ordered the Female Relief Society to begin a retrenchment program – an excellent label for the entire Cult of Domesticity itself – to reaffirm its basic values of piety, hard work, and collective struggle. Eventually, this drive to roll back or dig in became a sort of women's club movement of considerable vitality and initiative. Mormon women ran a grain-saving campaign that the men had not been able to maintain, created a silk industry that operated successfully for many years, and trained an astonishing number of women doctors and nurses in Salt Lake City.[3]

Brigham Young's feelings on the subject of women's work were blunt; in his view the functional housewife is the true lady: "I differ from the world generally; for the lady of the world is not supposed to know anything about what is going on in the kitchen; her highest ambition is to be pure and be in the fashion, at no matter what cost to her husband or father. . . . Let the beauty of your adorning be the work of your hands" (B. Young 1925, 329–30). To this, Mormon elder Heber C. Kimball added an attack on women's fashions that unwittingly echoed the contemporary feminist dress reform movement: "Th[e]y lace themselves up and carry such a load of Peticoats across their hips that it destroys the kidneys and the St[r]ength of their loins and causes them to dege[nera]te and thereby destroys their very existen[ce]" (Lee 1955, 139).

That these men felt it necessary to order Mormon women to "retrench" indicates that the larger culture had considerable appeal, though remote from the everyday life of Mormon women. Yet women tended to be obedient to the church, and shame about idleness was still a common value. Anti-polygamy tracts portrayed Mormon women as house slaves and drudges, but perhaps the imagery is better understood when one considers again the middle- and upper-class critics' disdain for women's doing any sort of manual labor. For example, in Bowles (1966, 107), "Their polygamy . . . means only

18. Mormon silk workers. *Courtesy of Utah Historical Society.*

the degradation of women. By it and under it she becomes simply the servant and serf, not the companion and equal of man."

Between 1870 and 1890 (from the first Protestant church established in Utah to the banning of polygamy by the Mormon church's Woodruff Manifesto) the antipolygamy campaign took on national significance as a battle against the last of those "twin relics of barbarism," slavery and polygamy (Larson 1971, 22), a phrase that also appeared in the Republicans' 1856 party platform. Lurid accounts of Mormon life, and especially of the degradation of Mormon women, began to filter back east, outraging many who read them. The Anti-Polygamy Society, in its first monthly newspaper edition (1880), featured a letter of support by Harriet Beecher Stowe, known around the world for her polemics against the other of the twin relics of barbarism. *The Fate of Madame LaTour* (Paddock, 1881 and 1900), a melodramatic exposé, endorsed by the society, ran to 100,000 copies in its second printing (see also Froiseth 1882; Stenhouse 1881; Ward 1856). In 1887, partially in response to the 250,000 signatures collected by the Anti-Polygamy Society, Congress passed the Edmunds-Tucker Act, which made plural marriage illegal and disenfranchised women—but not men—in the Utah Territory. (The territory of Utah had enacted woman's suffrage in 1870, probably to gain women's votes in an ultimately unsuccessful attempt to forestall federal interference in Mormon affairs. Not until statehood came in 1896 did

IN MEMORIAM BRIGHAM YOUNG.
"AND THE PLACE WHICH KNEW HIM ONCE SHALL KNOW HIM NO MORE."

19. "Exit Brigham Young," a cartoon from *Puck,* September 5, 1877, on the occasion of his death. This cartoon illustrates the hostility of outsiders to Mormon plural marriage.

the women of Utah regain the vote.) Mormons, of course, did not submit quietly to this barrage of abuse. At various times the Mormon women of Salt Lake City gathered to protest the antipolygamy campaign, both locally and in Washington. On a more formal level, they drafted memorials to Congress, one of which in 1870 charged the government to reconsider passing a bill that, by outlawing polygamy, would "bastardize innocent children and make harlots of virtuous women" (U.S. Congress 1869–70).

This latter sentiment of moral rectitude raises a final point about the relative positions taken by each group of women on what has come to be known as the Cult of Domesticity. Women back East preferred not to think of what their husbands did if they could not restrain their sexual impulses. The Mormons felt they were not so squeamish and had, in fact, solved the problem. John Taylor, president of the church, cried, "Oh you Gentiles . . . would you introduce all the institutions of pseudo-Christianity, with its prostitution, the houses of assignation, its social evil, foeticide and infanticide and the political and social hypocrisy and depravity and its debauching, demoralizing and corrupting influence, and call this a fair return for virtue, purity, honor, truth and integrity?" (Larson 1971, 44). George Q. Cannon added: "Our crime has been: we married women instead of seducing them; we reared children instead of destroying them; we desired to exclude from the land prostitution, bastardy and infanticide" (Larson 1971, 79). To plural wives, however, belonged "the right and privilege of every honorable woman to be a wife and mother, which in monogamy, under existing conditions, preponderance of women over men, disinclination of men to marry, etc., was virtually denied" (Whitney 1892, 212). This justification runs throughout the many attempts to defend Mormon polygamy: unofficial polygamy was practiced across the nation by gentiles and Mormons alike. The Mormons felt that only they were honest about it.

Two groups that had started out with very different needs, middle-class eastern gentiles and lower-class Mormon pioneers, found themselves condemning each other on the basis of which group best honored the purity and integrity of its women. Both cultures felt mistrustful and threatened by social change. What is striking is that these two cultures, which saw their respective values as being antithetical, should choose roles and values for women so fundamentally the same. Starting as a utopian experiment in the East, Mormonism quickly set limits on what would and would not be experimental about the Mormon community. Spatial organization of towns would be different. Membership status in church affairs would be different. Sexual options for men would be different. Women's work would be different. But woman's role would be what it had always been: whatever male leaders defined it to be. Polygamy was merely a variation on the theme of women's value for society as reproducers, workers, and socializers. The furor over what form this role took (monogamy vs. polygamy) pales before the consistent nineteenth-century conviction that its content should never be altered.

Notes

1. For example, from the *Godey's Lady's Book* of August 1831: "To suffer and be silent under suffering seems the great command she has to obey" (quoted in Welter [1966, 105]).

2. Nancy Cott, in the introduction to *Root of Bitterness* (1972), describes "the emergence of an American 'cult' whose goddess was the woman at her household hearth."

3. Claire Wilcox Noall (1939, 16–17) says that "no concentration of women in medicine ever occurred proportionately to equal the number of women doctors among the pioneers of Utah."

Works Cited

Bowles, Samuel. 1966. *Across the Continent.* Ann Arbor: Univ. Microfilms.

Brodie, Fawn. 1971. *No Man Knows My History.* New York: Knopf.

Cannon, Charles A. 1974. The Awesome Power of Sex: The Polemical Campaign against Mormon Polygamy. *Pacific Historical Review* 43, no. 1:61–82.

Cott, Nancy, ed. 1972. *Root of Bitterness: Documents of the Social History of American Women.* New York: Dutton.

Cross, Whitney. 1956. *The Burnt-Over District: The Social and Intellectual History of Enthusiastic Religion in New York, 1800–1850.* Ithaca: Cornell Univ. Press.

Ferris, Mrs. B. G. [1856] 1971. *The Mormons at Home.* Reprint. New York: AMS.

Froiseth, Mrs. Jennie Anderson. 1882. *The Women of Mormonism: or the Story of Polygamy as Told by the Victims Themselves.* Detroit: Paine.

Furniss, Norman F. 1960. *The Mormon Conflict, 1850–1859.* New Haven: Yale Univ. Press.

Gallichan, Walter M. 1915. *Women under Polygamy.* New York: Dodd, Mead.

Larson, Gustav. 1971. *The Americanization of Utah for Statehood.* San Marino, Calif.: Huntington Library.

Lee, John D. 1955. *A Mormon Chronicle.* Los Angeles: Anderson, Richie and Simon.

Lowry, Nelson. 1930. The Mormon Village: A Study in Social Origins. *Proceedings of the Utah Academy of Sciences* 7:11–37.

Marshall, Walter G. 1881. *Through America, or Nine Months in the United States.* London: Sampson, Low, Marson, Searle, and Rivington.

Merriam, Florence A. 1894. *My Summer in a Mormon Village.* New York: Houghton Mifflin.

Mulder, William, and A. Russell Mortensen, eds. 1958. *Among the Mormons.* New York: Knopf.

Noall, Claire Wilcox. 1939. Utah's Pioneer Women Doctors. *Improvement Era* 42:16–17.

Paddock, Cornelia (Mrs. A. G.). 1881, 1900. *The Fate of Madame LaTour: A Tale of Great Salt Lake.* New York: Fords, Howard and Hulbert.

Smith, Joseph. 1830. *Book of Mormon.* Palmyra, N.Y.: Grandin.

———. 1891. *The Pearl of Great Price.* Salt Lake City: Cannon.

Stenhouse, Fanny (Mrs. T. B. H.). 1881. *An Englishwoman in Utah: The Story of a Life's Experiences in Mormonism.* London: Sampson, Low, Marson, Searle, and Rivington.

Udall, David King. 1959. *Arizona Mormon Pioneer.* Tucson: Arizona Silhouettes.

U.S. Congress. 1869–1870. *Senate Miscellaneous Documents.* 41st Cong. 2d sess. No. 1408, 1870, Doc. 112.

Ward, Maria. 1856. *Female Life among the Mormons.* New York: Derby and Johnson.

Welter, Barbara. 1966. The Cult of True Womanhood, 1820–1860. *American Quarterly* 18 (Summer): 151–75.

Whitney, Orson. 1892. *History of Utah*. Salt Lake City: Cannon.

Young, Brigham. 1925. *Discourses of Brigham Young, Second President of the Church of Jesus Christ of Latter Day Saints, Selected and Arranged by John A. Widtsoe*. Salt Lake City: Deseret.

Young, Kimball. 1954. *Isn't One Wife Enough?* New York: Henry Holt.

11

Family Love, True Womanliness, Motherhood, and the Socialization of Girls in the Oneida Community, 1848–1880

MARLYN KLEE-HARTZELL

AT THE ONEIDA COMMUNITY in Madison County, New York, in 1848, John Humphrey Noyes attempted to fashion a collective family of 250–300 people. He envisioned himself as a modern Abraham who was the spiritual father of a new tribe of Bible Communists. He was the archetypical patriarch from whom all authority flowed. Throughout the community's history he was known as "Father" Noyes. He took unto himself all the power of the tribe. Until declining health forced him to withdraw from the everyday spiritual administration of the community, Noyes dictated the substance and form of spiritual orthodoxy for all members. He decided what economic activities the community would engage in and who would work where; he suggested which members could have children and when; and for some time he kept a close eye on sexual combinations in the community.

Into this collective patriarchal structure Noyes integrated a few leading men whom he deemed worthy to carry out his directives.[1] They were rather like younger brothers with whom the patriarch shared power. These men had several qualifications that fit them for the privilege. First, they were men. They were better educated or more spiritually developed, in Noyes's judgment, than most community members. Most important, they were loyal to Noyes's vision of the "holy family." Sometimes community members referred to these men as Noyes's "apostolic deputies" or "lieutenants," terms indicating a belief that the men were similar to Christ's disciples in function and prestige. The male leading members counseled with Noyes in his private living quarters concerning important decisions for the community. They spoke at evening meetings of the Oneida family and wrote ideological articles for the Oneida publications. They took a prominent role in mutual criticism sessions and controlled, through their appointed representatives, the indoctrination of the children in spiritual matters.

In addition, Noyes consulted with a few leading women who occupied relatively powerless, but nonetheless prestigious, positions as "mother" and "aunts" to the Oneida family. These women were, in fact, Noyes's wife, favorite lover, and two sisters, whose task it was to interpret Noyes's ideology and decisions to the Oneida women and to secure female obedience to them.[2] Both male and female leading members seem to have been exempted from the more mundane community work assignments, but the nature of their contributions to Noyes's rule was dramatically different. Whereas the leading men were party to the decision-making process of the community, the leading women relayed these decisions, made by the men, to their female constituency.

At the bottom of this family hierarchy was the vast majority of adults of both sexes at Oneida; they functioned as children in the collective family. They gave up their independence to Father Noyes, who, in their own best interests, directed their work and play, their education, their religious development, and their sexual activities. They believed implicitly in Noyes's wisdom as a prophet of God and understood, as do most children, that obedience to the father's authority insured their economic security as well. Until the inevitabilities of Noyes's declining physical vigor and the consequent challenge to his first husband privilege by dissident men combined with the restive energies of Oneida's second generation of children in the last decade of the community's existence to challenge the rule of Oneida's patriarch, Noyes was amazingly successful in forging unity and obedience from his communal family.

At the same time, Noyes made certain concessions to the relative power of all men over all women at Oneida. For example, individual men, no matter how insignificant in the total power relations of the community family, retained the privilege of initiating sexual relationships with women in the practice of "complex marriage"—a system of heterosexual relations between all adult women and men in the community. They also dominated, as workers and supervisors, the income-producing labor activities of the community.

Central to an acceptance of Noyes's vision of the biblical, communist family was his insistence that all true communists love each other equally. They were exhorted to enlarge their feelings of love and loyalty from a small family unit to include several hundred family members. Undoubtedly, many Oneida members at first found it difficult to unlearn their previous socialization and training concerning proper familial love. Some, perhaps, held moral objections to plural sex. Mrs. Jonathan Burt, for example, whose husband and neighbors offered Noyes their land in the Oneida Reserve for the site of the original community, balked at Noyes's complex marriage scheme. She eventually relented, however, and joined the community with her husband and children (Parker 1935, 161–64). Another woman, Louisa Easton, testified that she had trouble ridding herself of "an idolatrous love for my husband" and prayed to God "to remove all idols from my heart" (*Daily Journal*, Nov. 20, 1866).

On the other hand, according to one source, the men pleaded "hard and long" (presumably with their wives) for community membership, only to find themselves hard-pressed to give up "the petty authority that they had been accustomed to exercise in their family circles." This source hints rather delicately that these men could not concede "an enlargement of affectional happiness" to other family members, while "ready" for it themselves. Some men also found it painful to submit to criticism in which former wives participated (Estlake 1900, 33–34). Even though both men and women joining the Oneida Community experienced pain and difficulty in adhering to community family standards, the men held one major consolation. They were, by explicit community ideology, superior to women, and from this superiority accrued specific benefits in prestige, work roles, and sexual initiatives. While it was perhaps a relief to some women to get out from under the rule of a particularly tyrannical individual husband, community women simply exchanged one smaller, patriarchal family structure for a larger, collective one.[3]

Noyes's ideological pronouncements hammered constantly on the theme of the secondary, supportive role expected from women toward men in the Oneida family. In the "ascending/descending fellowship" at the heart of community ideology, women were enjoined to accept Paul's remonstrance of Corinthians 11:3 that "the head of the woman is the man." Community writings frequently attributed family quarrels, discord, and jealousy to two factors: first, that man was estranged from God and, therefore, could not fulfill his God-given duty to "inspire" woman; and second, that woman was overstepping her "natural" boundaries by attempting to rule and lead man. According to community ideology, the first dislocation had to be corrected before man could put woman in her rightful place.[4]

The ideal woman/wife in the Oneida family was perhaps best described in an obituary for Charlotte Noyes Miller, Noyes's sister, who died in the community. Miller was praised as a *"true woman"* because "there was not a suspicion of strong mindedness" about her. "She gave man his true place as head of woman, and felt no suppression or infringement from his superiority." All community accounts mentioned Charlotte Miller's beauty and instinctive grace. Despite her many talents and contributions to the community, which included receiving outside visitors, serving as a member of the Criticism and Stirpiculture Committees, and as "mother" to the class of younger girls, the strongest praise she drew was that "she would not have provoked your envy" (*Oneida Circular [OC]*, May 10, 1875 [emphasis in the original]). Here was the unmistakable message to Oneida women of their proper social role. They had to accede to an explicit male superiority and leadership and hide any talents or ambitions that might threaten the patriarchal assumptions of the community.[5]

Whether Oneida women had difficulty adhering to this standard of true womanliness in relation to men, they certainly had problems, judging from the number of references in the community literature, in dealing with feelings of special love for their children. Affection for and control over one's children, often a source of comfort and power to women in patriarchal family structures, were removed from the hands of individual mothers in the Oneida Community and entrusted to the authority of adults judged particularly capable of molding children to community ideology and behavior.

It was a community woman, Mary E. Cragin, a favored lover and devoted disciple of Noyes, who first articulated Noyes's rejection of "sickly, family" love to Oneida women. While living at the Brooklyn branch commune with Noyes and their young son Victor while her three older children remained at Oneida, Cragin penned a letter to Oneida women on the dangers of "philoprogenitiveness." She argued that excessive love of children prevented women from loving God wholeheartedly. Philoprogenitiveness kept women's hearts "in a bleeding state, to the weakening of our whole character." This weakness could be fatal because it interfered with woman's salvation. Cragin suggested that as a tree needed pruning to grow vigorously, so might God take away children from mothers who were blinded by the passions of philoprogenitiveness. Cragin quoted the biblical passage, "When I am weak, then I am strong," and exhorted her sisters to put God first. She concluded with a persuasive call: "I confess Christ my savior from the undue exercise of philoprogenitiveness. Who will join me?" (*OC*, Oct. 5, 1868). Apparently her exhortation won many female recruits. Mary Cragin subsequently became a leader and teacher in the newly organized Children's House at Oneida where she and Noyes's wife, Harriet Holton Noyes, zealously socialized the children into Noyes's communal family.

Cragin's agrument against philoprogenitiveness was buttressed by a variation of the ascending/descending fellowship theme developed by Noyes. The correct hierarchy of family inspiration under Bible Communism, according to Alfred Barron, then editor of the *Oneida Circular,* was the following: children should look up to the mother, the mother to the father, and the father to God. Barron warned of "false and divided counsels" in governing children when mothers diverted their love and attention "from husbands to sons" (*OC*, Apr. 1, 1867). An early community statement of "general principles" regarding the relationship of parents to children declared that love between adult men and women was a "superior passion" to love between adults and children. Parents "should not look so much to their children, as to the object of *pleasing God*" (*OC*, Jan. 29, 1863 [emphasis in the original]). Another article discovered "two poles of influence" in parent/child relations: "the father's exacting and truthful severity," and the "mother's and grandmother's indulgent tenderness." It seemed that the Oneida children were getting too much of the female influence and not enough of the male, resulting in "insubordination and untruthfulness" among the children. To correct this intolerable imbalance, the article concluded that "children governed by mere motherly feeling [are] like a wheel with the hub left out. There must be masculine power and execution at the center and the mother's philoprogenitiveness must be loyally organized into that" (*OC*, Nov. 5, 1863).

Depending upon specific conditions, community militancy against maternal philoprogenitiveness waxed and waned during the twenty-one years before the stirpiculture experiment ("race-culture," or scientific breeding) began in 1870. Mr. Hatch, who worked in the Children's House in 1866, gave testimony that previously, when children were sick or irritable, their mothers would come to the children's quarters to give them special attention and care, probably because the women who worked in the Children's House "had a great deal more respect for the mothers . . . than for Mr. Noyes's instincts." Hatch allowed that this permissiveness "worked in the wrong direction . . . but . . . we have learned better now." He concluded that the children's "department" was paramount to "the motherly spirit" and that all community members "should feel that every child . . . belongs to the Community and not to the mother" (*Daily Journal*, Apr. 18, 1866).

The advantages of community care for children, particularly in relation to its effects on mothers, were often emphasized. Community literature pointed out that communal child care freed mothers from anxiety and fatigue that they would have suffered had they been wholly responsible for rearing their children. The main advantage of communal child care, however, was always that it freed mothers to pursue their highest calling—serving God. On one occasion Aunt Harriet Noyes Skinner solicited for publication in the *Oneida Circular* testimony from mothers about the advantages of community care of children. Alice Ackley offered her opinion: "I now realize . . . that the old way of each mother caring for her own child, begets selfishness and idolatry; and in many ways tends to degrade woman . . . I appreciate the opportunity [communal child care] affords me of not only joining in public work but of self-improvement and 'going-home' to God every day." She also felt released from a constant "anxiety and worry lest [my daughter Corinna] should be sick" (*OC,* June 23, 1873).

In 1870, at the dedication of the new children's wing planned for the expected stirpiculture children, Augusta E. Hamilton spoke of the special advantages to mothers of community care of children. She emphasized: "The prosperity and happiness, nay, salvation even, of our children, are insured to us, so far as the best of spiritual surroundings and instruction, . . . can secure it. . . . Our children have, as it were, a hundred loving fathers and mothers. . . . We mothers, too, are ennobled by the thought that we bare [sic] our children, not for ourselves, but for the good of the church" (*OC,* Oct. 3, 1870). Another woman, "S.B.C.," emphasized woman's duties to man, and the unnatural interference that children often inserted into that relationship. She related that though she "struggled hard and long" against philoprogenitiveness toward her firstborn, "God found a way to have his truth." The child died. Through this experience she learned that it was "wicked to appropriate any of God's gifts" and concluded: "This propensity in woman to have pets and worship them, seems barbarous to me now. It belittles her, distracts from her charms, her power of usefulness, and above all is an abuse of God. The desire of my heart is to rise out of this liability and separate myself entirely from the spirit of idolatry, and be what God designed woman should be–a true helpmeet to man" (*OC,* May 18, 1868).

Philena B. Hamilton emphasized yet another theme. She wrote that she was grateful for community child rearing because "I should never be able, myself, to secure in my children that obedience and respect necessary to their improvement and my happiness." She found that separation from her children better prepared her to accept them as God's gifts. After an absence of one year from her youngest daughter while Hamilton lived at the Wallingford branch, she noted that her child was "healthy, buoyant, and affectionate. I can see how a mother's fondness may be like a close, hot room to a child." She concluded that community care released her from all anxiety about her children's futures and enabled her to "devote myself to the cause of the truth we have received, which is dearer to me than life" (*OC,* Dec. 16, 1867).

It is not surprising that these testimonials from Oneida mothers closely resembled Noyes's ideas of correct family relations under Bible Communism. These appraisals were solicited for publication in the *Oneida Circular* to prove to a skeptical outside world that all was well in the Oneida family. Curiously, however, several children's memoirs report that their mothers were considerably more ambivalent in carrying out the lofty principles of the holy family than the official community pronouncements indicated. Harriet M.

Worden, for example, once wrote of the "sickly, maternal tenderness" which damaged both mothers and children, but her son, Pierrepont, reported that she felt anguished by her separation from him. He believed that she surreptitiously gathered toys in her room for his weekly visit with her and remembered that she sometimes interrupted his play in her room to ask: "Darling, do you love me? . . . I remember how tightly she held me and how long, as though she would never let me go." Pierrepont Noyes felt that his mother was "trying to make up for lost opportunity, lavishing affection on me until . . . I half grudged the time taken from play." Several times Pierrepont Noyes heard his mother criticized for "idolatry" toward him and remembered periods of separation from her because of it. Occasionally, her tenderness turned abruptly to severity if she feared he would be "sticky" at the end of a visit with her; this change of demeanor confused the child, who remarked years later, "the turbulence was mine, but the greater tragedy was my mother's" (P. B. Noyes 1951, 65–67).

    In his boyhood memoirs, Pierrepont Noyes tried to evaluate how community militancy against philoprogenitiveness and separation from his mother had affected his development: "My conception of the grown folks' ideal was undoubtedly vague, but their antagonism to excessive human affection was neither vague nor meaningless. It came to us in the form of oppositions and prohibitions which affected our daily lives and whose intent even children would understand. A child has little capacity for loving that which it can neither see nor touch. Hence, the pressure to elevate the love emotion reacted with us as a suppression and, at least in my own case, oriented my interest toward material things" (P. B. Noyes 1951, 72).

    Although the community reported that toddlers went to their communal nurseries "with eager zest" in a "real atmosophere of content" (*OC*, Oct. 20, 1873), Corinna Ackley Noyes, daughter of Alice Ackley, remembered a less idyllic occasion of separation from her mother. Her own emotional reaction to the situation was undoubtedly heightened by her mother's ambivalence, which she communicated to the tot by some unspoken emotional mechanism. Corinna Ackley Noyes recalled "one two-week period of separation [when] I caught a glimpse of [my mother's] passing through a hallway near the Children's House and rushed after her screaming. She knew—what I was too young to know—that if she stopped to talk with me another week might be added to our sentence. Hoping, I suppose, to escape, she stepped quickly into a nearby room. But I was as quick as she. I rushed after her, flung myself upon her, clutching her around the knees, crying and begging her not to leave me, until some Children's House mother, hearing the commotion, came and carried me away" (C. A. Noyes 1960, 16).

    Even grandmothers were not immune from community militance against philoprogenitiveness. Just as mothers were instructed to turn their primary attention to serving God and being "helpmeets" to men, so were grandmothers particularly enjoined to "recover [themselves] from the disorders" that years of family cares had brought upon them. A grandmother's highest duty was to bring upon her grandchildren "the care of God. In saving her own soul from the disorders of philoprogenitiveness, she becomes a medium of heavenly spirits to her descendants" (*OC*, May 2, 1864). This advice notwithstanding, Corinna Ackley Noyes remembered her grandmother's love and care as a predominant force in her early life. In her memoirs she related a touching early memory of her grandmother's holding her in her arms, singing hymns with a "faith and fervor" that communicated "safety and peace" to the child (C. A. Noyes 1960, 8).

It is difficult to generalize about the cooperation Oneida women gave Noyes's ideals of the communist family. Certainly they tried courageously, if occasionally unsuccessfully, to separate themselves from feelings of philoprogenitiveness. Unfortunately, so far only two written memories of Oneida childhood, those of Pierrepont B. Noyes and Corinna Ackley Noyes, who married each other in 1894, provide much material on children's reactions to the practical and emotional ramifications of Noyes's prohibition against excessive maternal love.[6] As stirpicult children, their experiences were limited to the last decade of the community's life, when probably the rules of child care were most rigidly enforced. Although both autobiographies seem sensitive and honest, one must keep in mind that they were written from the hindsight of adulthood, after both authors had lived many years outside the community. Nonetheless, the clarity and poignancy of Corinna and Pierrepont Noyes's accounts of early childhood emotions lead one to trust them. If true, these accounts, at the least, indicate that Oneida mothers resisted giving up their children to the community–the greater good of the church and their own spiritual development notwithstanding.

By contrast, no references to paternal philoprogenitiveness can be found in the community literature. Corinna Ackley Noyes made no mention of her father in her memoirs and wrote of her grandfather, Joseph Ackley, that "during my early years in the old Community I seldom saw him and felt scarcely acquainted with him" (C. A. Noyes 1960, 5). Likewise, Pierrepont B. Noyes had almost no contact with his father: "I revered him, but he was much too far away, too near to heaven and God. He lived somewhere upstairs and, whenever I saw him, was usually surrounded by men . . . who were associated in my mind with the Apostles" (P. B. Noyes 1951, 70). Sometimes children developed close emotional ties with men who were not their biological fathers, as did Pierrepont Noyes with Abram Burt, the father of his half-brother.

Fathers were free to visit with the children in the children's quarters and occasionally took care of their offspring for short periods of time, but they apparently did not feel the pain of separation or the desire to control their children closely in the same way that mothers did. Clues about why the burden of philoprogenitiveness fell so much more heavily on mothers lie in several concrete realities of male and female parental experiences in the community.

First, Oneida women had exclusive care of their babies for the first year of the children's lives. They nursed their infants and watched over their waking and sleeping hours. From the intimate contacts of this first year of care, mothers developed strong ties with their children, who were totally dependent upon them for physical and emotional nurture. The abrupt change from their around-the-clock personal care of their children to their relinquishment to the Children's House probably caused a serious dislocation in the mothers' emotions and daily routines.

Secondly, women at Oneida were nearly powerless, submitting to a male-dominated regime in ideology, work, and sexual relations. It is, therefore, not surprising that they might resist loss of control in the one sphere in which they felt needed and responsible—care of their children. On the other hand, for Oneida fathers the care of children was but a minor aspect of community life. They enjoyed some compensating privileges and responsibilities that mothers did not have.

In evaluating the concept of the Bible Communist family at Oneida, the small amount of evidence available suggests that women were reluctant to give up special feelings of love for their own children. In fact, they did not. They suffered for it, and perhaps the children did, too. On the other hand, communal child care enabled Oneida women to enter the Community work force and to avail themselves of leisure time for study and cultural improvement. These advantages, however, were secondary to the ones most often mentioned in the Community literature, which instead stressed women's greater accessibility to God and women's service roles as "helpmeets" to the men.

In all, 135 children were brought to the Oneida Community by their parents or born there before 1869 (Carden 1971, 63). The fifty-eight stirpicults born in the last decade of the community's existence brought the total number of children whom the community reared to 193. After scientific breeding, the education of community children became paramount. This priority was explicitly stated in the *Oneida Circular* of June 8, 1874: "As we value the future of Communism we must see to it that our children . . . are brought up in 'the nurture and admonition of the Lord', else they will some-day rise up against us and become a curse."

Generalizations about Oneida children's education are difficult to arrive at for two reasons. References to the Bible Communists' program for children are scanty and scattered, found mainly in isolated articles in the *Oneida Circular* and in three published accounts of Oneida childhood. Secondly, conditions changed in the community during its forty-four years of existence, and with them the particulars of Oneida children's socialization. The material conditions of the community, for example, dictated how long the children received formal schooling. In the lean years children left primary school and entered the adult work force of the community at age ten. When the community became more prosperous, they continued their classroom work until age twelve. The changing emphases of Noyes's interests also contributed to organic growth and changes in the children's program. At the same time, a continuous commitment to Bible Communism and its indoctrination in the minds and hearts of the young permeated the children's education throughout the community's history. In particular, the following discussion will examine how community education socialized girls to the community standard of "true-womanliness."

Female and male children attended school together at Oneida until ages ten to twelve. They were usually graded according to age into three groups: toddlers, preschoolers, and primary school. For the primary school children, ages six to twelve, formal classroom time was limited to the mornings, during which time they learned the three Rs, geography, and science, as well as "obedience, manners, and prayer" (*OC,* Sept. 4, 1862). The afternoons allowed ample time for work, outdoor play, and a regular children's religious meeting. At the religious meetings Oneida children learned the idea of a "Providence"–"somebody bigger and wiser" who watched over them and their community family. They received criticism from their elders on their behavior and attitudes and occasionally administered criticism to each other. They often concluded their discussions by "confess[ing] Christ a pure heart" (*OC,* Jan. 4, 1869, May 13, 1872).

In the early 1850s, when the community was at the height of its religious fervor, the children's secular education was heavily infused with religious themes. Mary Cragin, Noyes's enthusiastic lover and disciple, relied on Bible stories, pictures, prayer, and moral lessons in her teaching. During her tenure as Children's House leader, Cragin instituted an infamous purge of dolls, which provided the girls with their first lesson in the roles they would be expected to assume as community women. The community campaign against girls' dolls coincided with community efforts to combat maternal philoprogenitiveness. Mary Cragin explained that she gave the girls dolls so that they would teach themselves to sew by making doll clothes (Robertson 1970, 331–32). The playthings, however, soon brought trouble to their young admirers. Harriet Worden, then one of the little girls who loved dolls, reported: "The grown folks soon discovered that we were idolaters, worshiping our little waxen images, and becoming very heedless of our variously appointed chores about the house, as well as inattentive to the Bible and more serious matters" (Worden 1950, 80).

In typical community style, Mary Cragin promptly formed a committee of herself and two girls, Sarah Burt and Mary Prindle, to study the "doll-question." Little Sarah dutifully reported that she was often late for breakfast because she tarried to dress her doll. Her doll drew her attention away from Christ, making her "frivolous" and inattentive to her studies. Mary Prindle testified that her doll offered similar temptations, and "then I have to be criticized" (Robertson 1970, 331). Cragin summarized the trouble with the dolls in a four-point report submitted to Noyes, Erastus Hamilton, and others, "who heartily approved of it." First, playing with dolls as though they were living beings "is acting and speaking a lie, and we do not mean to speak or act lies." Secondly, dolls encouraged philoprogenitiveness, whereas the "fear of the Lord" should be the beginning of education "before we try to learn to become mothers." Playing with dolls, furthermore, encouraged baby talk and baby thoughts and tended to make the girls forget "that our tongues belong to God." Finally, the "doll-spirit" seduced the girls from community work tasks and diligent study. It was, Cragin concluded, the "same spirit that seduces women to allow themselves to be so taken up with their children that they have no time to attend to Christ, and get an education for heaven" (Robertson 1970, 332).

Noyes accepted Cragin's report and in his response likened the girls' attachment to their dolls to the "worship of graven images." The solution to the problem came swiftly. Cragin suggested burning the dolls. The *Oneida Circular* reported that the "little boys were loud in their clamors for the great massacre" (Robertson 1970, 333). Harriet Worden recalled the subsequent ceremony in this way: "We all formed a circle round the large stove, each girl carrying on her arms her long-cherished favorite, and marched in time to a song; as we came opposite the stove-door, we threw our dolls into the angry-looking flames, and saw them perish before our eyes. . . . It was some time before we could think of this wholesale slaughter without a slight emotion" (Worden 1950, 80). Thereafter no dolls were permitted in the community.

This incident very dramatically illustrated to girls one of their most important lessons in becoming community women. God and the community spirit came before everything else. Maternity was not an inevitability, but rather a privilege which a girl might attain after sufficient community preparation for her womanly role.

In his memoirs of Oneida childhood, Pierrepont B. Noyes recorded the fullest details of life in the Children's House during the 1870s. From his descriptions one can conclude that boys and girls attended school and religious meetings together, with very little differentiation between the sexes, though he noted that the primary school teacher, Mr. Warne, was especially fond of boys (P. B. Noyes 1951, 100) and often took them on nature hikes while the girls stayed behind. In outdoor play the children seemed to have segregated themselves voluntarily according to sex, for Pierrepont Noyes's descriptions of his childhood, with minor exceptions, mentioned only boys as companions. Yet Pierrepont Noyes cited no adult pressure for separation of the sexes in play. Boys seemed to have had more latitude for recreation and mischief than girls. In the class of boys six to twelve years old, for example, each was promised a coconut if able to swim across the creek by the end of the summer of 1877 (P. B. Noyes 1951, 88–89). If girls had any part of the bargain, Pierrepont Noyes did not mention it, though one community source noted that the branch commune at Wallingford did teach their girls to swim (*OC,* Mar. 6, 1866). Likewise, Oneida girls were excluded from the July 4, 1873, children's celebration. Mr. Woolworth gave each of the little boys a bunch of firecrackers; they also launched sky-rockets and Roman candles from the top of the Mansion House's tower (*OC,* July 14, 1873).

Some toys, books, and facilities of the Oneida Children's House were regarded as the exclusive province of one sex or the other. The rainy-day playroom, for example, contained a "carpenters bench, where the boys can learn the handling of tools" (*OC,* Dec. 1, 1873). The bookshelves in the children's quarters segregated reading material by sex. For the boys Pierrepont Noyes recalled the "Castlemon series of adventure stories, *Frank on the Prairie* and *Frank on the Gunboat.*" Although he did not name the girls' books, probably because he never read them, Noyes noted that the boys "despised or at least affected to despise" the girls' books (P. B. Noyes 1951, 90).

Oneida boys and girls dressed simply but differently. The girls wore dresses covered by calico aprons; the boys, "pants-and-jackets" buttoned together (C. A. Noyes 1960, 49–50). One wonders why the little girls did not wear cotton pants, as adult women at Oneida did. The sleeping and dressing quarters of the children were also sex segregated (*OC,* Apr. 8, 1867). Pierrepont Noyes noted that "only the Girls' Room showed any attempt at decorative furnishing and for this very reason it always remained exclusively a girls' room" (P. B. Noyes 1951, 37).

Children performed daily work for the community as an integral part of their education. Sometimes the children helped at the various bees orga-

20. Oneida Community members at their Summer House, 1866. This photograph shows the unusual dress and pantalets costume and simple hair style that all Oneida women adopted. Founder John Humphrey Noyes *(seated, wearing white jacket)* encouraged these simplified styles in early 1848, arguing that contemporary fashions kept women in "spiritual and moral captivity . . . something like a churn, standing on castors!" *Courtesy of Oneida Community Collection, George Arents Research Library at Syracuse University.*

nized by the community to gather potatoes or butternuts (Robertson 1970, 312). They pared and sorted apples, and once, in the animal trap shop, sorted hundredweights of iron in a few hours, "a piece of work which would have

21. A bag bee at the Oneida Community. Women sewed these bags, which were sold commercially to travelers and tourists. The Oneida Community often used bees to accomplish urgent or onerous tasks. Note the man reading to the workers. *Courtesy of Oneida Community Collection, George Arents Research Library at Syracuse University.*

occupied as many hired boys all day" (Robertson 1970, 332). In the 1870s the children worked for an hour each day after lunch, making chains that were later attached to the steel traps manufactured by the community. Older boys each had a "stent" of one hundred chains to be completed before they could be excused. The girls and younger boys picked over the links, untangling them for the chainmakers (P. B. Noyes 1951, 101). At some time during this busy daily schedule one can conclude that the girls were taught sewing, since after age twelve they took full responsibility for making their own clothes as well as those of other community members.

If the sexual distinctions of early childhood at Oneida were somewhat subtle and restricted to certain activities and facilities, after graduation from primary school boys' and girls' experiences diverged sharply. After ages ten to twelve, depending upon the period of community history one examines, children became adults and moved into the adult quarters of the Mansion House. From that time until their middle twenties, young women and men were systematically separated from each other in work, study, and recreation by deliberate community policy, which feared too much sexual attraction or, as the Oneida Communists called it, "horizontal fellowship." Moreover, for young women, opportunities for self-expression and growth shrank as they moved into the protecting arms of the "family circle" and the world of women's work, whereas young men's educational and work activities continued to expand, offering opportunities for intellectual growth and leadership training.

At about age twelve, girls were introduced into the sexual practices of the community. It was a sharp departure from life in the Children's House. Probably, Oneida children knew little of the sexual arrangements in the community, for they lived apart from the adult population and had little contact with adults other than their child care workers. Likewise, Oneida children had no instruction in the rudiments of sex education or reproduction. They did not know where babies came from. The *Oneida Circular* printed an incident in which some curious outsiders tried to learn from a four-year-old boy who his parents were.

> "Where are your parents, little boy?"
> "My Papa Noyes and Mama Miller are at Wallingford."
> . . . .
> "Miller! That's a nice name; and what is your own name beside Miller?"
> The reply had such amplitude, such rolling fullness, such *naïveté* and simplicity, that we record it: "My name is Temple Noyes Dunn Burt Ackley!" (Robertson 1970, 321 [emphasis in the original])

The community described this encounter approvingly, because it verified their considerable efforts to teach the children that they had many communal "pas and mas."

Because Oneida children were sheltered from opportunities to see adults in social situations, they were probably quite uninformed about sex. Transition into adulthood was, therefore, more dramatically marked by initiation into complex marriage. Regrettably, one can learn little from extant public sources of how and by whom complex marriage was explained to community girls. In her later years, Jessie Catherine Kinsley wrote that "we [girls] were simply told that we were old enough to be good citizens of the big Community and were to go often to Mr. Noyes's sister, Mrs. [Charlotte] Miller, or to . . . Harriet Joslyn, for *counsel.*" Another mentor was "Miss B.," who instructed: "We are all brothers and sisters, and the wiser ones lead the less wise through 'Ascending Fellowship' into love." Kinsley remarked that Miss B. was "very serious, simple and loving, and we were blind young things." Of the young girls' sense of sexuality, Kinsley said: "That I was truly innocent, simple and modest, I believe for a certainty. Other girls may have had exciting experiences. I may have been a prig. I was a Puritan *trained* to seek first the Kingdom of Heaven in every action." She admitted that when she began the "strange, mysterious, uncomprehended" practice of complex marriage "no sex instinct was consciously awake in me, nor was any apprehended for a long time. Perhaps this will seem strange, but it is true. There was obedience and loyalty and some curiosity." Kinsley's final evaluation of complex marriage hewed closely to standard community ideology: "to make *desire legitimate* was, I believe, the purpose of those in authority . . . while in our hearts was innocence and struggle for unselfishness, and toward Mr. Noyes, loyalty as to one almost *divine.*" (Rich 1983, 32–40, [emphasis in the original]).

Noyes initiated each virgin into sexual intercourse shortly after her first menses, and thereafter, from approximately ages twelve to twenty-five, young women had sexual relations exclusively with much older community men who had learned the practice of "male continence" (*coitus reservatus*). According to one disgruntled older female member, some young women had intercourse with men daily, or even oftener (Van de Warker 1884, 789). By consenting to sexual "interviews" with older community men, young women supposedly demonstrated their understanding of and cooperation with a correct community spirit. Sexual relations with older men also provided girls with spiritual tutelage in accordance with Noyes's "ascending fellowship" principle. Similarly, boys from approximately ages twelve to twenty-five had sex with postmenopausal women until they mastered "male continence." This is the only community instance where (older) women took the "ascendant" spiritual position relative to (adolescent) males. This arrangement was practical, for it prevented conception even if a young man could not control his ejaculation.

The other abrupt departure from the Children's House routine for girls was their work. From puberty they spent a majority of their time in the women's world of work at Oneida—home, laundry, printing office, and silk spool factory. The *Oneida Circular* reported candidly that, upon graduation from primary school, girls took up "household duties" (*OC*, Oct. 29, 1851). At this time a young woman also began to make her own clothing and possibly those of a child as well. Eventually, she became "mother" to a man, mending and altering his clothing.

When Oneida girls moved into the adult world of work and sexual practices, their opportunities for education became limited to after-work hours. Formal educational instruction for young men continued, however, at least in the 1860s when the sons of the original community members were in their twenties. Harriet Worden noted that "most of the boys continued their attendance at the school while the girls pursued their studies under special instructors, or attended the various evening classes" (Worden 1950, 66). The *Oneida Circular* of November 22, 1860, noted a school for young men ages fourteen to twenty-six where they studied "reading, spelling, grammar and composition, arithmetic, algebra, and Latin." In 1862 Noyes inaugurated "an Insititue with a system of professorships" for young men ages twelve to twenty that met three to four hours daily. They studied elocution, reading, spelling, geography, composition, mathematics, astronomy, and languages. Noyes admonished the male scholars that they "should not consider their education finished when they had graduated from the school. . . . They could calculate to go on and become professors themselves" (*OC*, Sept. 4, 1862). Eventually five community young men were sent to college, two earning degrees in medicine, two in engineering, and one in law (Robertson 1970, 173). No community women attended college, nor did they receive formal classroom instruction after age twelve. Evidently, the community felt primary school education adequate for women.

Shortly before her death at age eighty-six, Polly Hayes Noyes, mother of John Humphrey Noyes, objected strenuously to the limited opportunities for young women in the community. She wrote: "I observe the young men in the Community are called out in various ways to new businesses and positions, and have new inducements and prospects to stimulate their activity, and I ask, is there anything like this for the girls? Is not the range of their operations very uniform and the extent of their opportunity for display of talent and genius too much confined?" (*OC*, June 18, 1866). Polly Hayes Noyes correctly perceived that woman's sphere at Oneida constricted the abilities of young women.

Although the community printed the indomitable old woman's criticism, it did nothing to correct the inequities she deplored. When community girls entered womanhood, the boundaries of their existence were defined by home, women's work, and female participation in complex marriage. An article in the *Oneida Circular* of August 11, 1873, perhaps best summarized the goals of female socialization in the community: They [young women] are such a comfort to us; instead of being a trouble and a worry, they add so much beauty, harmony and happiness to our home. Obedient, industrious and enthusiastic for the Community, we have no fear for them, but everything to hope."

Conclusion

At Oneida, childhood appears to have been highly structured but not oppressive for the young. Following the strictures of community ideology, Oneida children were not pampered or romanticized; rather they seem to have been cherished because they would someday become adult Bible Communists and carry on the social vision of their adult family. Boys and girls were raised and educated together until puberty; gender distinctions among the children were present but not particularly emphasized.

For an Oneida girl, the turning point in life was puberty and her initiation into adult status, which included obligatory heterosexual activity, and dropping out of school into the world of women's work at Oneida. From then on, comely cooperation and "community spirit" were to be her main virtues. Through criticism sessions, evening meetings, and her relationships with leading adults, she learned that her primary responsibility was to serve God, and man, as a "helpmeet." To become a mother required patience and training in community ideology. An Oneida woman did not control her own fertility or raise her children, were she awarded the privilege of becoming a mother. From the evidence available, the prohibition against philoprogenitiveness seems to have been the most difficult challenge to Oneida women.

Notes

1. George Cragin, John Miller, Theodore R. Noyes, William Woolworth, Erastus Hamilton, and Theodore Pitt.

2. Harriet Holton Noyes, Mary Cragin, Harriet Noyes Skinner, and Charlotte Noyes Miller.

3. Two recent studies of women in the Oneida Community (Foster 1991; Wayland-Smith 1988) differ from mine in emphases and interpretation.

4. *Oneida Circular,* Sept. 5, 1865. This same source reported a male discussion in the community that compared family disequilibrium to the U.S. Civil War; it referred to the Confederacy as the female half of the nation, bent on promoting discord in the country. The community published a weekly newpaper throughout its history. From 1851–1870, the newspaper was known as the *Circular,* from 1871–1876, the *Oneida Circular* (hereafter *OC*).

5. This "true woman" of the Oneida Community was strikingly similar to the prevalent nineteenth-century "Cult of True Womanhood," the chief characteristics of which were obedience, submissiveness, piety, and virtue (Welter 1966).

6. Another memoir (published posthumously) of the life of Jessie Catherine Baker Kin-

sley, who was born in the community in 1858, provides some details of her Oneida childhood (Rich 1982).

Works Cited

Carden, Maren Lockwood. 1971. *Oneida: Utopian Community to Modern Corporation*. New York: Harper.

Daily Journal of the Oneida Community. 1866–1867. 1–3. Oneida, N.Y.

Estlake, Allan. 1900. *The Oneida Community: A Record of an Attempt to Carry Out the Principles of Christian Unselfishness and Scientific Race-Improvement.* London: George Redway.

Foster, Lawrence. 1991. *Women, Family, and Utopia: Communal Experiments of the Shakers, the Oneida Community, and the Mormons.* Syracuse: Syracuse Univ. Press.

Noyes, Corinna Ackley. 1960. *The Days of My Youth.* Kenwood, N.Y.: Author.

Noyes, Pierrepont B. 1951. *My Father's House: An Oneida Boyhood.* New York: Farrar & Rinehart.

Oneida Circular. 1851–1876. (Published as *The Circular* (1851–1870) and *The Oneida Circular* (1871–1876) Oneida, N.Y.)

Parker, Robert Allerton. 1935. *A Yankee Saint: John Humphrey Noyes and the Oneida Community.* New York: Putnam.

Rich, Jane Kinsley, ed., with the assistance of Nelson M. Blake. 1982. *A Lasting Spring: Jessie Catherine Kinsley, Daughter of the Oneida Community.* Syracuse: Syracuse Univ. Press.

Robertson, Constance Noyes. 1970. *Oneida Community: An Autobiography, 1851–1876.* Syracuse: Syracuse Univ. Press.

Van de Warker, Ely. 1884. A Gynecological Study of the Oneida Community. *American Journal of Obstetrics and Diseases of Women and Children* 27, no. 8 (Aug.): 755–810.

Wayland-Smith, Ellen. 1988. The Status and Self-Perception of Women in the Oneida Community. *Communal Societies* 8: 18–53.

Welter, Barbara. 1966. The Cult of True Womanhood, 1820–1860. *American Quarterly* 18 (Summer): 151–75.

Worden, Harriet M. 1950. *Old Mansion House Memories. By One Brought Up In It.* Kenwood, N.Y.: Privately published.

12

Pronatalism, Midwifery, and Synergistic Marriage

Spiritual Enlightenment
and Sexual Ideology on The Farm (Tennessee)

LOUIS J. KERN

ALTERNATIVE SOCIETIES HAVE, by their very nature, been fundamentally engaged in the social reconstruction of the self and community and in the reconstruction of emotions, beliefs, and values. Such reconstructionist activity has required close attention to a wide variety of issues centering on sexuality and gender. Indeed, as Rosabeth M. Kanter has demonstrated, modern communitarian movements (post-1965) have tended to define themselves in terms of affectivity rather than of socioeconomic reorganization. Whereas "communes of the past called themselves 'societies'," she noted, "today's groups are more frequently called 'families'" (Kanter 1972, 165).

In this paper I examine women's experiences in a single modern community–The Farm (Tennessee)–during its communal phase (1971–1983). Here was a group whose social construction of gender relationships ran counter to contemporary trends. Whereas mainstream society was challenged (some argued threatened) by an apparent revolution in sexual behavior and the demands for women's liberation, The Farm, led by a charismatic male guru, established an ostensibly retrogressive social order predicated upon monogamy and pronatalism. How were women affected by the ideological structures and behavioral norms that defined life in this community? To what extent was there gender equality or female status enhancement at The Farm? What were the fundamental bases of female identity there? Were feminist concerns agitating society outside the community extinguished by the central importance the community assigned to maternal functions? What was the quality of emotional life for women at The Farm? To answer these questions we will need to consider the evolution, ideology, and social practice of this commune.

The Farm, founded in 1971, was a largely self-sufficient, strictly vegetarian, rural venture grounded in religious communitarianism. Located two hours south of Nashville, two miles outside Summertown, Tennessee, it was generally considered to be "the largest working commune in America" by the late 1970s (Wenner 1977, 80). As a "family monastery," its spiritual base rested on a rather diffuse, syncretistic set of principles combining Eastern mysticism, tantric telepathy, and Western spiritualism in a matrix of evangelical enthusiasm. Its guiding principles were dedication, order, and control.

The Farm's roots run back to Stephen Gaskin's days as a graduate student in semantics at San Francisco State University and to the Haight-Ashbury summer of love, 1967. During this period, Stephen began to teach classes called "Group Experiments in Unified Field Theory." By 1970, he had emerged as a significant spiritual force in the Bay area (upwards of 2,000 people were attending these weekly sessions), and he was invited to speak at colleges and churches across America. The result was the "Astral Continental Congress"–a call to a spiritual revolution based on Stephen's revelations–that took the form of the Caravan, a five-month (October 1970–February 1971), nationwide evangelical tour, involving a group of converted school buses and 250 of Stephen's followers. The Caravan experience was a cohesive one for this seminal group, and shortly after their return to San Francisco, they decided to establish a commune in Tennessee.[1]

By all accounts, the commune flourished during the 1970s. In early 1973 there were reportedly 500 members, an increase of nearly 100 percent in two years; by 1974, total population was 1,000. The Farm's population peaked in the late 1970s with 1,200 to 1,250 permanent residents and as many as 100 casual visitors on any given night. The population of the ten satellite communities that had spun off the original settlement by 1980 seems to have reached its highest level in the early 1980s, when there were an estimated 1,400 adherents in these affiliates. In the latter part of 1978 and 1979, The Farm experienced a sharp population decline; after 1983, the decline became precipitous. The population leveled out at about 200–220 by 1985 and has hovered between 250 and 300 since. Currently, the population is 280 with a rough parity of males to females.

In the late 1970s, Stephen relinquished his patriarchal position at The Farm and the community assumed a more populist polity. Serious ideological consideration of restructuring and reorganizing the community was also initiated. By 1982, restructuring had been completed, and in 1983 The Farm was decollectivized. Barter was replaced by money as the medium of exchange; The Farm was incorporated and issued stock as a means of generating capital; and all affiliate communities became independent units. In 1982, "the gate was closed," and a limitation was imposed on the length of time visitors could remain in the community. The practical effect of this policy was to discourage new members. Since 1982, only about a dozen people have been accepted into the community.[2]

As a social entity the commune had originated with a group marriage— an extension of Stephen's marriage to a "four marriage" in 1967 and then to a "six marriage" shortly before the foundation of the community. This group marriage was considered a permanent social unit grounded in mutual commitment. And yet, within two years of the establishment of The Farm, a mixed marital system had been instituted there that included only some four or five multiple marriages. This would have meant that between 6 and 8 percent of the adult population was living in multiple marriages, and that by 1973, over 90 percent of the men and women of The Farm were living either singly or in strictly monogamous relationships. By 1975, only the original multiple marriage remained. The original "six marriage" had become a "four marriage" by 1983, and in 1984 Stephen and Ina May Gaskin became a monogamous couple. Strict monogamy had become both the demographic norm and the ideologically sanctioned marital institution for the community.[3]

It is important to emphasize here that The Farm was founded with the presupposition that a plural marriage system would continue to characterize its social relations. It was also an important part of early community ideology. Therefore, the initial "four marriage" structure was exported in the early 1970s to the various satellite communities established in this period. The move to a monogamous structure was largely predicated on pragmatic considerations. A public announcement of the community's commitment to monogamy was made as early as 1972, while several multiple marriages still existed. Because of their rural lifestyle and more conservative values, The Farm's neighbors frowned on a more liberal expression of sexuality, and because the community needed the assistance of these neighbors, it was thought best to conform in appearance and in public pronouncement to the prevailing norm. While a minority continued to live in multiple marriages, the community seems to have decided at this time that a monogamic social order promised greater long-term social stability, and so monogamy became an essential element of internal community ideology.

Students of historical and contemporary communes as well as members have frequently observed that the persistence of the dyadic unit has been detrimental to the development of a broader sense of community loyalty in a communal setting. Many communities have sought some strategy to wean the affections of the couple away from each other; to tame the dyadic bond; to both defuse and diffuse the erotic drive. Yet, though Stephen had earlier warned about the dangers of "being married in two" (a relation he felt all too often led to parasitism on one side and emotional starvation on the other), it was under a monogamous system that The Farm enjoyed its period of most dynamic growth (S. Gaskin 1970, n.p.).

In his earliest revelations, Stephen recognized the centrality of love as the basis for a revolutionary, affective social order. Love was an elemental natural force that bound together individual aspirations and the power of collective moral authority. It was at once a source of personal empowerment and a therapeutic tool of extraordinary social potential. It is one thing, however, to talk about love as a means of individual and social salvation (a kind of generalized expression of the hippie ideals of the 1960s), and quite another to work out a system for its use as a principle of social organization. The systematization of communal affection lay in Stephen's perception of love as a mediating principle that provided access to the "astral plane" and to the "aura." In essence, love provided the essential link between the medium (telepathic "soul communication") and the message (the power of the cosmic energy that sustains the universe).[4]

The sexual ideology of The Farm was grounded in this cosmological view. The physical world was seen as an expression of the cosmic energy force ("the juice"), and as such, it manifested a gender-based dualism. Stephen believed that male and female energy, while complementary, are different in kind, and perhaps also in intensity and in duration. For the community to exist in harmony and balance, both kinds of energy had to be nurtured, and most importantly, shared. The juice was love transmitting energy; its expression was personal and collective attention focused on interpersonal relationships. As Stephen expressed it,

> "Now it ain't like you can go on your trip and freak out and hurt yourself without mattering to someone else. We are all interdependent, and we are all taking care of each other. And we have to use our good judgment and our good love and our good courage to do it. What you're supposed to do is just to love folks un-self-consciously and wholeheartedly and do not define yourself to them, but let them experience you, and don't tell them what to think about you or tell them how to treat you or anything like that. Just put it [your attention] on them and let them have some [juice]" (S. Gaskin 1980, 129).

But for individuals to be able to creatively affect the reality of their personal and social experiences, the community must find institutions that both transmit and combine energy. The institutions that embodied Stephen's religion of "energy and love that pass in the here and now" (Thorndike 1979, 42) comprised the trinity of sacraments at The Farm—sex, marriage, and childbirth. At the center of this sacramental order lay the conjugal pair. After 1972 or early 1973, the overwhelming majority of members of The Farm practiced monogamy, with prohibitions on promiscuity and premarital sex. Reportedly, there was no homosexuality, and sex with or between minors was prohibited. Divorce, though not absolutely forbidden, has been rare. In the first five years of community life, breakups averaged about one per year.

Until 1978, all artificial means of birth control were rejected (though even during this period there seem to have been some few instances of uses of IUDs) (Ina May 1975, 142). That community members had no objection to birth control per se was made patent with its publication of a book on planned parenthood entitled *A Cooperative Method of Natural Birth Control* (1977), by Margaret Nofziger, which made their early position on contraception clear. No reliance on artificial intervention or drugs was recommended. Close attention to basal body temperature and cervical mucus discharge combined with a traditional rhythm method summed up the preferred method of contraception. But after 1978, there were no longer any community restrictions on contraception; any contraceptive means were acceptable.

Abortion was prohibited in the community and, indeed, it was widely known on the counter-cultural grapevine in the 1970s that The Farm served as a secure refuge and a supportive birthing environment for young unmarried women. A standing offer had been made to single pregnant women: "Don't have an abortion. You can come to The Farm and we'll deliver your baby and take care of it, and if you ever decide you want it back, you can have it" (Ina May 1975, 375). Between 1971 and 1979, about one hundred unwed mothers gave birth at The Farm, but only three subsequently left their babies. In addition, some three hundred women came to The Farm for natural birthings during this period (Thorndike 1979, 39).

While standards of sexual behavior at The Farm were definitely more restrictive than those of contemporary American society, they did not reflect a repressive attitude toward sexuality. Stephen's epigrammatical statement to courting couples was characteristic: "If you're sleeping together you're engaged; if you're pregnant you're married" (Thorndike 1979, 39).

Sexual relations were legitimized by the community ritual of marriage, which took place before the assembled commune at Sunday morning meditation. But the sex act as an expression of love and a means of generation and sharing of "the juice" was believed to be inherently sacral. "You can feel the presence of the Holy Spirit," Stephen wrote, "while making love. You can see the presence of Divinity on the material plane because if you do it right, the person you're making love to will become so beautiful that you can see Divinity right in them" (Ina May 1975, 284). The sex act was a eucharistic experience; it provided the basis for self-transcendence.

According to Stephen, the sexual relationship also had a cosmological-ecological function. The rough, aggressive energy of the male must find its completion in the gentler, beautiful energy of the female. In *Hey Beatnik!* he likened these two types of energy to electrical charges. Neither should be allowed to predominate, or the ideal order of nature (expressed by the couple in microcosm) would be disrupted. In order to preserve the natural balance of energy or, perhaps more accurately, to reinstitute a balance that had been tipped in modern America toward a predominance of male energy, Stephen recommended more aggressive female self-assertion during intercourse. In practical terms, this meant that "the male should see to it that his partner achieves orgasm, and he is instructed that his own orgasm is not of primary importance" (Pfaffenberger 1982, 203).[5] Sex at The Farm, therefore, was not solely sacramental; it was also to be pleasurable. The logic of the latter perspective was carried through to an endorsement of sexual relations during pregnancy: "Lovemaking [at this time] is okay if it's Tantric [energy channeling] and gentle" (Ina May 1975, 343).

Sexual relations were essentially a question of investment of energy; primary energy was given to the couple. As Stephen put it, "I choose to put my energy into this relationship and try to bring it to fruition, and in order to do that, I will avoid starting such other heavy relationships that they will tend to make me unable to pursue this one to the fullest. Isn't that telepathic back there in the marriage contract?" (S. Gaskin 1980, 76).

The ideology of marriage at The Farm during this period might most appropriately be called synergistic marriage. Couple love created the plenitude of communal affection, but only when it guided and channeled the erotic drives of individuals. It was through couple love that a communal "aura" was created, an encompassing, enlivening energy flow that moved in many different directions throughout the community and affectively bound each discrete individual to the whole. In a communal setting, Stephen warned, "you have to be very careful and very kind and very full of love, which means very moral about how you arrange those energy relationships. . . . You honor other people's relationships. It's the subtlety and the depth of the way we love each other that makes it possible for us to have a lot of love and a clean mind" (S. Gaskin 1980, 77).

It is clear that the spiritual and interpersonal skills necessary to make such a system work needed to be continually refined, that love and enlightenment were in a delicate balance. To ensure equilibrium in the couple relationship and thereby communal stability, a system of complex households was instituted in the late 1970s that ensured affect density (concentration and amplification of mutual affection) and social oversight of the dyadic unit. The Farm welcomed these denser domestic units because "they found that couples managed better if they related closely with other people—someone who shared their space and could say, 'Wait a minute, one of you is out of line on that.'" As one member of the community put it, "We get along in our households, and it keeps us from being self-indulgent" (Thorndike 1979, 38). Large households also allowed women to share child care responsibilities (although women remained the primary care givers) and fostered a psychological sense of extended familial structure, a kind of "little community" within the larger communal setting. If warnings about selfishness were ignored, one member of the couple might be asked to leave the community for thirty days to "get back in sync" with the flow of community "juice," to submit to the authority of the collective community will. Despite these disciplinary procedures, there is evidence of serious stress within the ideal of synergistic marriage at The Farm.

On one occasion, Stephen asked at a Sunday morning service how many women were intimidated by their husbands. At a meeting held later in the week, to explore the prevalence of male domination in the community, forty women showed up. This group comprised less than 10 percent and probably closer to 5 percent of the married women in the community at the time. They aired grievances ranging from verbal to psychological abuse. They argued that the emphasis on the obligation of women to set the moral tone of the community and to maintain its emotional balance weighed too heavily on them. When things went wrong, when there were inevitable disagreements and dissatisfactions, women tended to be blamed. Stephen, who chaired the meeting as spiritual leader of the community, expressed sympathy for the women but pointed out that the intimidation they felt was in some sense owing to their failure to liberate themselves from a subordinate mind-set rooted in the vestiges of their precommunal life-styles. Stephen asserted that "intimidation is un-sane; un-sane because you have the most help and the best chance to get out from under it here; this is where you're going to find the most people dedicated to not being that way" (Pfaffenberger 1982, 206). As the meeting broke up, Stephen underlined his role as personal counselor and informed the group that if there were further interpersonal problems the women could always appeal to him for help. In a particularly resistant case, where the husband did not respond either to community pressure or to Stephen's lead, the couple might be separated for a time. The husband would be disciplined by being sent to live with the single men where he might learn humility, where his rough, macho crudeness could be ground down by the abrasive force of the all-male environment of the "rock tumbler" (Pfaffenberger 1982, 205–7).

While sexual and marital practices provided only imperfect and sometimes grudging support for The Farm's vision of an ideal alternative life-
style, the ultimate sustenance of communal life was the queen of the sacral
trinity–natural childbirth. Birthing claimed central importance as a physical, emotional, and spiritual ritual at the heart of community life. It was
a communal rite of renewal that recreated and redirected the energies of the
dyadic unit and reforged its bonds to the whole. The "spiritual midwives"
who guided the couple through the birth had both a hierophantic and an
educative role. They stood in place of the entire community at the birthing, because only the parents and the midwives (and in a few exceptional
cases, Stephen) were present during childbirth. While training the couple
to achieve higher levels of intimacy and a deeper sharing of their experience,
they reasserted the primacy of the community over the dyadic unit. The
sanctification of the couple occurred in its reabsorption into the communal
energy field. Through the transcendent, telepathic sensitivity of the process
of natural childbirth, communal commitment was recreated, and the couple's consciousness was anchored in the community through the support
system provided by the midwife network.

The midwife network constituted a female community that embodied
community spiritual ideals and the mastery of the practical techniques of
natural childbirth. The qualifications for midwives were consequently both
spiritual and practical. "To be a real midwife," a community publication
affirmed, "it is necessary to be spiritual. Compassion has to be a way of life
for her. The midwife must be able to consider someone else's viewpoint,
and in her daily life take care of those around her" (Ina May 1975, 338).
The midwife also had to be married and to have had at least one child by
natural childbirth. Relations with both husband and children had to be exemplary. She represented, then, an ideal type of both wife and mother.
Her role as midwife required no less, for to insure the proper channeling
of physical and spiritual energy at a birthing, "she must be able to teach
a couple to be tantric, if they need help. To do all this, she has to really
know and love her husband, be his best friend and know how to give him
some [juice]" (Ina May 1975, 339).

Technical training for midwives came from two sources–texts and on-
the-job experience. Midwives were enjoined to be avid students of an ancient feminine craft that exploited the most modern scientific and medical
knowledge. The Farm midwives also learned from a local male doctor who
was sympathetic to natural childbirth practices and who delivered at a nearby
hospital the few community children with unusual birth complications. The
normal period of training for a new midwife was between one and two years,

22. Ina May Gaskin and other Farm women share the community aura with an infant, 1970s. *Courtesy of Farm News Service.*

and during this period a woman could expect to assist at about twenty-five births, assuming increasing responsibility as her mastery of basic physical skills grew and her spiritual karma with the birthing mother intensified. During boom times, a head of a midwife team could deliver as many as thirteen babies in two weeks (Ina May 1975, 67–68, 76).

The terms most frequently used on The Farm to describe birth were sacral. As one woman described her experience: "It was a miracle. I really know in my heart of hearts that choosing to be spiritual instead of bummed out was what got me together enough to have a baby" (Ina May 1975, 58). Another couple testified to the effect of the experience in recalling them to communal values and in renewing their marriage. Before the birth they had not been getting on too well, but afterwards, as the wife reported, "we felt literally married and quite telepathic. I saw that we could get along real well if our attention was focused outside ourselves and available to each other and not on our own desires" (Ina May 1975, 251).

Most frequently, communal testimony from the mid-1970s emphasized the role of the midwife in "straightening up" one or both members of a couple, and in drawing on the communal energy field to dissipate negative energy concentrations or "hassling." For example, one couple reported that two midwives who came to assist at the birth sensed that the couple's relationship was far from harmonious. They "started to sort out mine and Eugene's relationship pretty intensely," the wife related. "The outcome was that we practically felt like we had to start over again. They said I didn't give Eugene much real juice, that I needed to really give him some . . . and also said that I came on low key and whiney to him which made him come on macho and cold" (Ina May 1975, 267).

In another case, William, Linda's husband, was "out of sync" with the emotional energy field of the birthing, and when his wife looked to him for support he felt confused and challenged. "He got huffy with Linda," and when one of the midwife team pointed out the inappropriateness of his behavior, "he got angrier." William was sent outside to run off some of his aggressive energy. When he returned he was questioned by one of the midwives, who found his anger had not yet dissipated. Linda was consulted to see whether she felt his presence would be a positive one at the birth, and she concurred with the midwives' recommendation that William be sent away again. In this instance, the midwives were unable to achieve the proper emotional balance and affectional relationship between the parents, and the husband was banished from the birthing (Ina May 1975, 34–35).

The psychology of the midwives' role in maintaining adherence to the communal marital ideal through a dual process of criticism and enlightenment is clear in these examples. Focusing all attention on the baby being born reenforced the communal value of self-transcendence. Midwives routinely counseled women about to give birth to "stop being self-indulgent." The midwives also stood in the front ranks to battle against the most besetting sin that threatened communal life – becoming "attached." For an individual to become attached or selfishly fixated on some purely personal goal put a drain on the energy of the whole community. Self-absorbed obsession closed off options; it destroyed the openness that provided access both to one's own feelings and to the emotional flow of the whole community. Attachment blocked energy; it put the dyadic unit out of joint and thereby threatened communal stability. The role of the midwives in this instance was an equilibrating one.

An illustrative example was the case of the young mother with a responsible position in the community whose newborn began to lose weight and soon "looked like a sour old ascetic–resigned to a life of none." At work the mother was worried about a lack of money coming into the community. The midwives looked into the case and decided the mother had an attachment–she was having difficulty nursing the child because it was male, and she had guilt feelings about feeling good while he suckled at her breast. The case illustrated the degree to which midwives, who comprised an elite female leadership group at The Farm, had internalized the community's spiritual-ideological values, and more particularly, the teachings of Stephen. It was in fact Stephen who finally provided the key to resolving the situation when he said to the mother, "Look, Mildred, a little incest is cool up to about age twelve. Somebody's got to give him some" (Ina May 1975, 279). The mother's attitude and behavior changed, and the balance of energy within the familial unit was restored. Once that level of energy flow had been therapeutically reestablished, the broader communal problem troubling this woman was also resolved–"the money started coming in again" (Ina May 1975, 280). This sequence of events may well have been purely coincidental, but on a popular level of belief such stories had the power of moral tales that served as vehicles for framing and transmitting communal values to Farm members.

Those values embodied behavioral prescriptions as well as community ideals. Given the emphasis on the equivalence of male and female energy in The Farm's ideology and the central role of women in maintaining communal harmony and a healthy flow of affectivity, an important question is, Did this ideational structure cause a significant alteration in traditional sex roles in the community? The primary feminine role was maternal; the community's prescriptive norms were thoroughly pronatalist. As one woman expressed it, "Having a baby is your ultimate fulfillment" (Ina May 1975, 191). Broadly speaking, Farm members believed that female energy prescribed roles that were domestic and moral for women, while male energy was more assertive and was channeled into manual labor and the direction of community affairs. As Stephen put it, women were supposed to suffuse their environment with their energy, to create a "field" "that's nice and smells good and feels good and is clean and a good place for a baby to be" (S. Gaskin 1974, n.p.).

Despite this emphasis on the maternal function, some women worked outside the home, and a few had positions of real importance at The Farm. In the mid-1970s, a woman was financial manager of the community, a position described as "one of the more high-pressure, demanding jobs one can have" (Ina May 1975, 278). In the same era, one woman served as banker and another as housing officer. On the other hand, traditional attitudes toward the division of labor along gender lines prevailed for most women.

Most of the food preparation, child care, and cleaning functions still fell to women. Both visitors and ex-community members have testified that women at The Farm enthusiastically accepted this sexual division of labor. Community men claimed that women were not excluded from holding any position at The Farm but that lack of opportunities and fundamentally conservative gender attitudes in the surrounding community inevitably meant that fewer women than men were able to work off communal property. Women did work in the fields with the agricultural crew, in the community medical lab and health clinic (they comprised about one-quarter of the total staff), in the community publishing business (the Book Publishing Company), and in the various extracommunity relief and support activities undertaken by Plenty, The Farm's nonprofit, international social service agency. Women did not generally work as carpenters, electricians, mechanics, or drivers. Despite the evidence that some women held a variety of positions at The Farm, such women clearly constituted a minority of the female population and may have been predominantly single women. The sacral value of the domestic sphere was evident in the comment of one of Stephen's wives, who "considered it to be a holy duty to cook for them [her family] and keep them healthy and keep them clean and keep it sanitary and clean and together for my family" (Pfaffenberger 1982, 204).

In a pronatalist community, motherhood was a sacred trust that combined childbirth and child rearing. The nurture and education of children were also predominantly female responsibilities. Women typically raised three or more children, some of whom may have been adopted, as approximately one-quarter of the children living in the community in the late 1970s were fostered.

While the family was the basic unit of social organization, by the late 1970s most households at The Farm were extended, with a single structure sheltering from twenty-five to sixty people. Each household was multigenerational and may typically have encompassed handicapped and emotionally disturbed adults as well. A mature couple headed each household and insured that the domestic unit collectively provided care and attention for all its members (Thorndike 1979, 40).

Farm ideology held that a child should remain with its mother for the first year or eighteen months. While parental affection was valued, the telepathic bond of nursing child and mother was considered primary. Early child care took place largely within the home, but there was a community nursery where professional nurses (all female) provided care. The values the community considered essential were conveyed in two educative environments—the family and the school. In order to sustain and transmit communal values, The Farm maintained its own school. In the late 1970s, some three hundred students from kindergarten through high school were in attendance (Thorndike 1979, 41–42). Many women worked as teachers in the school. Children were socialized to community life through the inculcation of the ideals of love, order, and control. Open expressions of affection between children and parents were encouraged, but children were taught at an early age that they were not the central focus of community life. While they might expect a reasonable amount of attention, they could not rightly monopolize their parents' or other adults' "juice." Beyond this fundamental lesson of the primacy of community needs over individual desires, Stephen summed up the educational goals of The Farm: "Teaching the children to be good, teaching the children to be honest, teaching the children to stay away from bad dope and alcohol, teaching the children not to be promiscuous sexually, can all be done within the school system" (S. Gaskin 1981, 219). Farm women had an essential role to play in transmitting and reenforcing those values.

But by far the most important female role as well as the most prestigious female occupation at The Farm was that of midwife. While economic decisions were made by a board of fifteen men and women – heads of work crews, leaders of the school, the lab, the clinic, the publishing business, and so forth – social and ideological power and crucial decision making lay with Stephen, the midwives, the gate crew, and the women who oversaw housing arrangements (Thorndike 1979, 41) Midwifery was an elite profession, though; in 1975 there were only seventeen women on the midwife crew. They had delivered 350 babies between 1971 and 1975 (Ina May 1975, 8). These women played a central role as well in the process of spiritual enlightenment and behavioral modification through criticism that ranked them among the most powerful people at The Farm.

Midwives saw their practice as revolutionary because, as they expressed it, "it is our basic belief that the sacrament of birth belongs to the people and that it should not be usurped by a profit-oriented hospital system. . . . [We] feel that returning the responsibility for childbirth to midwives rather than a predominantly male medical establishment is a major advance for women. The wisdom and compassion a woman can intuitively experience in childbirth can make her a source of healing and understanding for other women" (Ina May 1975, 6–7). Indeed, Ina May Gaskin argued that "birth is a time of transformation and empowerment in women's lives." Through "spiritual midwifery," she asserted, "we have unlocked the great riddle of birth and in doing so, we have found a way that women can live with men without being exploited" (I. M. Gaskin 1989, 27, 28).

The implications of the appropriation of a role traditionally reserved for male professionals in the modern medical community are clear. That the birth process required a telepathic sensitivity that inverted sex-role expectations that prevailed outside the community was underscored by Stephen's advice to an expectant mother. "At the birthing," he said, "the man is supposed to be open and receptive so the energy can flow, and . . . the midwife should be the yangest thing in the room" (Ina May 1975, 120).

The techniques of natural childbirth the midwives taught mothers and the female support network (a communal sisterhood) they organized that sustained the flow of energy, that kept everyone "stoned" (charged with spiritual energy), represented a form of female empowerment. "Spiritual midwifery" allowed birthing mothers to retain control over their physical, mental, and emotional states during pregnancy and parturition and thus valorized natural, communal childbirth as a basis for the reclamation of maternal dignity. Unlike childbirth in a hospital setting, where women were usually given local anesthesia, spiritual midwifery enabled women to retain complete control over their bodies during the birth.

In a broader context, modern midwifery represents a challenge to male cooptation of prenatal care, the birth experience, and postnatal care of both mother and infant embodied in professional obstetrical and gynecological care, physician-assisted hospital births, and analgesic intervention in the form of the epidural or pelvic bloc. As practiced at The Farm, "spiritual midwifery" reenforced the alternative communal life-style by mounting a direct assault on contemporary social values and established technological practices in their most fundamental expression–the male management, manipulation, and control of women's bodies and the process of childbirth. Birthing became gynecentric again, sororal and maternal centered.

The emotional bonding of the midwife-mother team and the centrality of childbirth to the sustenance of the community (both demographically and emotionally) assured an essential role for the women of The Farm that reaffirmed the communal as well as the personal value of their feminine identity. As the process of birth had become again a source of feminine empowerment ordered and controlled by women, the role of the father at the birth was determined by the community of women–the mother-wife, and more importantly, the midwife, who reconstituted the spiritual and ideological significance of childbirth through her personal embodiment of community centeredness. Men were encouraged to open themselves to the more nurturing side of their personalities, not simply to support their wives during childbirth but to share the sacral experience more directly. This required conscious attention to changing traditional male role expectations, especially in the areas of expressive and affective behavior.

The ideological concern for maintaining a balance in the gender-based energy flow and the spiritual value attached to the maternal, nurturant role led to a negative evaluation of macho tendencies. Community norms frowned on the aggressive male sexual swagger that led a man to think "that his erection is his lightning bolt . . . that he's the cat with the juice" (S. Gaskin 1974, n.p.). Men needed to strive to overcome the tendency to treat women as sex objects and come to enjoy a more mutual sharing of energy (Ina May 1975, 299). To some extent, the community practice of using only first names, which deemphasized both patriarchal preeminence and the nominal significance of the marital unit, reaffirmed the sense of individual identity with the broader household unit and with the more inclusive family of the entire community and thereby reenforced the idea of gender equality.

Nevertheless, most contemporary observers of The Farm from mainstream society in the late 1970s found that its ideology of sexual differentiation led to sexual inequality. Given this body of criticism, what satisfactions did women find in a community whose ideology made no claim to abolish sex role distinctions, and whose marital system, while it sought balance and harmony, could not have been described as liberated by contemporary standards? Was The Farm just another patriarchal community where women were controlled by a male theology that reenforced traditional sex roles and female subordination through a sanctification and reification of the maternal instinct? The reality of women's experiences in this community, it seems to me, was rather more complex.

Certainly, under a system of pronatalism, the maternal role was preeminent. Midwives and mothers alike spoke of "the Holiness of birth" (Ina May 1975, 176). The child-mother relationship was paramount. Yet, while women's opportunities for work outside the domestic environment were limited, professional openings seem to have been more available to women than openings in skilled trades. Perhaps those who had acquired useful skills before joining the community found a ready acceptance of their competence; there seems to have been little philosophical commitment to equalizing access to all jobs to both men and women. The composition of the staff that worked on the community's book on "spiritual midwifery" underscores this point. The editors of the volume were evenly split—two men and two women. Of eleven printers, only one was female.

For midwives, there had clearly been status enhancement. Although admission to the midwife crew was theoretically open to any woman who had undergone natural childbirth in the community, what seems to have most characterized Farm midwives was their mastery and internalization of community theology and social ideology. Midwife power originated in thorough conviction of the truth and efficacy of Stephen's teachings. It may have been that, especially in the early years of The Farm, closeness to the community's spiritual teacher conferred special status on women. The fact

that Ina May, Stephen's first (and later monogamous) wife, remained the
acknowledged leader of the midwives, and that she claimed to have learned
much of what she knew about birthing from Stephen, is particularly significant in this connection (Ina May 1975, 8).

But it would be a serious misapprehension, it seems to me, to assume
that midwives were little more than pale reflections of a dominant male
ideology. Their importance in the community, given the centrality of the
pronatalist position, made them role models in both a spiritual and a practical way for much of the female community at The Farm. They represented
the ideal as wives, mothers, and sisters. Indeed, they created the basis for
a community of women at The Farm, a sisterhood that not only linked
community women but that united them with a more universal, affective
female community that transcended the boundaries of The Farm. Community women described birthings as powerful channelings of love between
women and analogized them to psychedelic experiences of personal tran-
scendence. Describing her birthing experience, one woman said, "I found
it easy to do what she said. It was like making love to Ina May." Another
testified that "Mary Louise and I got stoned [a state of heightened, transcendent consciousness] together. I felt in love with her real heavy. She felt real
soft, but strong and sure at the same time. She really felt the baby's presence
a lot. She was very compassionate with me. I could feel her feeling what
I was feeling." The link to a broader community was clear in a third woman's
assertion that her birthing had been "holy, and pure and I felt telepathic
with all mothers before me and knew that we were one thing, and all come
to that same place" (Ina May 1975, 173, 179, 241).

The hundreds of noncommunity women and unwed mothers who have
given birth at The Farm and who have received pre- and postnatal care, food,
and shelter are a broader testimonial to the more extensive female community created by the midwives. The books published by the community on
natural contraception and natural childbirth have also served to provide a
service, grounded in midwifery, to noncommunity women, and thus to
broaden the community of women.

The degree to which The Farm addressed feminist concerns agitating
the outside world is a complex question. In regard to conception, its contraceptive techniques (given male subordination to the female cycle) placed
control of pregnancy in the hands of women. Indeed, one reviewer of the
community's birth control handbook described it as explicitly "non-sexist"
(*Booklist* 1977, 254). Given the pronatalist position of the community, natural contraception coupled with breastfeeding, which often continued for
a year, allowed women to exercise control over their reproductive lives
through limiting and spacing births. The fact that the community took in

unwanted children and fostered others suggests a fundamental emphasis on the value of children but a less than maximum exploitation of the childbearing capacities of community women.

While the goals of the community can be more accurately described as restorationist than as progressive and can certainly not be described as liberationist from a feminist point of view (except, perhaps, within the sphere of the maternal), The Farm did offer women a power and a security that were often lacking in the lives of their more liberated sisters in the outside world. If the pronatalist position was central to the community, it must be seen in the context of synergistic, monogamous marriage. Women secured greater control over their heterosexual experience by way of male solicitude for their sex partners' orgasms, control of conception and thus of the timing and frequency of intercourse, and control of the physical and emotional experience of childbirth. In a culture where divorce and sexual promiscuity were the norm, women at The Farm were provided these not insignificant controls in the context of ideologically and theologically sanctioned marital stability. Although the available evidence suggests that those marriages sometimes fell short of the ideal, and although there were divorces in the community, the great majority of marriages seem to have remained stable.

The Farm, then, sought through its ideology and social organization to reconstruct gender-based power as it related to sex, marriage, childbirth, and child rearing. The community overturned the male-dominated practices of childbirth, emphasized the predominance of female pleasure in the sex act, inverted the emphasis on patriarchal models in child rearing, and moved toward a marital relationship defined in terms of fundamental female rather than masculine psychological and emotional needs. For a community led by a charismatic male spiritual figure, these were substantial achievements that might quite appropriately be interpreted as a movement toward a feminization of the social and emotional relationship between the sexes. The identity of women at The Farm was with a new order of love, mediated by the sacral female principle expressed sacramentally through sex, marriage, and childbirth. The old man (the male principle) was being sloughed off in the community's social environment. Some women, particularly the most powerful in the community, found the experience of this new social role highly invigorating and transcendent—a "stoned" experience, one "charged with spiritual energy, which raises the consciousness to new levels of perception" (Ina May 1975, 10).

Pronatalism inevitably led The Farm to a social reorganization of what Gayle Rubin called the "sex/gender system," those "systematic ways [societies devise] to deal with sex, gender, and babies" (Rubin 1975, 168). While reorganization of the "sex/gender system" does not preclude and has occasionally been accompanied by changes in a society's organization of production, that has not typically been the case. As Nancy Chodorow has observed, "In the modern period . . . the development of capitalism, and contemporary developments in socialist countries, have changed the sex-gender system more than the reverse" (Chodorow 1978, 8–9). It should come as no surprise, then, that a communal society like The Farm should have found it easier to reassess and reorganize its social life in areas related to sex, birth, and child rearing than in the realm of gender roles related to work.

For women who found a pronatalist stance acceptable, The Farm provided a strong sense of female identity, a supportive and revered community of women (the midwives), an extended familial environment with shared child care, an elevation of status (insofar as motherhood and the domestic sphere were elevated in community ideology above the realm of the public work world), greater stability of relationships, and more substantial female control of sexuality and conception. But in many ways these gains for women required implicit renunciation of more thoroughgoing feminist objectives through acceptance of a social order that seemed to replicate the patterns of nineteenth-century gender experience—a division (though not categorically prescriptive) into domestic and public spheres of activity and an apotheosis of the female as maternal, moral, and child-centered that reflected the Victorian ideology of the "true woman."

While The Farm's social reorganization of the "sex/gender system" was reactive to practices in contemporary American society, it did produce some gains for women who had a strong spiritual commitment to community ideology. For those women who sought more progressive change, who sought transformation of the social order through a radical reorganization of gender that would potentially eliminate sexual inequality, the direction and pace of social change at The Farm would have been sorely disappointing. For women like these, the path to a more thoroughgoing gender equality led back through the community gate that swung out onto a less secure and less predictable world.

Notes

1. The events of the evolution of The Farm are described in three of Stephen Gaskin's books: *Monday Night Class* (1970), *The Caravan* (1972), and *Hey Beatnik! This Is The Farm Book* (1974). The 1970 and 1974 publications have no pagination. The events are also summarized in "A World of Husbands and Mothers" (Pfaffenberger 1982, 184–86, 198–99). The Caravan recalls the Merry Pranksters' voyage six years earlier in their bus, "Further," with Neal Cassady at the wheel and Ken Kesey as spiritual and chemical navigator chronicled in Tom Wolfe's *Elec-*

tric Kool-Aid Acid Test (1969) and reexamined as the archetypal sixties experience in Kesey's *Further Inquiry* (1990).

2. I am indebted to Albert K. Bates, attorney, member of The Farm, and director of the Natural Rights Center, Summertown, Tennessee, for much of the demographic data presented here.

3. These details on marital arrangements at The Farm were provided by Albert K. Bates in a telephone conversation on January 10, 1991, and in comments on an earlier version of this paper presented at a national Communal Studies Association conference at Canterbury, N.H., Shaker Village, October 10, 1986.

4. The terms *astral plane* and *aura,* though loosely understood in the 1960s, have specific meanings in Stephen's philosophy. The *astral plane* refers to the spatial dimension in which direct telepathic communication between souls takes place (S. Gaskin 1980, 119). *Aura,* as used on The Farm, refers specifically to "the field of spiritual energy that surrounds all living things" (Ina May 1975, 10). Because Stephen was a serious student of semantics, the conclusion I have drawn here, that in the communal setting love was seen as a primary facilitator of communication, seems justified.

5. See also Stephen's statements on heterosexual relationships at The Farm in *Hey Beatnik!* Despite the prevalence of monogamy at The Farm during this period, male solicitude for female sexual pleasure provides an interesting parallel with some aspects of the sexual practices that prevailed in the Oneida Community (1848–1880) under the system of "male continence." See *An Ordered Love* (Kern 1981, 240–46).

Works Cited

Booklist 74, no. 3 (Oct. 1, 1977). Review of Margaret Nofziger, *A Cooperative Method of Birth Control.*

Chodorow, Nancy. 1978. *The Reproduction of Mothering: Psychoanalysis and the Sociology of Gender.* Berkeley: Univ. of California Press.

Gaskin, Ina May. 1989. Midwifery and Women's Power. *Woman of Power* 14 (Summer): 27–28.

Gaskin, Stephen. 1970. *Monday Night Class.* San Francisco: Book Farm.

———. 1972. *The Caravan.* New York: Random House.

———. 1974. *Hey Beatnik! This Is The Farm Book.* Summertown, Tenn.: The Book Publishing Co.

———. 1980. *Mind at Play.* Summertown, Tenn.: The Book Publishing Co.

———. 1981. *Rendered Infamous: A Book of Political Reality.* Summertown, Tenn.: The Book Publishing Co.

Ina May and The Farm Midwives. 1975. *Spiritual Midwifery.* Summertown, Tenn.: The Book Publishing Co.

Kanter, Rosabeth M. 1972. *Commitment and Community: Communes and Utopias in Sociological Perspective.* Cambridge, Mass.: Harvard Univ. Press.

Kern, Louis J. 1981. *An Ordered Love: Sex Roles and Sexuality in Victorian Utopias—the Shakers, the Mormons, and the Oneida Community.* Chapel Hill: Univ. of North Carolina Press.

Kesey, Ken. 1990. *The Further Inquiry.* New York: Viking.

Nofziger, Margaret. 1977. *A Cooperative Method of Natural Birth Control.* Summertown, Tenn.: The Book Publishing Co.

Pfaffenberger, Bryan. 1982. A World of Husbands and Mothers: Sex Roles and Their Ideological Context in the Formation of The Farm. In *Sex Roles in Contemporary Communes,* edited by Jon Wagner, 172–210. Bloomington: Indiana Univ. Press.

Rubin, Gayle. 1975. The Traffic in Women: Notes on the "Political Economy" of Sex. In *Toward an Anthropology of Women,* edited by Rayna Reiter, 157–210. New York: Monthly Review.

Thorndike, John. 1979. The Farm: Where Self-Sufficiency Means More than Mere Subsistence. *Country Journal,* Feb., 36–43.

Wenner, Kate. 1977. How They Keep Them Down on The Farm. *New York Times Magazine,* May 8, 74, 80–81, 83.

Wolfe, Tom. 1969. *Electric Kool-Aid Acid Test.* New York: Bantam.

13

Female Education in the Lubavitcher Community

The Beth Rivkah and Machon Chana Schools

BONNIE MORRIS

CROWN HEIGHTS, BROOKLYN, is the present-day headquarters for a two-hundred-year-old sect known as Chabad Lubavitch. These ultra-Orthodox Jews take their name from Chabad, a doctrine of Jewish missionary activism popularized by eighteenth-century Hasid Schneur Zalman, and Lubavitch, the Russian village where the sect took root. Oppressed and exiled by both Tsarist and Soviet authorities, then persecuted by anti-Semitism in Eastern Europe, the Lubavitchers looked to the leadership of each successive Rebbe throughout one and one-half centuries of wandering. During the 1920s and 1930s, with the encouragement of the reigning Rebbe, the Lubavitchers began to resettle in Crown Heights, Brooklyn. Though the Holocaust diminished their remaining numbers in Europe, the American Hasidic community grew steadily in both pre- and postwar generations. Today, followers of the seventh Lubavitcher Rebbe point with pride to his power and influence in the American Jewish community as a spokesman for traditional Jewish education and practice.

Education and instruction form the core of Hasidic philosophy, and the Crown Heights community has become a living laboratory for the adaptation of Hasidic law and worship to American institutions. Within the strictly regulated world of higher Talmud study, schooling for women has always been separate from, and a lesser priority than, male learning. Historically, the Orthodox Jewish woman learned only the religious dicta governing her own responsibilities, all other education being considered superfluous to her preparation for marriage and direction of a religious household. Hasidic women in Eastern Europe freely consulted male authorities or their Rebbe for advice on religious, domestic, and community issues,

221

but remained outside the male scope of *yeshiva* activity. In the United States in the twentieth century, however, it was no longer possible for Lubavitcher authorities to ignore the need for female education.

Beth Rivkah

In 1940 the sixth Lubavitcher Rebbe, Joseph Yitzchak Schneersohn, arrived in the United States and settled permanently in Crown Heights. While the Rebbe and his followers had devoted two decades to the establishment of male religious academies in Brooklyn, there were no companion institutions for Lubavitcher women and girls beyond a small study group in Riga, Latvia (Jacobson 1967, 11). Female religious study was still anathema in the eyes of Hasidic authorities, although the Bais Yaakov girls' schools founded by Sara Schenierer in Poland demonstrated the possibility for a female parochial system under Hasidic auspices (Weissman 1976, 139–48). The transplantation of the Lubavitcher movement from Eastern Europe to the United States forced the issue of female education onto the Rebbe's agenda, for in America all schoolchildren learned state-mandated secular subjects. This extensive modern curriculum, plus the availability of college education for young women, gave the Hasidic community its final push to provide religious academies for girls. With mingled amusement and resignation, the Rebbe called upon his aide, Rabbi Israel Jacobson, to begin the inevitable: "Yisroel, organize Beth Rivkah schools, one or two, for girls. Our mutual concern has always been the study of Torah and Chassidus with boys in yeshivos, but here in America, we have to do everything" (Jacobson 1967, 13).

The Beth Rivkah school system thus began not as a recognition of female academic ability but to hold the line against the onslaught of secular forces in American education. While most supporters of the Rebbe and of the Lubavitch movement appreciated the concept of insulating religious girls against the winds of public schooling, Rabbi Israel Jacobson found that very few congregations or philanthropists were interested in pledging financial support to a female academy. In his memoir "Chassidus Study for Girls," Rabbi Jacobson recalled that "it was no easy matter at the time to persuade even religious congregations to give the use of their premises for a girls' school, so strange and new was the concept of comprehensive Jewish education for girls, even for observant Jews" (Jacobson 1967, 13). Because no congregation or *yeshiva* would allocate space, the first Beth Rivkah elementary school, with an enrollment of thirty pupils, began meeting in a Brooklyn storefront in 1942.

No member of the Lubavitcher community painted a more vivid portrait of those early years than Sudy Rosengarten, a graduate of Beth Rivkah's first class. In seven short stories written for the Lubavitcher women's magazine, *Di Yiddishe Heim,* during the 1970s, Rosengarten described the poor conditions, ill-equipped teachers, and haphazard curriculum endured by the pioneer students of Beth Rivkah in the 1940s.

> By some strange miracle, thirty children had been recruited and Girls' Yeshiva was launched. Teachers ran from group to group in classes that were doubled up for warmth and economy. Often we sat in darkness, the electricity turned off because of non-payment. The desks were broken, the plaster was peeled, a puddle was always forming where some pipe had suddenly burst; entire floors roped off till some charitable plumber would fix it gratis. . . . All thirty of us, though looked upon with pity by all our former school-mates and teachers as being the sacrificial lambs for the nation, were fired and fused with Rabbi Newman's enthusiasm. For it was not merely a school that we would build; we were rebuilding a nation. (Rosengarten 1973, 21)

Despite their fervor for continuing unique Hasidic traditions in America while the war in Europe devastated Jewish communities abroad, these American-born girls keenly felt the inferiority of Beth Rivkah's first curriculum. One problem was that the Beth Rivkah elementary school did not expand to include a high school until 1955. Nor was there a Beth Rivkah Teachers Seminary until 1960. As a result of this acute shortage of trained women teachers throughout the 1940s and 1950s, Beth Rivkah relied upon young public high school graduates to do the lion's share of instruction. This pattern of assigning eighteen-year-olds to teach fifteen-year-olds created predictable discipline problems in the postwar Lubavitch community.

Rosengarten wrote frankly of her classmates' frustration: "Feelings of being cheated were defined in disobedience: playing pranks on teachers, organizing the class into situations that made it impossible to teach what might have been attempted" (Rosengarten 1973, 22). At the Lubavitcher boys' *yeshivoth,* where venerated rabbinical scholars taught seminars on the intricacies of Jewish law, a harsh scolding from a learned sage instantly restored order in the classroom. But at Beth Rivkah, students were only too aware that their teachers lacked qualifications and status. Contempt, rebellion, and intellectual lassitude created a host of morale problems at Beth Rivkah that were unheard of in the prestigious male academies.

With the passing of Rebbe Joseph Schneersohn in 1950 and the succession of his dynamic son-in-law to Lubavitch leadership, the Crown Heights community began a new era of adjustment to American culture. One result was the establishment of the Lubavitcher women's periodical, *Di Yiddishe*

Heim (The Jewish Home). From 1958 on, this quarterly journal of essays and neighborhood anecdotes gave women in the Crown Heights community a forum for addressing Beth Rivkah's needs. Countless articles by timid or angry novice teachers noted the lack of support for female education and demanded changes in the Beth Rivkah system. In 1963, community educator Chana Heilbrun contributed a controversial three-part article, "Can We Improve Our Schools?" to *Di Yiddishe Heim.*

In part 1 of her series, Heilbrun critiqued the level of scholarship in teacher preparatory courses, the inability of the Hasidic school system to provide for special-needs students, and the shocking lack of *derech eretz* (respect and good manners) in a student population representing Lubavitch Hasidism's oldest families. Although she upheld the positive influence of Hasidic ideology in the Beth Rivkah program, Heilbrun felt that Torah for girls in America was taught tepidly and ineffectively. She recalled the Bais Yaakov schools of prewar Europe, where women teachers, usually rabbis' wives, were respected and beloved role models for Hasidic girls (Heilbrun 1963, Pt. 1, 12). Heilbrun's own memories of her student days informed her views as a parent and a teacher. She placed much blame upon the male instructors intermittently assigned to Beth Rivkah, whom she accused of disparaging female scholarship even while acting as mentors to girls. "Theoretically, the need for formal Torah schooling for Jewish girls has been established and encouraged. At the same time, there still exists that negative feeling about 'too much learning.' Many a time has that little chuckle and a joking 'What do you girls have to learn so much for anyway,' on the part of a teacher, revealed his true attitude" (Heilbrun 1963, Pt. 1, 13).

Having laid the groundwork for fundamental criticism of the attitudes and agenda impairing Beth Rivkah, Heilbrun turned to the students' own irresponsibility. In part 2 of her series, she called for "discipline without apology" as a necessary tactic in the era of progressive educational ideals (pt. 2, 17). Heilbrun's striking anecdotes revealed how student awareness of teacher inadequacy greatly undermined the structure of authority upon which academic progress depended. "A novice teacher enters her first class assignment—a third grade of *yeshiva* girls. All goes smoothly until she reprimands one of the more talkative students, who answers in tones of furious rage, 'You're a new teacher and you won't last a week here. Just wait until I tell my father you pick on me and you'll get fired like this,' and the 8-year-old rebel snaps her finger in the air" (Heilbrun 1964, pt. 2, 17).

The problem of misbehavior led one Lubavitcher mother to recommend that all children attend annual seminars on the importance of *derech eretz.* A more pressing concern was the low status and low self-esteem of Beth Rivkah's teachers. Heilbrun merely opened the discussion with her articles, and *Di Yiddishe Heim* continued to publish a painful dialogue of other correspondence – from teachers forced to resign after a few weeks, teachers afraid of their own students, and teachers bitter over their minimal seminary training, which had in no way prepared them for professional interaction with adolescents.

Despite the unresolved issues of student-teacher friction and irregular coursework, Beth Rivkah continued to grow as an institution. Its expansion during the 1960s and 1970s reflected both the high birth rate of the Hasidic population and the added arrival of refugee children from Jewish communities in Iran and the Soviet Union. By the early 1980s, the school in Crown Heights boasted three buildings, six hundred students, and eighty-one teachers (Beth Rivkah High School 1986, 7).

In 1986, after years of campaigns led by concerned mothers, the Lubavitcher community purchased the old Lefferts General Hospital and two adjoining properties, totaling nearly one square block, for a new Beth Rivkah site. The *Neshei Chabad,* the Lubavitcher women's organization newsletter, announced in December 1986 that "architectural plans have been drawn to – G-d willing – completely renovate the building to house a modern yeshiva for 1,000 girls in kindergarten through eighth grade and to level the adjacent properties to build a playground" ("Neshei News" 1986, 19). The projected cost for this new facility was $3 million.

In spring 1987, another article in the newsletter mentioned that Beth Rivkah's financial battle should include an adjustment of teacher salaries, which lagged far behind metropolitan standards. Why was Beth Rivkah still ignored as a priority charity by its own people? This article's anonymous author suggested that Lubavitcher men had a responsibility to pitch in as fundraisers; did not fathers have a role in supporting the school where their daughters were instructed in Hasidic ways? The author hinted, "And you know the 'they' we're all waiting for? You know: 'they' should do something about Bais Rivkah? Well, these gentlemen are the 'they'" ("Bais Rivkah" 1987, 3).

Today, Beth Rivkah students learn Bible, Hebrew, Midrash, Hasidic philosophy, Jewish history, Shulchan Aruch (the code of Jewish law), the works of the Rebbe, and secular studies in English, geography, science, American history, French, and business. The girls attend school six days a week, Sunday through Friday; the latter is a half-day because the Sabbath commences at sundown after many hours of meticulous preparation. Despite the community's mistrust of secular academic subjects, the Beth Rivkah high school library contains the works of Austen, Dickens, Mann, Steinbeck, Stevenson, Swift, Tolstoy, and Twain. Hasidic literature dominates the shelves, but students may also browse through texts on black history,

urban sociology, psychology, women's studies, Greek philosophy and logic—
and even Christian-oriented novels such as the children's classic *Prince Caspian* by C. S. Lewis. Despite some evidence of censorship of the books,
such as the removal of nude images in art and photography texts, the inquisitive student at Beth Rivkah today does not lack access to the tools of
a liberal arts education.

As the first and second waves of Beth Rivkah high school graduates
married and started families of their own between 1965 and 1975, a change
occurred in Lubavitcher women's writing. Articles on female education in
Di Yiddishe Heim no longer focused on Beth Rivkah's limitations but expressed nostalgia and gratitude for the school. Young mothers, isolated and
overwhelmed by the demands of housework and child care, wrote wistful
essays about the climate of academic challenge they had enjoyed (or failed
to appreciate) in their school days. Such articles praised Beth Rivkah for
sharpening its students' intellectual skills and lamented the lack of adult
educational outlets for Lubavitcher mothers. Women whose artistic or literary talents had found sanction at Beth Rivkah now wrote to *Di Yiddishe
Heim* in despair: Were there no roles for intellectual women in the Lubavitcher movement?

In response to this new genre of writing, *Di Yiddishe Heim*'s editor,
Rachel Altein, and male authorities urged "unfulfilled" women to become
activists in the Lubavitcher women's organization, Neshei Chabad. Learning for its own sake was permissible, but more important was outreach to
less learned women who were not fully observant Jews. Those Lubavitcher
women who expressed dissatisfaction with their limited roles as wives and
mothers were warned that, as adults, they now had a moral obligation
to foster learning in others. The campaign to incorporate literary and articulate women into the Rebbe's outreach programs, in order to attract
American Jewish women to the Lubavitcher movement, partially resolved
the dilemma of the alienated homemaker. Ideally, the "selfish" desire of
many women for more learning could be justified as necessary to their "unselfish" capacity as Hasidic representatives. This argument was sufficiently
flexible and expedient for one writer to daringly acknowledge the influence
of American feminism.

A Jewish wife and mother, a Woman of Valor, knows of and discharges
the moral obligation to her husband and children inherent in her role. Yet
what about her moral obligation to herself? Since the end of her formal
schooling, has she made a similar attempt to increase her own knowledge?
It is not merely passivity, but a failure in duty, to refer the intellectual and
seeking questions of children and guests in the home to those whose "job

it is to know." Furthermore, even with the cries of Women's Libbers comes this quiet voice with the same message—what of the G-d-given talents that were so evident in your younger years? (Schusterman 1972, 11)

The Lubavitcher woman's high school education could not match that of her male, *yeshiva*-educated counterpart. Yet she still possessed more religious knowledge than the assimilated and nonobservant American Jewish woman. The obligation to act as mentor to new Hasidim thus brought many Lubavitcher housewives into the public sphere as teachers of *baalot teshuveh* (women returning to orthodoxy after living secular lives).

Just as female education at Beth Rivkah had created an army of women sufficiently conversant in Lubavitcher philosophy to proselytize, so the resultant flow of incoming pilgrims created the need for more adult education in the community. Before the Beth Rivkah graduate could request continuing education for her own peer group, she found herself pressed into service, helping to create school facilities for Jewish women just arriving in Crown Heights.

Education for Baalot Teshuveh: Machon Chana

There was a time several years ago, when every day was a challenge to me, to conquer my old ways and live by the Torah. . . . At that point in time, I had an amazing thirst to learn more . . . and I can remember my angry frustration over the cancellation of a class (this was before Machon Chana, the new school for women from backgrounds like mine), for it seemed I would never to able to fill the void of 21 years. ("A Chance Meeting" 1974, 19)

The intensive outreach efforts organized by the seventh Lubavitcher Rebbe after his takeover in 1950 spawned a new generation of observant American Jews. Attracted to, or affected by, the Chabad houses established on their college campuses by young Lubavitcher representatives, Jewish students throughout the 1960s turned to Judaism for the answers secular society failed to provide. To assure the swift matriculation of interested young men in Lubavitcher-sponsored *yeshivoth,* the Rebbe created Yeshiva Hadar Hatorah in 1962. This institution was the first *baal teshuveh* school designed for American Jewish men who lacked an Orthodox background but were eager to become religious as adults (Goldberg 1982, 37). After several years of remedial study at Hadar Hatorah, young men transferred into traditional Hasidic academies and continued their learning there. After Israel's victory in the 1967 Six-Day War, which culminated in the Jewish occupation of

the Western Wall in Jerusalem (Judaism's most holy site), a strengthened
sense of Jewish pride and identity led other young American men to examine their religious roots. To serve the needs of this group, the Rebbe
established a second *baal teshuveh* school, Yeshiva Tiferes Bachurim, in the
Lubavitcher complex at Morristown, New Jersey. Jewish men who craved
intensive but basic preparation in Hebrew and Talmud were rewarded for
their newfound dedication with instruction and counsel from some of the
most erudite rabbis in Lubavitch Hasidism.

While newly observant men were being courted during the 1960s, the
plight of the female penitent went ignored by most Crown Heights educational administrators. Women, too, were attracted to Hasidic traditions and
came to Crown Heights to seek instruction, but the female experience of
adjustment to a new life in Lubavitch differed strikingly from that of the
male *baal teshuveh*. The young male, generally recruited from college, transferred from one academic environment to another. The familiar routine of
attending classes, engaging in lively seminar discussions, and receiving feed-
back from male role models resembled the secular college experience. Of
course, at *yeshiva*, young men also found a highly structured environment,
conducive to self-discipline and the reinforcement of new group values. Re-
wards were plentiful for diligent *yeshiva* students; in the Hasidic world male
status was measured by a scholarly, not an economic yardstick. Nor was the
learning regimen dry and pedagogical. Young men who had participated
in the alternative political or spiritual movements of the late 1960s found
that Jewish scholars and philosophers in every century had also been obsessed
with questions of justice, oppression, fulfillment, and mysticism. This sense
of identification with Jewish forebears also helped to integrate the male *baal
teshuveh* into his new family of Hasidic pietists.

For women, however, the transition to *baalot teshuveh* status meant isolation and struggle. The group learning experience and institutional reinforcement of shared values could not occur without a school or regular tutorials.
While young men who entered Lubavitcher academies were fed and housed
by their institutions and eligible for scholarships as well, young women who
moved to Crown Heights undertook a self-imposed regimen of individual
study while struggling to survive financially. In the small community,
crowded with both wealthy and impoverished Hasidic families, affordable
housing for unknown single women was nearly impossible to find. Adult
baalot teshuveh women were not able to room with unmarried Lubavitcher
women at the dormitory of the Beth Rivkah Teacher Training Seminary;
the Rebbe was concerned that the more wordly outsiders might have a ques-
tionable influence upon the sheltered, vulnerable Lubavitcher-raised students. Forced to pay expensive Brooklyn rent on the typical workingwoman's

salary of the late 1960s, the female newcomer to Crown Heights was often poorly fed, exhausted, and lonely. If her decision to embrace Hasidism baffled or angered her family and old friends, she also lost the emotional and financial support of those relationships. Because she usually lacked a husband and children, the focal points for mature Lubavitcher women, the newcomer sought to marry and begin a family as soon as possible. But even formally arranged matchmaking was forbidden until the Rebbe, or a close mentor, pronounced her ready. Until she mastered Hasidic legal and social codes, she remained single, an oddity in her age group in the Crown Heights community.

The Lubavitcher women's journal *Di Yiddishe Heim* offered an outlet for the confusion and alienation felt by some *baalot teshuveh*. Their poems, stories, and letters were modest rather than plaintive. Tactfully, these new writers did not use the magazine to criticize lack of community support for their own subgroup. Instead, authors reflected on their former lives in secular society and praised the Rebbe for rescuing them from drug abuse or spiritual searching. A variety of women contributed confessional-style essays with lurid descriptions of their experiences in cults, abusive sexual relationships, and bureaucratic universities.

The pattern of *baalot teshuveh* articles published in *Di Yiddishe Heim* reflected editorial decisions beyond the actual spectrum of submissions; letters suggesting better facilities and assistance for *baalot teshuveh* would embarrass the community, whereas essays depicting the evils of secular culture upheld the view of Lubavitcher superiority and morality. Clearly, most *baalot teshuveh* did share a common experience of disillusionment, search, and rebirth, and these similar experiences created the potential for solidarity and mutual support among newcomers. But because of the secular, feminist, and countercultural connotations of women's support groups at that time, no comparable format was sanctioned or organized by Lubavitcher authorities as an aid for incoming women.

By 1972, the conflict between an escalated proselytizing agenda and a total lack of facilities for *baalot teshuveh* forced the issue of adult women's study groups. One Lubavitcher matron, Sara Labkowsky, opened her home to an informal group of new Lubavitchers interested in regular Torah study. According to another Lubavitcher spokeswoman, Nechama Greisman, "There was no school yet available to satisfy their needs. Without a command of Hebrew, all doors of existing schools were closed to them. And then someone said, 'If Lubavitch has a Yeshiva for boys beginning Torah, why not one for women?'" (Greisman 1975, 25).

Thus, more than ten years after the establishment of Yeshiva Hadar Hatorah, *baalot teshuveh* women began their own school in the basement of a private home – a beginning as humble as that of the first Beth Rivkah elementary school in 1942. From 1972 to 1975, Torah classes for women operated without a budget. All teaching was provided on a volunteer basis by mothers, rabbis, rabbis' wives, and young Beth Rivkah Teacher Training Seminary students (Greisman 1975, 25). The lack of formally appointed faculty compounded the irregularity of the academic program. Because most students were self-supporting and worked full time, classes met on weeknights and on Sundays. This arrangement quickly depleted the reserves of non-compensated instructors, who as mothers of large families needed evenings and Sundays to themselves. Teachers also expressed frustration when enthusiastic students brought friends to classes, thus requiring a continual review process for each guest unfamiliar with the previous lesson. Despite these setbacks, the student population grew, and the Rebbe authorized the purchase of two buildings for an official school in 1974. The new institution was named Machon Chana Women's Institute for the Study of Judaism, in honor of the Rebbe's late mother, the Rebbetzin Chana.

Machon Chana included a classroom building on Eastern Parkway and a dormitory on President Street near the Rebbe's own home. During the Sabbath, students ate meals with neighborhood families and enjoyed Lubavitcher hospitality. By 1975, the Rebbe also began to arrange meetings between the families of Machon Chana students and representatives from the Lubavitcher community. Nechama Greisman presented a short history of Machon Chana at the twentieth annual convention of Neshei Chabad in 1975 and declared: "It's not enough to reach the students – we must reach their families, too. And so, to date, three 'farbrengens' have been held . . . these have done much to promote a feeling of acceptance and friendship where there might have been resentment and bitterness" (Greisman 1975, 26). Of course, this statement reveals that bitterness and resentment did, in fact, exist in many families. Experts at public relations, Lubavitcher authorities did not wish to appear to be the agents of estrangement between young women and their parents. With family orientation as the primary value taught to all Hasidim, the Machon Chana administration sought to build bridges between students and their less religious relatives. Unfortunately, the dismay felt by many parents over the defection of a daughter to an ultra-Orthodox sect was not always pacified by an outreach tea.

With the establishment of the official women's school, *baalot teshuveh* who had previously brooded in isolation now restructured their time around rigorous group study. Machon Chana classes, held from 8:30 in the morning until 9:30 at night, offered beginning, intermediate, and advanced instruction in Hebrew, Yiddish, prayer, Psalms, Talmud, Jewish history, Mishna, Midrash, Hasidic philosophy, Jewish law, and Jewish women

(Machon Chana Institute 1983). A financial aid program gave students the option of evening and Sunday courses at a reduced rate. One program led to the teacher's certificate in higher Jewish studies, preparing *baalot teshuveh* for academic positions in the Crown Heights school system. The 1983 brochure described Machon Chana in glowing, mystical terms:

> Direct, total immersion into the depths and intricacies of the eternal Torah, in the original, leads to the discovery of the greatness of woman and the luminous future that is her destiny.
>
> Machon Chana provides exactly this opportunity. An intensive women's Yeshiva, it was founded by the Lubavitcher Rebbe Shlita, on the premise that Torah education for women may be more significantly important than for men. Machon Chana, through the teachings of Chabad Chassidism, fuses the Revealed and the Mystical into a vital, living Judaism, enabling each woman to become knowledgeable in her heritage and secure in her place and purpose in the cosmic entity. (Machon Chana Institute 1983)

This dramatic passage contains an obvious reference to the *mikveh*, the ritual bath required of adult Jewish women after each menstrual period. By offering "direct, total immersion" in Torah, Machon Chana hinted that a student just reborn after a lifetime of secular contamination might well need purification. The same brochure provided extraordinary course descriptions designed to excite those women who were interested in learning more about their stalwart foremothers. One course was devoted entirely to the scrolls of Ruth and Esther and promised "dramatic testimonies to the unique power and greatness of woman!" Another seminar, on Jewish faith, had this note: "Special emphasis will be placed on developing the student's capacity for learning a Maamor in conjunction with a study partner," thus offering women the ancient system of pair studying fostered among male *yeshiva* students. The combination of original text study, Jewish women's history, and academic techniques once reserved for men gave Machon Chana's curriculum a look that was both innovative and traditional.

In reality, however, the financial status of the institute and the social status of unmarried women students dovetailed to distract most *baalot teshuveh* away from study and into volunteer work. Service projects, fundraising, babysitting, and similar responsibilities occupied most of the students' free time. The community justified its exploitation of a free labor pool on the grounds that such involvement was the best way to integrate and endear newcomers to the Crown Heights social structure. Another brochure declared: "Machon Chana students are embraced by the community and, during their course of study, become a vibrant force in every aspect of community life. This coupling of classroom study and community interaction results in a deeper understanding of what being a Jewish woman means" (Machon Chana Institute 1986).

When the community needed eye-catching banners for a children's religious parade, Machon Chana students stayed up until 3:00 A.M. to cut and paste. This would be an unheard-of frivolity in a male *yeshiva*—a *bittul Torah*, or waste of time better spent in Torah study. As future mothers, however, Machon Chana "girls" (as they were universally referred to) viewed such job assignments as evidence of the Rebbe's trust and favor. Work-study students eagerly accepted jobs as babysitters and librarians for the community's children; this contact substituted for the family life that long-established Lubavitchers enjoyed.

All courses at Machon Chana focused on the relevance of the subject matter to woman's role in Jewish law and tradition. The larger frame of reference was reduced to content that women were required to know in order to fulfill their particular obligations under Jewish law. The male *baal teshuveh* student would use intellectual skills throughout his adult life in the culture of rabbinical dialogue and scholarship; but for women at Machon Chana, the goal was to accumulate as rapidly as possible the basics of Hasidic belief and practice—in order to proceed with marriage and child rearing.

By 1985, Machon Chana had discontinued the early brochures that stressed the school's academically intensive curriculum and the joy of learning for learning's sake. The promotion campaign of the mid-1980s capitalized on traditionally feminine themes from the non-Jewish world: fashion and cosmetics. Machon Chana advertisements borrowed concepts from popular women's magazines as a way of packaging Jewish topics. One flyer for a summer session coaxed, "Get to know your true Jewish colors!" and listed courses under such headings as "Tone," "Makeup," "Balance," and "Color." The sum of these studies would "increase your face value" (Machon Chana Institute 1985). The workshop titles on this poster continued the metaphor with "The Spiritual Beauty of the Jewish Woman," "Color Your World with Kosher Cuisine," and "Professional Wares and Personal Cares." For the 1986 season, Machon Chana brochures also included references to *Vogue, Cosmopolitan,* and *Mademoiselle* magazines. Whether such approaches were intended as a satire of 1980s consumerism or as reassurance that Hasidic authorities were in touch with modern pastimes, the shift away from intellectual rhetoric was stark. In fairness to Machon Chana, this shift was hardly limited to the Lubavitcher periodicals; by 1985 even *Ms.* magazine included fashion columns and dress-for-success tips from feminist professional women.

It is no coincidence that both Machon Chana and its sister school in

23. Hasidic women dancing at a Succos festival, 1990, Brooklyn, New York. *Courtesy of Bonnie Morris.*

Minneapolis, Bais Chana, emerged in the early 1970s. The Rebbe was well aware of the burgeoning feminist movement, and this threat to Hasidic values, coupled with the glaring lack of educational choices for Lubavitcher women, hastened the development of the *baalot teshuveh* schools. The entire Crown Heights community used the waning youth movement and the rising divorce rate to attract disoriented single women in search of a spiritual anchor. Machon Chana's ads suggested, "Give yourself the opportunity to think Jewish, feel Jewish, be Jewish—and put an end to spiritual and emotional chaos forever!" (Machon Chana Institute n.d.).

Conclusion

Today, female education is accepted as a vital, essential part of Lubavitcher culture at all age levels. Ongoing institutional fundraising and publicity, corresponding to rising enrollment, assure the future of the Beth Rivkah and Machon Chana schools. The development of both school systems has also fostered a new spectrum of employment opportunities for Lubavitcher women. *Baalot teshuveh* women who enter the Lubavitcher movement as adults with advanced professional degrees or technical training are welcomed as assets, for their expertise enhances the directory of Hasidic-observant specialists serving Crown Heights (Grossman 1981). Beth Rivkah graduates, too, now have a wider range of options, as mentors to newcomers or as outreach activists sent by the Rebbe to promote Hasidic women's programs on college campuses. These changes in female opportunity correspond to the leadership of the seventh Rebbe, Menachem Schneersohn, since his predecessor's death in 1950. The reigning Rebbe has assured a place for intellectual women in his following while defining and maintaining the limits of their intellectual ambition. The scholarly woman in this Hasidic sect is expected to serve as an educator within the existing facilities for other pious women.

Although Lubavitcher women do not question the authority of the Rebbe and his policy decisions on female education, open periodicals such as *Di Yiddishe Heim* permit a broader range of opinions to flourish in print. This ongoing dialogue among Lubavitcher women reflects both acceptance of and dissatisfaction with the curriculum of female education in Lubavitch Hasidism. It remains to be seen whether the growing *baalot teshuveh* population, college-educated and career-oriented women, will affect the Lubavitcher prohibition against college for Beth Rivkah graduates. The present stategy within Crown Heights of publishing those *baalot teshuveh* essays most critical of the secular university experience suggests that incoming women have a conservative rather than liberal impact. The great irony in the postwar Hasidic community is that, having overcome centuries of male disapproval in order to gain access to classroom, print, and podium, most Lubavitcher women must use their limited opportunities as scholars to uphold the male interpretation of woman's role in Judaism.

Works Cited

Bais Rivkah. 1987. *Neshei Chabad* 13, no. 4 (Apr.–May): 3.

Beth Rivkah High School. 1986. Crown Heights, Brooklyn. Brochure.

Chance Meeting, A. 1974. *Di Yiddishe Heim* 15, no. 4 (Spring): 19.

Goldberg, Daniel. 1982. The Lubavitcher Rebbe: Eighty Years. In *The Rebbe: Changing the Tide of Education,* edited by M. Rivkin, 20–60. Brooklyn: Lubavitch Youth Organization.

Greisman, Nechama. 1975. Machon Chana. In *Souvenir Journal of the Twentieth Annual Convention of Neshei Ubnos Chabad.* May: 25.

Grossman, Miriam. 1981. Ginger Ale, Cake . . . and Truth. *Di Yiddishe Heim* 22, no. 3 (summer): 7–10.

Heilbrun, Chana. 1963. Can We Improve Our Schools? Part 1. *Di Yiddishe Heim* 5, no. 2 (Fall): 12–14.

———. 1964. Can We Improve Our Schools? Part 2. *Di Yiddishe Heim* 5, no. 3 (Winter): 17–18.

Jacobson, Israel. 1967. Chassidus Study for Girls. *Di Yiddishe Heim* 8, no. 3 (Winter): 11–13.

Machon Chana Institute. N.d. G-d Is Not For Men Only. Brochure.

———. 1983. Get in Touch with Over 5,000 Years. Brochure.

———. 1985. For Women Only. Poster.

———. 1986. Where Women Who Are Jewish Learn to Be Jewish Women. Brochure.

Neshei News. 1986. *Neshei Chabad* 13, no. 2 (Dec.): 19.

Rosengarten, Sudy. 1973. The Girls' Yeshiva. *Di Yiddishe Heim* 14, no. 4 (Spring): 21–24.

Schusterman, Rivka. 1972. One Small Still Voice. *Di Yiddishe Heim* 14, no. 1 (Summer): 11–12.

Weissman, Deborah, 1976. Bais Yaakov: A Historical Model for Jewish Feminists. In *The Jewish Woman: New Perspectives,* edited by E. Koltun, 139–48. New York: Schocken.

PART FIVE

Women's Voices
Personal Experiences of Community

Introduction

THIS SECTION PRESENTS the personal experiences and observations of women in a communal setting. In the first instance we have a discussion of a tight-knit patriarchal religious community, and in the second, the experience of an outside observer in a commune self-consciously concerned with feminism.

The Hutterites, or the Hutterian Brethren, were Anabaptist sectarians first organized by a Swiss minister, Jacob Hutter (d. 1536) in 1528. Practicing radical pacifism, insisting on the absolute separation of church and state, and operating their own system of schools, they encountered persecution everywhere in Europe. From 1770 to 1870 they found religious freedom in the Ukraine, but when persecution began there too, the entire community (some one thousand people) emigrated to the United States (1874–1877). About half the group established three colonies (Bruderhofs) in South Dakota: Bon Homme (today the Schmiedleut), Wolf Creek (today the Lehreleut in Montana), and Elmspring (today Dariusleut in Silver Lake, South Dakota). The rest of the original group settled on individual farmsteads in South Dakota. By 1920 there were twenty-one Hutterite colonies in the United States. Communities are usually limited to 150 members and are governed by a five-man council (elected for life) and the minister. In this strictly patriarchal community, women are not permitted to vote and are relegated to domestic and maternal duties. Hutterites live communally in longhouses (modeled on sixteenth-century archetypes), each family having its own apartment. Doors remain unlocked and members often enter each other's apartments without knocking. Privacy is thus deemphasized, and communal oversight is enhanced. Premarital sex is proscribed as are all contraceptive practices. Families are consequently very large by contemporary U.S. standards. Hutterites, unlike Old Order Amish, use modern, labor-saving devices and welcome technology but still consider movies and television and other forms of popular entertainment and recreation too worldly. Communities are largely self-sufficient–they raise their own food and make most of their own clothes. There are today approximately forty thousand Brethren in the three families—the Lehreleut has 82 colonies, the Dariusleut (the most widespread geographically) has 133 colonies, and the Schmiedleut has 138 colonies. Best sources on the Hutterites are John A. Hostetler, *Hutterite Society* (Baltimore: Johns Hopkins Univ. Press, 1974) and Victor Peters, *All Things Common: The Hutterite Way of Life* (Minneapolis: Univ. of Minnesota Press, 1965).

Twin Oaks is an egalitarian, secular community governed by a planner/manager system (compulsory rotation of planners). It was established in 1967 to implement the psychological system laid out in B. F. Skinner's *Walden Two* (1948). Located on a farm of 123 (today 483) acres outside Louisa, Virginia, it initially employed positive reinforcement techniques to achieve behavioral modification. By 1970, behavioralism was abandoned, and Twin Oaks evolved into a diversified, eclectic, cooperative New Age community. Members are called by first names only, indicative of their intent to phase out the nuclear family and replace it with a communal one. Originally agricultural, today Twin Oaks relies for support on a hammock business, visitors' fees, an editorial service, and members' jobs outside the community. A labor-credit system of accounting determines the contributions of individuals to the communal economy. The community supports sexual freedom and diversity of sexual expression. All members are considered "singular," and there has been an active program of recruitment of gay and lesbian members, with limited success. A Child Program is used to determine whether prospective parenthood should be allowed by the community in view of the current communal economic situation. Twin Oaks practices natural childbirth assisted by birthing crews. Children are reared communally, with special adults called child managers playing a prominent role. The community has self-consciously attempted to break down stereotypes about gender roles and continues to strive for a nonsexist social order. Twin Oaks has both male and female consciousness-raising groups. Television is excluded, and the community prohibits any form of pornography on its premises. By 1980 there were 71 members of the community. Best works on the community are Kathleen Kinkade, *A Walden Two Experiment* (New York: Morrow, 1973) and Ingrid Komar, *Living the Dream: A Documentary Study of the Twin Oaks Community 1979–1983* (Norwood, Penn.: Norwood Pubs., 1983).

14

Colony Girl

A Hutterite Childhood

RUTH BAER LAMBACH

BECAUSE MY FATHER MARRIED MY MOTHER with the intention of having many children and I was the firstborn of fifteen, my life was destined to be engaged with community of some sort. My parents were deeply religious, and my father in particular was attracted to the idea of living in a religious community. He knew his Bible well, having read it from cover to cover a dozen times. During my childhood and adolescence, we lived in several different religious communities, all of them of the German pietistic persuasion. "Colony Girl" describes my childhood among the Hutterites of the northern plains, where I lived from the ages of seven to thirteen, 1949–1955.

In 1942 I was born into the Mennonite faith in Bright, Ontario. My uncle, Moses N. Baer, was a bishop in the conservative branch of the Mennonite church. He farmed with horses all his life. When I was four years old our family and two sets of aunts, uncles, and cousins began living together in a big stone house, sharing resources, work, meals, and spiritual expression. This meant that we got a double dose of religious education every Sunday: once in English from my uncle Moses and the second time, for good measure, in German, from my father. From an early age we children took our religion seriously. I remember my baby sister Myrtle's funeral; she had smothered in her crib at age nine months. My cousin David and I stood on the mound of dirt looking at the puddle of water in the bottom of the open grave and argued about whether she was going to go to heaven or hell. David insisted that Myrtle was going to hell because she had a bad temper and had screamed. I insisted that she didn't know how to talk yet, so had to scream to get what she needed. David was four and a half and I was three and a half at the time.

Across the field from our farm was the Julius Kubasek Colony. This was in essence like a Hutterite Colony but because of the egomaniacal eccentricities of its leader, the Hutterites had not accepted him as a full member into their fold. In 1946 our family began spending Sundays at the Kubasek Colony. Our parents sat in rooms with other adults and we played outside on the porch. On especially hot afternoons I remember being told to swing the door to create a cool breeze for the black-clothed adults who sat inside discussing religious matters.

In 1947 our family spent about two months at the Kubasek Colony. I can still repeat part of the Lord's prayer in Hungarian. According to my father, we had to learn Hungarian in order to get to heaven. Because the purpose of our lives on earth was to prepare us for heaven, it was clear to us that we had to learn Hungarian as soon as possible. Papa delighted in teaching us the new words he learned.

Being placed in a group with other children my age rather than having the adventure of following my father around throughout the day was a distinct loss of status for me. I resented the big, fat kindergarten teacher when she tried to correct me. I called her a *diszno* which in Hungarian means pig. She reported this to my father. It was his duty to make sure that I became socialized. One day he took me on the truck, and we drove far out into the fields leaving the colony in the distance. The wind stroked my hair as I stood up straight on the back of the truck. I felt free once more. I thought things were back to normal. All of a sudden my father stopped the truck and took me off the back and told me that he had to give me a spanking because I had called the kindergarten teacher a pig. This was the beginning of my hatred and mistrust of fat, usually pregnant women who were to be my authority figures and models throughout my life in the colony.

Fat women were all over the place in my Hutterite life. They exerted their influence and authority by virtue of their position as married women – fat, complacent, long-skirted, and usually pregnant. Once they gave birth to their child, which happened about every nine months, they stayed home for nine weeks, pampered with extra-rich food cooked by a special cook in the kitchen. For the first six weeks they did not do any work in the home or in the colony. After nine weeks of vacation they entered the general work force; by that time some of them were already pregnant again. Once I remember being told by one of these bossy pregnant ladies that all we had were warts for breasts. It was clear that the prime status to achieve was adulthood. Even our bodies had to wait to be accepted.

After a trip to the "real" Hutterites in Manitoba, my father returned and announced that we would join the real ones near Portage La Prairie, Manitoba. He convinced us that we were engaged in a grand adventure and that we would have to do many new things such as fix our hair in tight french braids and wear long, dark dresses and black caps. Gone would be the big braids hanging down the back with pretty ribbons at the ends. Before leaving we had a big auction sale. Everything not essential or permissible in the colony was sold or destroyed. My mother still has photos from this time which show evidence of having been crumpled up and thrown out. Many of them were burned but some of them she rescued and gave to her sisters to keep. Our Mennonite relatives had a taffy pull for us before we left Ontario. It was a sad farewell. I remember walking among our somber, long-skirted relatives as we said good-bye. I felt as though my mother were preparing herself to go to a far distant land, somewhere about as remote as a prison in Siberia from which she did not know if she would return or ever see any of her family and friends again.

Few people from the outside ever join the Hutterites. They had no visitation policy. My father was prepared to do whatever was necessary to fulfill the requirements of being a real Hutterite and my mother had in her marriage vows made a commitment to him. It was clear that our father was the absolute authority in the family. Once, when I was just over three years old, I talked back to my mother. She did not punish me but waited until the evening when my father returned and then reported my mouthiness to him. I got a spanking. As a result of this incident I was sure that I did not like the position of being female. As a woman, my mother could not deal with me directly but had to call on my father's authority.

In April 1949 we arrived at New Rosedale Colony near Portage La Prairie, Manitoba. I was six years old, and there were six children in our family. My father did nothing by halves. He joined, bringing $15,000 in hard cash, and committed himself completely to becoming a Hutterite. The highest compliment anyone could pay me was that one could not tell I was from the outside. As children we learned the Tyrolean dialect easily but labored under the burden of our parents' "horse" language, as the other children called the Pennsylvania Dutch we had been used to speaking as Mennonites. My mother introduced raw salads and greens as edibles; this aroused some controversy among some children who said that only animals ate weeds and grasses. I couldn't share with these children my fondness for dandelion green salad, which we used to eat in Ontario.

With peer pressure and whippings at school and at home we were soon completely socialized and as happy as children anywhere. Over and over again we learned the lessons of collective responsibility. One day, under the instigation of fourteen-year-old Rebecca, the oldest girl at school, all of us girls skipped school instead of coming back after recess. We knew little about the specifics of the tension between Rebecca and Jack Jantzen, our young English teacher from the outside, but we did know that Rebecca hated him with a vengeance and that she was going to get even with him. In the bitter cold winter we walked several miles to visit an old Indian woman we affectionately called Maggie Tobacco, who lived in a shack by the edge of the Assiniboine River. My sister Miriam and I were among the youngest girls in school. It took me a long time to convince Miriam to go along. She was sure that we would get punished. This incident was a serious break from our well-practiced good behavior as new Hutterites.

At Maggie's all twenty-three of us huddled into her shack. We warmed ourselves around her pot-bellied stove. She offered us tea in two tin cups which we passed around politely–afraid to drink, but also afraid to hurt her feelings. She knew where we were from, and we knew her as the friendly Indian lady who came around at Christmastime, greeting each family with a hasty "May I Kiss?" as her pronunciation of Merry Christmas. A simple story or funny expression like this provided us endless hours of laughter and comment. In the Hutterite colony we would not use such a worldly greeting. For us Christmas was just another Sunday on which we had an exceptionally long sermon. The other longer sermon was at Easter time. We did not exchange gifts or have trees or decorations.

Our walk back to the colony was more difficult than the walk away from the colony. We knew what we faced. The boys warned us about the punishment we would get that afternoon from Jack Jantzen. We pretended we didn't care and acted as though our adventure was well worth any spanking he could give us. We had stories to tell: stories about what a real Indian shack smelled like, stories about how Maggie cooked big goose eggs and offered us some to eat. For us, goose eggs were only for hatching goslings. We cringed at the thought of somebody eating the whole baby gosling, beak, eyes, and all. The nearby Indians were a curiosity to us, and none of the boys had ever been inside their shacks.

That afternoon at school Jack Jantzen matter of factly asked that all the girls stand by their desks. The boys sat and snickered. Each girl, in turn, held out her hands and took the black leather strap. Jack meted out the punishment according to how much responsibility he thought we might have had in the decision to skip school. He started by spanking the youngest and moved up the line. When he got to Rebecca she fought back. They struggled in the front of the room, and the next thing Jack was pulling back, straightening his crumpled hair and tie and blindly groping on the floor for his broken glasses. Rebecca moved triumphantly back to her seat. We contained our smirks and attended to our work. That night, my father, according to his stated policy, insisted on giving Miriam and me a spanking for good measure. Miriam complained that no one else would get a double spanking, but he wanted to make sure we would learn our lesson: as converts we had to be super-Hutterites. This extended also to our dress. My mother dyed the cloth with which she made our dresses. We pointed out that the other girls wore brighter, more colorful dresses than we did, but she shut us up, saying simply: "Talk to Papa."

When a Hutterite colony grows to more than 125 people, it divides, much as a cell divides. A minister is chosen by lot, and each department selects a new boss: for the pigs, cows, farming, German school teacher, chickens, geese, ducks, turkeys, and shop. Women have no say in this division of property except what they might say to their husbands in private. After only two years at New Rosedale Colony we experienced this branching. Before we went to bed at night we did not know which side we would be on. Excitement and anticipation animated every activity in the colony because that evening the men and two ministers would choose, by lot, which colony they would go to. The new colony would move across the border near Grand Forks, North Dakota. At breakfast the next morning all of us kids knew where we were going. We began counting up the advantages for our respective lots, each putting forth grand arguments for why we got the better deal.

Forest River Colony, our new place in North Dakota, was hundreds of miles from any other Hutterite colony. Our living quarters lay nestled in a valley, halfway surrounded by the winding Forest River, a tributary of the Red River. Almost every year we had the excitement of a serious spring flood, which caused anxiety and often forced the adults to fetch us from school to help move chicks out of the houses that were too close to the river. We welcomed any excuse to get a couple of hours out of the daily school routine. In October we got several weeks off school to help harvest potatoes. During the slaughtering season or when thousands of new chicks, goslings, or ducks arrived we were asked to come and help. We all knew the priorities of colony life: food, shelter, clothing, and religion, all of which came ahead of schooling.

Formal education was something of a luxury, something we did in order to fulfill the demands of the state. Not only did we have six hours a day of regular school to attend, we also had an hour of German school every day before and after the regular school day. After school we had half an hour of daily evening church services. On Saturdays we had German school all morning. Since none of the Hutterites were educated beyond the eighth grade, "English school," as we called the state-oriented curriculum, was taught by outsiders. Even the German school teacher had only an eighth-grade education. We basically learned reading, writing, and memorization from religious texts.

The river was a constant part of our lives. Several times a week during the summer I took a bucket of dirty diapers down to wash. Because we had no indoor plumbing, dirty diapers were collected in buckets of water. Usually several girls went together. We visited and played while getting the job done. We stood barefoot in the river and watched the fish gather on the diaper and then pulled it up quickly, each holding onto two of the four corners. We caught buckets of little minnows and snuck into the kitchen to fry them, guts, eyes, scales, and all. They were crunchy nuggets, and no one had to know what bait we used.

In the winter we used the frozen river as a shortcut to Annie Ustmos's house. Her name became a household word because she fed us cookies and milk. She and her husband were as strange to us as the Indians had been. We were curious, especially since we had never known a childless couple. In our culture children went with marriage. After her husband died and she could no longer take care of herself, she came to live at the colony until she died.

Among the Hutterites, the oldest daughter often does not get married, or she will marry late because of her primary position in her immediate family. As the eldest I was responsible for my younger brothers from the time they were about six weeks old. From the age of nine I was not able to go anywhere for too long without a little one. We got to be very handy at dragging babies along with us. Since almost all women had babies each year, most of us girls between the ages of nine and fifteen had these tots on our hips and in our laps. The second eldest daughter in a family babysat for another family that did not yet have any older girls. Being the eldest was an honor because you could pay attention to your own siblings. I was certain that my brother Amos, with his curly red locks, was the cutest baby in the colony.

We built playhouses in the woods and dragged along our younger siblings instead of dolls. These houses reflected the life in the colony in many ways. They were collective. Each house had one person assigned as the *Annehmer*, the person whose job it was to take in new members to the group house, and another person whose job it was to be the *Wegsprenger*, the person whose job it was to get rid of those we didn't want to play with anymore. While these functions were rarely exercised, we took these positions seriously. We made simple dolls by twisting and turning pieces of cloth. These dolls had no eyes but we made them in all sizes and created whole families extending through several generations. Often we placed these dolls in nests we dug in the ground. We carefully padded the nest with soft cot-

24. The Baer family, 1954, Forest River Colony, Fordville, North Dakota. *Left to right, front row:* Luke, Amon, baby Amos, and Zenas. *Back row:* "Papa" Allan Baer, Miriam, James, Ruth behind "Mama" Edna Baer, Moses, Naomi, and Mark. The Baer family subsequently included four additional sons: Joel, Jonah, Elam, and Eden. *Courtesy of Ruth Baer Lambach.*

ton layers of cloth and then wrapped and blanketed the dolls. Finally we put a jar lid on top and then filled over the top with dirt. If you really wanted to annoy someone you were angry with you would violently rip out her camouflaged nests from the ground. Card games of any kind were strictly forbidden, but we had a game that I have not seen among children anywhere else. It is a game of deceit and bluff—a variation of hide-and-seek. One group would hide somewhere while the others closed their eyes. A representative of the hiders would return and then give directions to the seekers about where to find them. These directions were explicitly scratched into the ground with a stick. The rules were that every scratch, except one, was true. Although boys and girls played separately most of the time, we played this game as well as ball games in mixed groups. We adhered strictly to the rule about boys and girls not swimming in the river at the same time, despite the fact that we went swimming fully clad. Only shoes and head-coverings were taken off. Getting to use the swimming hole was always a contest. Sometimes we even stationed one of our fastest girl runners so that we could claim the space for the afternoon.

Because the older daughters did child care, mothers were free to do the colony work such as taking care of the fifteen-acre garden, canning, cooking, baking, cleaning the kitchen, slaughtering animals, making soap, and sewing all the clothes for the family. Sewing entailed tedious work such as sewing hooks and eyes onto jackets. My first sewing assignment was to hem diapers and dishtowels. Spinning involved not only spinning the wool but carding, washing, and dyeing it and then knitting stockings, mittens, and scarves for the family. My first brassiere was made of a white flour sack.

Taking care of my brothers was my primary job. Every night I rounded them up, washed them, and tucked them in. Children in a Hutterite colony have a great deal of freedom. The entire colony including the shop, all the farming equipment, the animals, garden, woods, creek, other family homes, and common dining room, kitchen, and basement in the center of the place are theirs to play in. With so much freedom it is not uncommon to have major accidents such as getting run over by a tractor, drowning, getting caught in an auger, burning, or swallowing poison. Two of my siblings swallowed caustic soda thinking they were getting a handful of white sugar crystals.

Cleaning the house was my other major task. This involved a thorough Saturday scrubbing of the windows, walls, floors, and furniture as well as daily sweeping, straightening, and, of course, making all the beds. I took a great deal of pride in my work. My mother was known to have a clean and orderly house, and everyone commented about how lucky she was to have me. I was like a neurotic housewife who badgered everyone when I spotted the least splash in the sink, a smudge on the windowpane, or a mark on the floor that I had painstakingly scrubbed and waxed.

The proverb I remember best from the Hutterite Colony is "Cleanliness is next to Godliness." I learned this lesson early and well. It was on our first visit to the Hutterites when our parents sat in a room on straight-backed wooden chairs. At least fifteen adults crowded into the room, with more standing by the doors. We were a real anomaly: outsiders who wanted to join the Hutterites. Someone noticed black marks on the otherwise clean hardwood floor. A man came toward me, lifted up my shoe, and scratched the floor, leaving a black mark. He decided I was the guilty culprit. Next I was given a bucket, a rag, and some soap and told to kneel down in the middle of the room under the watchful, joking voices and eyes of the Hutterite men and women. They concluded that I would make a good Hutterite. I took in this message and surpassed their expectations. By the age of twelve I was given the nickname Kristel Katrina; she was a colony woman rumored to be so fastidious she insisted on having her sheets changed hourly on her deathbed. When I hung out the clothes I'd line them up so as to have a perfectly graduated look on the washline. The sheets came first, followed by the square diapers, the rectangular diapers, then slips, underpants, and socks. If by chance I missed one of the diapers I would go back and redo the whole line to make it look orderly.

My fifteenth birthday would be my escape to freedom, independence, and adulthood. At the end of the evening meal on this day, a Hutterite child stands up and announces this birthday to the entire childrens' dining room population. The German school teacher, under whose strict supervision the children's dining room has been kept in order, gives the departing child a lecture on what it means to be an adult. Paul Maendel, whose father, Paul, was our teacher, got a lecture about not grabbing for the biggest piece of meat on the plate! It was the dream of each of us to get out of the tightly supervised net of this man and his wife who had served us food for our entire childhood. One's fifteenth birthday marked the end of childhood, the end of spanking as punishment, and the end of German school. *Mandle* and *Dindla* (boy and girl) would now become *Bauh* and *Dieen* (young, unmarried man and woman), and we would take our place with the adults.

The children's dining room was modeled after the adults' dining room on the other side of the kitchen. The boys sat on one side of the room at long tables and benches while the girls sat on the other side. As in the adults' dining room, we sat according to age. Four people shared one serving dish. Because no meals were eaten at home, we got to know each other as well or better than you know members of your own family. We had no cooking facilities in the private homes. We knew each other's habits, and we kept each other in line. Especially at breakfast time we would watch out for each other because that was when the children's meal began with a recitation of a long memorized prayer, done while kneeling. If you arrived late you had to kneel and say the prayer silently. The trick was to arrive in time to catch the last few minutes of the prayer even if that meant kneeling by the door. We closely monitored those who did not manage to arrive in time for the prayer; we made sure they didn't just kneel there and think other thoughts. We estimated about how long it would take to say the prayer and made sure they knelt the required amount of time. Joining the adults also meant no more long kneeling prayer. They only had a short, four-line prayer that they said while seated.

The eight oldest girls in the children's dining room formed a kind of work force that was responsible for cleaning both the school and the children's dining room. Sometimes we spent hours telling tales, and sometimes we got into arguments. One day we had a serious battle about which row belonged to which girl, and the result was that two sections of the floor remained unswept but strewn with oiled sawdust. The unswept floor was visible to everyone attending the half-hour prayer service after German school. The next day all eight girls were called up in front of the tittering boys. We held out our hands and took our perfunctory leather strapping. This punishment reinforced the lesson of collective responsibility.

Lessons of collective responsibility and group activity were forever around us, but we still managed to retain a healthy sense of individuality. We could not express this by having different styles of clothing or a different pattern of dress or even a unique hairdo, but we could make tiny differences that distinguished us. I focused on my black-and-white polka-dot scarf, which I starched and ironed to perfection so that it sat on my head with the peak at exactly the most flattering angle. The folds at the sides flared out in a fullness that framed my face. At the back the fold began at the top of the head and was perfectly straight. I twisted my long hair casually in the usual manner being careful not to make the twist too tight or too loose. I paid equal attention to how I wore the apron. The long, well-ironed sashes went around my slender waist twice and then flowed down the sides.

The eight oldest girls formed a tight social club, although we knew we had no real status in the colony until we took our place in the adult dining room on the day after our fifteenth birthday. On that day the girls got a rolling pin and a wooden chest; the boys got a hammer and a chest. All of the furniture was handmade at the colony. The women took pride in painting their names in medieval German script on the rolling pins. We embroidered this same style lettering on our black-and-white polka-dot scarves and were criticized when this embroidery got to be too large and fanciful with extra little flowers.

Once you were fifteen you were relieved of the constant responsibility of being the second mother in the family; now you got to participate in the colony work. It was eminently clear to us that the most desirable state in a Hutterite colony was to be one of the Dieene, single women between the ages of fifteen and marriage. Marriage for Hutterite women took place sometime before age twenty-five; after that age you were considered to be an undesirable and unfortunate old maid. The Dieene even had a special bell ring – three rings, pause, three rings, pause, three rings. They were called whenever there was a project such as plastering and painting a newly constructed house, gardening, going off for an afternoon to pick wild grapes, june berries, or choke cherries, going to town to help the men with some salvage operation, doing spring cleaning in the central dining room, rolling buns on Saturday mornings, making sausage, rolling noodles, or making sauerkraut for the winter. The Dieene were also called upon during spring planting season to cut up the potatoes for planting. They gathered around a big bin of potatoes on a table around which sharp knives were fastened. The girls sat and pulled the potato through these knives several times, making sure each quarter contained some eyes. A scar on my chin still reminds me of my attempt to do this work before I was tall enough to keep my chin out of the sharp knife.

Every time the Dieene got together they sang or told stories. Sometimes we younger girls walked by with our arms full of babies and listened. We envied the Dieene who seemed so free, happy, and engaged. Because there were few books, no magazines, and certainly no radio or television, the Dieene passed around and practically devoured the occasional magazine such as *Reader's Digest* that found its way into a colony. The best reader read while the others worked. Sometimes they retold what they had read with embellishments. Working with other women while talking and singing was being in the center of the life of the colony. I couldn't wait to get there. Sometimes the girls would even discuss forbidden topics such as where babies came from. I remember hearing about how you could get pregnant through almost any opening in your body, including the ear.

Forest River Colony, North Dakota, was the only Hutterite colony for miles around. As a result there was more interchange with the outside through business dealings and with neighbors. Our colony must have been one of the sights to see in North Dakota because on some Sundays we had as many as a hundred cars of visitors. As children we delighted in giving tours to these curiosity seekers.

Greater contact with the outside world influenced our colony to think more seriously about education. Both of my parents enrolled in correspondence courses. My father took high school science courses, which he then taught to the young men, and my mother took a course in practical nursing. Every week she got a new booklet, which she shared with the Dieene. Miriam and I peeked down through the metal grating around the stovepipe to see if we could learn something or see some pictures of nudity. We grew up feeling that the adults' world contained secrets that we were not privy to.

One day, half a ton of water-damaged sanitary napkins in crushed boxes arrived at our house. This was one of the hauls the Hutterite men regularly made when they went to a fire sale. They were excellent scavengers. That night all the Dieene came to our house; my mother doled out boxes of napkins to each according to how many girls they had in the family. It was a big secret, and no one said anything about the boxes stacked in our front entryway. The next day I found one of those damaged boxes of pads on my shelf in the closet. Along with the box was a booklet about menstruation. That was my education on the subject. I felt very much excluded because my mother didn't say anything about menstruation to me, and I was jealous because all the Dieene knew about it. The pads were a luxury item, and the only reason we got them this time was that they were cheap. Usually women were literally "on the rag." My mother kept her stained rags in a bucket of water in her closet. She never let me touch or wash them.

I could not speak to my mother about anything personal. She was a closed book. One hot July afternoon in 1953 I saw her standing by the open window looking toward the cow barn. I thought there was a dark cloud around her so I went toward her to say something. She brushed me off as though I were a bothersome mosquito or a cat in the house that she shushed and stamped off to the basement. Later that day she went to the hospital to give birth to my brother Amon. My older brothers had all been born at home with the help of a midwife and my father. There must have been some complications with this birth, and she was worried. We were not informed about the forthcoming births into our family. All married women got fat, and babies just arrived at the rate of one per year to each family. It was something worth gossiping about if a woman did not have a baby each year.

Because I was unable to get close to my mother, I watched the Dieene closely. Two sisters, Rachel and Elizabeth Maendel, became my models. I knew them as well as I knew my mother. They were both attractive but in different ways. Rachel was quiet and exceptionally competent at all skills such as knitting, embroidery, sewing, finishing furniture, and printing. Her noodles, her pies, and even her buns had a smoother and more finished look about them than those made by other women. She usually sang the alto parts of the songs; her whole demeanor appeared to be in the minor key. It was difficult for me to emulate Rachel for even a couple of hours.

Elizabeth, on the other hand, was outgoing, vivacious, and generous. I could not imagine her sitting still long enough to finish knitting even one stocking. She told stories, read books, and was usually the vital force in any group. Her voice and her laughter were everywhere recognizable. She loved children. She worked enthusiastically at whatever she did, but her best feature was her singing voice. She sang soprano. It was easier for me to be Elizabeth. Some days I tried on one style, and other days I tried the other. What I really wanted was to combine the talents of Rachel and Elizabeth and be that person. I felt strange and a little apprehensive to think that I actually had the power to determine who I was. An identity that I had carved out for myself seemed so arbitrary and fragile. I wondered if there was not something more solid and real inside, something that would not be subject to my whims.

The individual mattered in the area of romance. The knowledge of who you were going to marry grew up gradually around you. For me this process began when I was nine years old. Had I remained a Hutterite I could have enjoyed at least a seven-year romance with Joshua Maendel, younger brother to Rachel and Elizabeth, before being permitted to marry. Marriage was possible only after baptism, and baptism occurred after age eighteen.

The relationship between Joshua and me began at school when he asked me to sweep the stove after he had filled it with coal. I was no longer just one of the girls. Evidently he and the other boys had a contest to see which of them could get my attention. All of them stuffed my desk with candy bars, which I took home and put in my drawer. My mother discovered them and went to the steward of the colony. First she thought I had stolen them, but when I told her where they came from she was even more worried.

I gave all the candy bars back to the steward. He gave them out again when the boys presented rat tails and buckets of glass that they picked up around the colony. Each tail merited a candy bar as did each small bucket of broken glass. In this way the colony grounds got cleaned up and we continued going barefoot.

Because Joshua's father had been killed in a tractor accident he hung around with my father, helping him in the dairy barn. Since husband and wife worked together in the barn, it was my mother's job to separate the milk from the cream and wash up in the milkhouse after the twice daily milking. Once again I got the job of being the second mother in the family, frequently substituting for my mother. I welcomed this as another chance to see Joshua at close range. One day my father was not there, and it was Joshua and I who did the milking. The thrill I got anticipating this event felt wickedly sinful. We exchanged glances but no words. At the end he took out a piece of Juicy Fruit gum and, eyeing it carefully, divided it so that I got by far the larger piece. We considered our future together sealed.

By 1955 my father was promoted from cow boss to business manager. Next to the minister, this is the most powerful position in a Hutterite colony. The business manager or steward is the only one who handles money and the only person whose house has a telephone. All contact with the outside world goes through him. He pays all bills and signs off on all purchases. My mother became the head cook, the most influential position in the colony among the women. Any lingering negative effects of our outsider status had clearly disappeared, and we were fully integrated. The only area in which there was some actual discrimination was that we had the outside English teacher living in a room in our house, because the Hutterites perceived our parents to be better equipped to deal with outsiders. Christine Cardinal, the so-called English teacher, was no more English than we were, but that was her label because, according to our view of the world, there were only two kinds of people: German and English. "English" referred to anyone who was not a Hutterite. Christine Cardinal lived with our family for three years, but she did not participate in our communal meals. She did her own cooking, and she was allowed to have a radio in her room upstairs. One day around Christmas I recognized "Silent Night" coming from the radio or "devil's box" as it was known to us. I was stuck in my tracks on the stairs. Part of me was telling me I should not listen to it while the other part of me was calling me to listen and sing along because it was so beautiful.

Christine Cardinal had a camera, too. As an outsider she was allowed to take pictures. She took a picture of the schoolchildren and one of baby brother Amon, whom she frequently took care of in the evenings. She also took a picture of me, alone. This picture I gave to Joshua. While pictures were not allowed in the colony, people were generally indulgent about little infractions. It was always so in the Hutterite colony. There were official rules about things, but many times the elders looked the other way because they themselves were often like curious children about things they had not seen before. It was only when things got out of hand, when the foreign item took over and became the dominant force and too much attention was given over to it, that it was stopped. Officially, musical instruments were not allowed, but no one ever stopped people from playing the harmonica. Even Joshua had one. He played it in the cow barn, he played it in the barnyard, and he played it when he rode off on his horse. He even played it in the living room at our house. It was a small thing that he carried around in his pocket, but it was a symbol of something daring, beautiful, and powerfully masculine. No girls played the harmonica. Girls would not dare flaunt the established rules as readily as the boys, but we would be the most ardent cheerleaders for the boys who dared to do so.

By the summer of 1955 I was a thoroughly socialized Hutterite girl. My future stretched out before me, predictable and secure. But by the winter of 1955 all hopes of announcing my fifteenth birthday and becoming a Dieen and then marrying Joshua were dashed. The Bruderhof arrived at our colony and changed things forever.[1] My teenage years were filled with tumultuous cultural and geographical shifts. First we joined the Bruderhof, then we left in strife and had our own small colony at Forest River. After a year of this we moved to Koinonia Farm in Georgia and, six months later, rejoined the Bruderhof in Pennsylvania. In Pennsylvania, after less than a year at the Bruderhof, they felt it best for my spiritual development that I experience the outside world. They took me to Pittsburgh, gave me twenty dollars, and dropped me on the street. I found a job and lived on the outside for nine months. In the meantime, my parents, unbeknownst to me, had decided to leave the Bruderhof. On the day I arrived back at the Bruderhof my father announced that our family was leaving the next day. I was taken to a sister Bruderhof in New York State. After a year, I left and rejoined my family in Minnesota where my father had committed his enterprising spirit and an abundant, free, trainable labor force to building the largest single-family chicken ranch in the Midwest.

Today, after thirty years as an adult in the outside world, I still struggle with the twin needs of individuality and community. I build community wherever I work, and it appears that I can't work effectively unless I feel myself part of a cohesive system. At the same time, I am usually drawn to the most eccentric individuals of the group. As I reflect on my experiences in communal societies I am aware that the person I have become was formed by communitarian values, by my position in the family, by the influence of my father who selfishly and courageously pursued his own inner vision to both the enlightenment and detriment of those around him, and above all by the influence of my mother who endured, adapted, and weathered all of the changes without losing either her sense of pride or her integrity.

Note

1. The Bruderhof, or Society of Brothers, was a visionary Christian sect that originated in Germany in the 1920s. The society founded communities in England and South America (Paraguay and Uruguay) in the 1940s, and established its first U.S. community at Woodcrest, New York, in 1954. The Hutterites and Bruderhof merged in 1973 and are currently known as the Hutterian Brethren.

15

The Power of Feminism at Twin Oaks Community

ZENA GOLDENBERG

THE MEMBERS OF THE WOMEN'S-ONLY Feminist Theory Discussion Group settled themselves in a makeshift circle of lawn chairs, hammock jigs, and wooden benches in the shade of a large oak tree and began their discussion. As hands busily worked braiding rope or weaving hammocks, a member asked if anyone had anything in particular to discuss. After a bit of conversation, a topic emerged. Two of the group members had been working in the hammock shop a few days before and two Twin Oaks men were complaining aloud that they felt left out of a recent activity held for women only. The group then discussed how individual women could address challenges to what they felt was the women's right to hold whatever exclusive activities they chose. The discussion continued, not leading to any particular conclusion, but allowing members to give voice to their frustration at having even to address the issue. "Just the fact that women's activities are challenged shows why we need them," one member stated toward the end of the discussion, and most members nodded in agreement.

Separate women's activities were not new to Twin Oaks, which held its first Women's Gathering in 1978, but a strong, multifaceted, and ongoing women's culture had only evolved during the last few years. During the summer of 1987, I visited Twin Oaks to study this culture and the community's feelings toward the growth of feminism there. I worked alongside members digging ditches, weaving hammocks, washing dishes, and collecting garbage; I also participated in many women's groups and activities and conducted formal interviews.

Based on my participation, observations, and interviews, I will illustrate the impact of feminism on Twin Oaks at that time. I use the term *feminism* to mean the elimination of women's "enforced subordination, limited options, and social powerlessness," and the provision of a place where women are empowered in their own terms, where what women have always done is valued, and where they are enabled to do everything else (MacKinnon 1987, 22).

Twin Oaks was founded in 1967 by eight people who were galvanized both by the counterculture and by B. F. Skinner's *Walden Two* (1948), a utopian solution to the alienation of modern industrial life. They were disenchanted with the isolation of the nuclear family, the dichotomization of work and family, and the general dehumanization of city life. While Skinnerian behaviorism played a role in the early years of Twin Oaks, little evidence of these ideas remained twenty years later. One of the founding members, Kat Kinkade, still lived in the community, whose population had stabilized at approximately seventy adults and fifteen children.

Despite this stability of numbers, turnover was constant, with four years as the average length of membership. People interested in joining spent three weeks as visitors, working with members in all areas and attending orientation meetings. After that time, the community decided whether the visitors would be invited to join. Members were generally white and middle class and attracted to the slower-paced rural life-style.

The community consisted of about four hundred acres of Virginia farmland, bordered by a small river. Woods, hills, pastures, and a stream lay within the boundaries. Almost all buildings were built or reconstructed by members. The layout of the community incorporated a sense of extended family and an integration of work and home. Residential buildings housed between twelve and twenty people and contained at least one work space (Komar 1986, 38). Each member enjoyed a private bedroom, regardless of marital status. All major buildings bore the names of historic communities such as Zhankoya, Harmony, and Oneida.

A booklet distributed to potential visitors explained that the aim of Twin Oaks was "to sustain and expand our community which values cooperation, sharing and equality; which is not violent, racist, sexist, heterosexist or competitive; which strives to treat people in a kind, caring, honest and fair manner; and which provides for the basic physical and social needs of our members" (Federation 1986, 3). Many of these values could be called "female values"—cooperation, sharing, and nurturance of individual members (Weinbaum 1984, 164). The rejection of all hierarchies implicit in racism, sexism, and heterosexism is decidedly feminist.

While members were reticent to classify their community by any ideology, many members spoke of egalitarianism as the key value. Egalitarianism had many manifestations at Twin Oaks: all members received equal compensation for their labors; regardless of family ties or academic credentials, no one was referred to by title (children called their parents by their first names); there was equal opportunity to work in all job areas; all members voted on issues facing the community; and women and men were considered capable of doing anything, regardless of their sex.

Of all these various forms, the one many members chose as the most important was equality between the sexes. Twin Oaker Allen Butcher wrote, in an article describing the foundations of egalitarian communities, that "equality is the term we cite as best representing our ideals, yet we may as correctly term ourselves feminist communities" (Butcher 1987, 50). Kinkade, who has written extensively on the community, described Twin Oaks as "theoretically nonsexist." In a letter to anthropologist Jon Wagner, she wrote that "absolute sexual equality is fundamental to our idea of equality, and equality is fundamental to our approach to changing society. There is no platform of our ideology that is more central." In his collection of essays on sex roles in contemporary alternative communities, Wagner concluded that Twin Oaks "may be among the most non-sexist social systems in human history" (Wagner 1982, 37–38).

An important part of the nonsexist nature of the community was the rejection of traditional definitions of masculinity and femininity and the tolerance of all sexual preferences. Oakers placed no value on marriage or monogamy, and some married members engaged in sexual relationships outside their marriages. In 1987 the majority of Oakers identified themselves as heterosexual, a vocal minority as lesbians, and some as bisexual women. A few married or monogamous couples lived in the community, but the majority of members would be considered single.

As the toleration of a variety of sexual preferences illustrates, Twin Oakers placed great value on individualism. This value also played a central role in shaping their political institutions. They decentralized leadership as much as possible; most decision making was in the hands of the appropriate work group, team, or residence. Individuals and small groups were thus empowered to take control of their own lives. For decisions that affected the community on a larger scale, Twin Oaks established a board of planners. Three people served on the board on staggered eighteen-month terms, with an additional stand-in planner, or planner-in-training.

Women as well as men have served as planners since the inception of the community, though it was often difficult to convince members of either sex to take on this responsibility. Planners held "overall executive power" and focused "the community's attention on issues and their long range effects." At the same time, members had constant access to planners through personal conversations, papers posted on a community bulletin board, and regular community meetings. After receiving adequate community input, planners made decisions that were then subject to overrule if 51 percent of community members disagreed (Federation 1986, 4). Such procedures allowed and even encouraged the involvement of all members in decision making.

The community was economically self-supporting, striving to meet as many communal and individual needs as possible; almost all work took place in the community. For the majority of their income Twin Oakers manufactured and sold handcrafted hammocks and hammock-chairs, distributed to small shops and to specialty import stores. Almost all members spent some hours every week making hammocks, out of both desire and a feeling of obligation to support themselves. A small income came from their indexing business.

The remaining community work did not generate outside income but certainly saved members a great deal of money as well as providing some satisfaction. Members grew organic vegetables, fruits, and herbs for consumption, as well as hay to feed their dairy cows that provided them with fresh milk and cream twice daily. A fully equipped auto shop enabled Oakers to service their own fleet of community cars, vans, trucks, and tractors. They cared for their children communally and tried to care for one another's physical and mental health needs, turning to outside resources when appropriate.

Everyone was required to work the same number of hours each week, which amounted to forty-seven hours in the summer of 1987. No one received wages, but instead all received "labor credits" for their work, with one hour of work equaling one hour of labor credit. Most members worked in numerous areas of the community rather than on just one job. Some members changed jobs often; others remained in the same jobs for years. The community decided some years ago to place a high value on achieving nonsexist workplaces, and everyone was encouraged to take on nontraditional jobs. Community members placed greater value on spending the time to train women in auto mechanics, for example, than on getting the job done quickly with already skilled men.

Twin Oaks was based on a feminist egalitarian ideology rooted in cooperation, nurturance, and antihierarchical values. Members collectively recognized that women had suffered oppression and that men had denied the feminine sides of themselves, and the community worked to counteract these realities. In the pursuit of full sexual equality, some tensions existed because of the sexism of some individual members and to the differences of opinion on how to address this sexism. A close examination of four areas of Twin Oaks life will more clearly illustrate the nature of feminism there: work, separate-sex activities, "wolfing," and nonsexist language.

Twin Oakers valued hard work. When visitors applied for membership, the question of whether they worked the required hours during their visiting period weighed heavily in deciding their acceptance or rejection. Oakers were interested not only in the quantity but also the quality of work. The community strived to radically change the nature of work by humanizing the workplace, integrating work and play, valuing all work equally by assigning an equal labor credit to one hour of any work, demystifying expertise, cooperating rather than competing to achieve success, and giving labor credits for work that is unpaid in contemporary American society (e.g., parenting, giving back rubs).

Hand-weaving hammocks, the economic mainstay of the community, incorporated many of the above values. Conditions in the hammock shop ranked high in importance. In interviews, almost all women mentioned enjoying the combination of work and socializing at Twin Oaks. Hammock weaving provided such an atmosphere. The jigs on which the hammock beds were woven were built so that two people could weave across from each other. Oakers often moved the lightweight jigs outside the hammock shop to enjoy the outdoors while weaving or to spend the time alone with a friend. Conversations and meetings took place during hammock production because the work was not mentally taxing.

As little mysticism enshrouded the procedures, newly arrived visitors spent many hours weaving hammocks and getting to know members while they worked. Such flexibility of place, time (with the shop open twenty-four hours a day), and people allowed moods and feelings to play an active role in determining how any individual worked. These working conditions enabled women and men to participate equally in the main income-producing work of the community, thus strengthening feminist egalitarianism at Twin Oaks.

Although some members described weaving hammocks as "women's work," most Oakers rejected such gendered depictions of work. During my interviews on the subject, most members did not contrast the "men's work" with the "women's work" they performed; rather, they distinguished between enjoyable, challenging work and repetitive, easy work. Nonetheless, much of what is traditionally called "men's work" came under the former category, and "women's work" fell into the latter. The notable exception was child rearing, a task that both women and men saw as important and fulfilling.

Excluding child rearing, men and women most enjoyed performing "men's work." And, although men found such work challenging, women experienced deeper and more far-reaching satisfaction in this work. They became more self-confident, competent, proud, and strong through their work. Many faced fear and total ignorance, which made the work frustrating

25. Twin Oaks women hauling the garbage, August 1987. They often prided themselves on serving as role models for other women. *Courtesy of Zena Goldenberg.*

and left them continually sensitive to community judgment. However, when they overcame their fears and successfully performed these jobs, women overwhelmingly expressed feeling personally empowered by doing "men's work." Once so empowered, they prided themselves on serving as role models for other women, especially on women-only projects. Women not engaged in construction, farming, auto maintenance, and the like still derived pleasure from seeing other women in these areas.

Women also enjoyed greater opportunities for growth and fulfillment through the extensive women's culture at Twin Oaks. This culture was feminist in form: women voluntarily shaped what they wanted to do as women. The fact that the community provided a place for women's culture increased the social power of women as a group and attested to the strength of feminism at Twin Oaks. Twelve separate women's groups, activities, and spaces rounded out women's culture at Twin Oaks. No one participated in all, and a number of women participated in none. But the variety and intensity of available activities provided women with many opportunities for personal and social growth. Women involved often spoke with excitement of breaking uncharted ground. They exuded the hopefulness of unlimited growth.

Women's culture included a women's living room that provided a place for weekly women's teas and housed the women's library, kept in order by a woman who received one-half of a labor credit for her work. A portion of the library books was given to the community in exchange for some indexing work Oakers had performed. The women's living room also served as a meeting place for the planners of the annual Women's Gathering, which took place at a secluded conference campsite within Twin Oaks grounds. Almost all the women at Twin Oaks, even those who did no other women-only activities, participated in some way in the annual event.

Most planners of the Women's Gathering also took part in two other women's groups. They lived in the six separate bedrooms that constituted the Women's Small Living Group (SLG). All residences in the community were divided into SLGs to provide both a sense of family and a legitimate voice for the people who lived there to decide on SLG membership and the use of public areas in their buildings. The Women's SLG members and others took part in the weekly Feminist Theory Group, a discussion group limited to invited members. Three separate support groups met weekly, and a women's co-counseling class met occasionally. Many women attended two special events that occurred that summer: a women's dinner and a women's sweat. Almost thirty women attended the dinner, called in honor of the return from vacation of two Oakers active in women's culture. In a more spiritual vein, a group of female "pagans" and other interested women held a sweat, a ritual borrowed from Native American culture that combined spiritual and physical cleansing and took place in an outdoor earthen hut.

In contrast to the active women's culture, exclusively male activities have rarely occurred in Twin Oaks history. In the late 1970s members formed three types of men's groups: one to play poker and competitive volleyball, one for intellectual discussions, and two support groups that continued for two years (Komar 1986, 204–5).

During the summer of 1987, two men's-only activities took place. In May, the community hosted its second annual Men's Gathering, a weekend-long conference and celebration. Approximately fifty men attended, including a handful of Oakers. One man organized the weekend with assistance from two others, and he was disheartened by the lack of interest from community members. After the Men's Gathering, five male Oakers took up temporary residence in a vacant building and called themselves a Men's Small Living Group. Meaning to stay together for a week, they ceased after three days. While individual men have benefited from and sought out these experiences, Twin Oaks men appeared uninterested in, and perhaps unskilled at, separating from women to work, play, or grow as men.

Over the past few years, many Oakers have been discussing the benefits to the community of separate-sex activities, with women's-only activities being the main focus. Some Oakers supported women's separatism because they saw it as a means to achieving deeper equality. As one woman who was involved in a number of women's groups told me: "It's good for women to do their things and men to do theirs; but we're doing this so that eventually we can all get together."

A male member of another egalitarian community, Sandhill Farm, published an article entitled "Personal Thoughts on Sexual Discrimination," which addressed the question of whether women's separatism discriminated against men. He differentiated between "discrimination that limits access to work or information," which he considered negative, and that which "is shown to be a stepping stone for growth leading to greater awareness and opportunities for all." He concluded that because separate-sex groups provided growth opportunities for the entire community, feminist separatism was a positive step (Sandhill 1987, 26).

Some members, however, felt that separatism clashed with egalitarianism by denying men access based solely on their gender. A small group of men reportedly have felt discriminated against (Greenwood 1987, 24). Such feelings were expressed by individual men in public only once or twice during the summer of 1987. Other Oakers felt that Twin Oaks men were not oppressive enough to call for separatism. Men choosing to live in a community that overtly prohibits sexism often behaved in a feminist manner.

Kinkade, the only original member, felt that community women were equal with men from the start and she "resented it" when, in the early 1970s, newer women held what she called "speak-bitterness" meetings to talk about male oppression. She attended an early women's meeting and challenged the women on whether it was Twin Oaks men who were oppressing them. According to Kinkade, the women rejected her challenge as hostile, and they walked out on her. As she explained to me, "They didn't want to discuss whether Twin Oaks men were oppressive, they wanted to discuss their feelings of oppression." In my interviews, some men concurred with this view. Although they supported women's rights to separate, they regretted that separatism prevented them from learning from women. Three men, two active in men's group organizing, each wished he could be "a fly on the wall" at women's activities.

The abundance of women's activities also created some tension in the community. Women's culture contrasted at that time with a dearth of other cultural options. Besides six parties, choir meetings, co-counseling, and pagan celebrations, no organized cultural activities took place during that summer. Women not interested in women's groups and all men had little to choose from. Interested women, meanwhile, could and did take part in the many women-only groups, meetings, and activities described earlier. Such a wide array of activities might reflect greater desire or need by some women. In any case, women's culture offered women richer social lives, took up much of women's spare time, and engendered negative feelings in some members. The fact that the community chose to favor women's desires for limited separatism shows the power of feminism at this time, but problems still existed.

The strength of feminism was also evident in the method of addressing a particular problem in female/male relations labeled "wolfing." When male Oakers aggressively persisted, consciously or unconsciously, in trying to get female visitors or new members to sleep with them, they were labeled "wolves." Within this dynamic, females were seen as sometimes lacking the assertiveness or power to make a free choice, as a result of cultural conditioning and their desire to be accepted within the community. Men had more power, as a result not only of norms of traditionally expected sexual assertiveness but also of their being on their home turf.

The growth of a feminist awareness within the community and the social power of feminists turned this behavior into a taboo at Twin Oaks. In the feminist tradition, just the naming of what is otherwise considered normal behavior is part of the process of changing sexist behavior. Giving male sexual aggressiveness the name "wolfing" forced people to view it as a social rather than as an individual issue. Oakers went beyond naming to a second feminist method, raising consciousness through semiformal women's meetings on the subject.

Concerned women took it upon themselves to inform visiting women of the possibility of encountering wolves during their visit. In the first week of each visiting period, all female visitors were scheduled to have a dinner meeting with one of these concerned women, who would describe women's culture in community, the opportunities for learning nontraditional work skills, and the phenomenon of wolfing. She warned that wolfing occurred occasionally and advised visitors to feel free to refuse any unwanted sexual advances. Women were empowered enough socially to take control of the situation in an unobtrusive way, through regular discussions with visitors. With the subject of wolfing constantly in the air, men at Twin Oaks were aware that such behavior was offensive to many women.

Finally, Twin Oaks took the simple but strong step of eliminating sexist language. Beginning in the mid-1970s, in addition to using "person" instead of a gendered noun, they replaced all gendered pronouns—*he, she, him, hers,* and the like—with "co" and "cos." While newcomers often found this cumbersome and members occasionally made mistakes, others quickly corrected them. "No other norm in the community is so vigorously enforced," according to Kinkade (Wagner 1982, 37). Oakers thus took the trouble·every day, in all conversations, to rid themselves of sexism.

The strength of feminism at Twin Oaks is clear. Women experienced empowerment through taking on "men's work"; a strong women's culture promoted social and personal growth; feminists exercised their political power in addressing wolfing; and all members had to use nonsexist language in public. While tensions existed in some of these areas, they were acknowledged and addressed by the community, not ignored or suppressed. Many members believed that the strength of feminism at Twin Oaks made it an exciting place for women.

Works Cited

Butcher, Allen. 1987. Foundations of Egalitarian Community. *Communities, Journal of Cooperation* (Winter): 48–52.

Federation of Egalitarian Communities. 1986. *Living in Community.*

Greenwood, Leslie. 1987. Women in Community. *Communities, Journal of Cooperation* (Winter): 23–25.

Komar, Ingrid. 1983. *Living the Dream: A Documentary Study of the Twin Oaks Community, 1979–1983.* Louisa, Va.: Twin Oaks Community.

MacKinnon, Katherine. 1987. *Feminism Unmodified, Discourses on Law and Life.* Cambridge, Mass.: Harvard Univ. Press.

Sandhill, Laird, 1987. Personal Thoughts on Sexual Discrimination. *Communities, Journal of Cooperation* (Winter): 26.

Skinner, B. F. 1948. *Walden Two*. New York: Macmillan.

Wagner, Jon. 1982. *Sex Roles in Contemporary American Communes*. Bloomington: Indiana Univ. Press.

Weinbaum, Batya. 1984. Twin Oaks: A Feminist Looks at Indigenous Socialism in the United States. In *Women in Search of Utopia*, edited by R. Rohrlich and E. H. Baruch, 157–67. New York: Schocken.

Index

Abolitionist movement, 32–33
Abortion, 205
Ackley, Alice, 186, 188
"Acrostic on Esther Markham" (Lyman), 111
"Acrostic on Mother Ann Lee" (Lyman, 111–12
Acrostics: by Shaker women, 6, 109–12
African-Americans, 11–13, 22, 23, 24, 25, 140, 146n. 4, 165
African-American women, 11–12; among Shakers, 140; and work, 23. *See also* Jackson, Rebecca; Kingdom, The; Truth, Sojourner
African Methodist Episcopal church, 25
Allen, Catherine (Sister), 125, 126
Anabaptists, 239
Anderson, Martha (Sister), 125, 126
Andrews, Edward Deming, 73, 127
Andrews, Faith, 73
Anti-Polygamy Society, 177
Anti-Semitism, 221
Apostasy, 9, 10
"Astral Continental Congress," 202
Atlantic Monthly, 33, 84
Avery, Giles (Elder), 139

Baalot teshuveh, education for, 227–32, 234–35
Baal teshuveh school, 227–28
Baer family, 247 (illus.)
Bailey, Laura, 105 (illus.)
Bais Yaakov girls' schools: in Europe, 222, 224
Barron, Alfred, 185–86

Baruch, Elaine Hoffman, 13
Bates, Paulina (Sister), 124
Bathrick, Eunice (Sister), 108–9
Battle Creek, Mich., 31
Bayley, Bishop James Roosevelt, 154
"Before I Went to Brook Farm" (Kirby), 79
Behavioralism, 240, 257
Belton, Tex. *See* Woman's Commonwealth
Belton Journal, 55
Benson, George, 18
Beth Rivkah schools, 222; effects of on education of Lubavitcher women, 226–27, 234; growth and improvement of, 225–26; limitations and low status of, 223–25
Bible Communism, 166, 185, 187, 190, 191. *See also* Oneida Community
Birth control. *See* Contraceptive practices
Bisexual women, 258
Blithedale Romance, The (Hawthorne), 75
Book of Mormon (Smith), 171, 173
Bowers, Lucy (Sister), 126
Bowery Hill community, 25–26
Briggs, Nicholas (Brother), 130
Brodie, Fawn, 173, 174
Brook Farm, 6, 71–72, 75–77; and Abby Morton Díaz, 84–87; and Marianne Dwight, 81–84; and Georgianna Bruce Kirby, 79–81
Brown, Elsa Barkley, 11
Bruderhof, 238, 254–55, 255n. 1. *See also* Hutterites
Bryant, Hannah (Sister), 137
Bullard, Harriet, 142–43
Burger, Martha, 101 (illus.)

Burt, Mrs. Jonathan, 183–84
Burt, Sarah, 192
Butcher, Allen, 258

Campbell, D'Ann, 10
Canaan, N.Y. (Lower Family, Shaker com-
munity), 137
Cannon, George Q., 179
Cannon, Martha Hughes, 174
Canterbury, N.H. (Shaker community),
73, 100, 121 (illus.), 141, 146
"Can We Improve Our Schools?" (Heilbrun), 224
Caravan, 202
Carney Hospital (Boston), 157
Catholic sisterhoods, 5, 117–18, 150; domestic work by, 154–55, 159; and
hospitals and charitable agencies, 157–
58; male authority over, 151–54; and
property disputes, 158–59; training
and salaries for parochial school teachers, 156–57
Celestial marriage, 165
Celibacy, 10, 19, 56; and the Shakers, 72,
106, 120, 123, 124, 127, 128, 133,
134; and "unwomanly" women, 139–
40
Chabad Lubavitch. See Lubavitcher Community
Childbirth: among the Mormons, 173;
natural, 166, 205, 208–11, 213–14,
216, 217, 240; and pronatalism at The
Farm, 211, 212; at Twin Oaks, 240. See
also Pronatalism
Childrearing: at The Farm, 207; and Hutterite rites of passage, 248–49, 250–51,
252; and maternal instinct in the
Oneida Community, 185–90, 192,
199; pre-natal maternal influence on,
80–81; at Twin Oaks. See also Philoprogenitiveness
Children, 4, 5; at Brook Farm, 71, 79 (Infant School); at The Farm, 166, 205,
207, 212–13, 216–17; in Franklin
Community, 45; in Lubavitcher culture, 167; and Mormons, 173, 175; in
New Harmony, 44–45; in Shaker
communities, 72–73, 146n. 2; at Twin

Oaks, 240; in Woman's Commonwealth, 57, 60, 64–65. See also Education; Hutterites; Oneida Community
Church of Jesus Christ of Latter-day
Saints (LDS), 5, 165; anti-polygamy
campaign against, 176–78; and defense
of polygamy, 178–79; early history of,
169–72; and importance of marriage
to men, 172–73; and importance of
women's work, 176; persecution of,
171–72, 175; and Smith's revelation
on marriage, 174; and women's acceptance of polygamy, 174–75
Civil War, 33, 53, 54, 55, 90
Class differences, 170, 172, 173, 176, 179
Collins, Sarah, 122 (illus.)
Colored Soldiers' Aid Society, 33
Communitarianism, 201, 205; and cultural activities, 77; and domiciliary arrangements, 62, 63, 65; and Hutter-
ites, 250; in The Kingdom, 26; and
Mormon society, 170; and outsiders,
254; and religion, 27; theory of, 3–4,
6, 8; at Twin Oaks, 257, 259
Complex marriage. See Marriage, complex
Contraceptive practices, 10, 166, 167, 197,
205, 216, 239
Cornell, Reynolds, 31
Cott, Nancy, 176, 179n. 2
Cragin, Mary E., 185, 191, 192
Crown Heights (Brooklyn), N.Y. See
Lubavitcher Community
"Cult of Domesticity" (Cott), 176, 178,
179n. 2
"Cult of True Womanhood" (Welter), 5,
55, 169, 184–85, 199n. 5
Custis, George W. P., 33

Damon, Thomas (Elder), 141
Dial, The, 77
Díaz, Abby Morton, 75, 79, 84–87
Diocesan communities, 152, 153, 154,
156, 157–59
Divine Book of Holy and Eternal Wisdom,
Revealing the Word of God, out of Whose
Mouth Goeth a Sharp Sword, The (Bates),
124
Divorce, 57, 167, 205

Dixon, William Hepworth, 10, 139
Di Yiddishe Heim, 223–24, 225, 229, 234
Dolls: condemned in Oneida Community, 191–92; in fancywork, 98–100; Hutterite nests of, 246–47
Domestic Problem: Work and Culture in the Household, A (Díaz), 85
Doolittle, Antoinette (Sister), 143
Doolittle, Mary Antoinette (Sister), 125, 126
Dow, David, 58
Dow, Matthew, 58
Dunlavy, John (Brother), 123–24
Durgin, Dorothy (Sister), 73, 100, 146
Dwight, John Sullivan, 75
Dwight, Marianne, 72, 75, 78 (illus.), 79, 81–84
Dyer, Mary Marshall, 9

Easton, Louisa, 184
Edmunds-Tucker Act, 170, 177
Education, 4; of *baalot teshuveh,* 227–32, 234–35; at Brook Farm, 71, 76, 77, 79, 80; at The Farm, 212–13; and feminine culture, 232; of Hasidic girls, 224–26; Hasidic male and female contrasted, 228–29; of Hutterite children, 239, 242, 243–44, 245–46, 251; of Lubavitcher girls, 167, 221–27, 234; in Oneida Community, 191–95, 198–99; in Owenite communities, 19, 41–42, 45; parochial schools, 156, 157, 159; and religious life, 231–32; sexual, at Oneida, 196–97; in Shaker communities, 72–73
Egalitarianism, 38, 39, 257–58, 263
Elkins, Hervey, 139–40
Emancipation Proclamation, 33
Emerson, Ralph Waldo, 71, 75, 76
Enfield, Conn. (Shaker community), 100
Enfield, N.H. (Shaker community), 9, 139
Englishwoman in Utah: The Story of a Life's Experience in Mormonism, An (Stenhouse), 170
Eugenic reproduction. *See* Stirpiculture experiment
Evangelicalism, 52; and Lubavitchers, 167; and Mormonism, 165; and revelations, 54, 62; and Woman's Commonwealth, 52
Evans, Frederick (Elder), 125–26, 127, 128, 139, 141
Evans, Jessie, 105 (illus.)
Evans, William (Brother), 137
Extended households: at The Farm, 206–7, 212; among Hutterites, 239
Ezrat Pleithm-Vesidurom, 167

Family: as basic social unit at The Farm, 212; multi-generational (extended), 62–63; in Oneida Community, 183–84, 185; reorganization of, 31, 49
Family violence, 6, 8, 53, 57
Fancy goods, 8, 71, 89–90, 102n. 2; attitudes toward production of, 100–102; colors used in, 97–98; form and iconography of, 98–100; functionality of, 95; poplar ware as, 92–93, 97; as a Shaker industry, 91–92
Fancywork, 90–91, 129. *See also* Fancy goods
Farm, The, 5–6, 166, 201–2; children's education and socialization at, 212–13; and feminist concerns, 216–18; natural childbirth at, 208–11, 214, 217; power of the midwives at, 213–14, 215–16; sexual and marital practices at, 203–8; and the sexual division of labor, 211–12
Female friendship, 6, 106
Female Relief Society, 174, 176
Feminism, 3–7; and community, 8–9; defined, 256–57; and female bonding, 104, 106, 112; and sexuality, 10; in Shaker communities, 119, 125–26, 141, 142; at Twin Oaks, 262–63, 264–65; and women-only communities, 11, 65–66. *See also* Twin Oaks Community; Woman's Commonwealth; Woman's rights movement
Fifteenth Amendment, 36
Fisher, Helen, 43
Flower, Eliza Andrews, 46, 48
Flower, George, 46, 48
Folger, Ann, 27, 28
Folger, Benjamin, 26, 28
Folger, Frances, 25–26

Forest River Colony, 245, 251
Fourier, Charles: and Fourierism, 29, 72, 76, 81, 82
Franciscan sisters, 157
Franklin Community, 42–44, 45
Fraser, Daniel (Brother), 126
Freedmen's Bureau, 35
Freedmen's Hospital, 33
Freedmen's Village, 33, 35
Fretageot, Marie, 41–42
Fuller, Margaret, 71, 76

Gaskin, Ina May, 203, 213, 216
Gaskin, Stephen, 166, 202, 211, 214; on educational goals of The Farm, 213; on marriage and sex, 203, 204, 205–6, 207
Gender roles: equality in at Twin Oaks, 258, 259, 264; at The Farm, 217–18; among Hutterites, 246, 248, 252; in The Kingdom, 6, 27–28; and men's culture at Twin Oaks, 263; among Mormons, 173, 176; at New Harmony, 43, 46; religious dimension of, 137–39, 151–52; in Shaker communities, 117, 123, 125–26, 130, 134–35, 143, 145–46; and women's culture at Twin Oaks, 262–63, 264. See also Labor
Gibbons, Cardinal James (archbishop), 154, 158
"Gift drawings," 138
Gifts, exchanging of, 104, 106, 112
Gilmour, Bishop Richard, 158
"Girl of Sixteen at Brook Farm, A" (Sedgwick), 77–78
Godey's Lady's Book, 96 (illus.), 98
Goff, Ann Maria (Sister), 138
Gospel affection, 104, 106, 108, 110, 111, 112
Gospel union, 7, 71, 72, 104, 108, 112
Green, Calvin (Brother), 134, 135
Green, Myra, 105 (illus.)
Greisman, Nechama, 229, 230
Grey Nuns of Montreal, 158

Hamilton, Augusta, 187
Hamilton, Philena B., 187

Hancock, Mass. (Shaker community), 141
Harbinger, The, 72
Harmonia, 31–32
Hart, Emeline (Sister), 100
Hasidic Jews. See Lubavitcher Community
Hasidic women, 233 (illus.)
Hawthorne, Nathaniel, 75
Hayden, Dolores, 12
Haymond, Ada McWhirter, 57
Healy, Bishop James, 153
Heilbrun, Chana, 224
Henry, Margaret J., 57, 59, 60, 63
Hey Beatnik! This Is The Farm Book (Gaskin), 166, 206
Hill, Samuel, 18
Hippies, 166
Hollister, Alonzo (Brother), 126
"Home Life of the Brook Farm Association" (Russell), 77
Homosexuality, 205, 258
Housework, 12, 18, 72, 239
Humez, Jean M., 12, 117
Hurston, Zora Neale, 12
Hutter, Jacob, 239
Hutterian Brethren. See Hutterites
Hutterites, 8, 239–40, 245, 254–55; children's play and responsibilities among, 246–49; education of, 245–46, 251; and establishment of new colonies, 245; and socialization of children, 241–45; transition to adulthood among, 249–53

"Importance of Keeping Correct Book Accounts" (Wells), 128

Jackson, Rebecca (Eldress), 12, 140–41, 146n. 4
Jacobson, Rabbi Israel, 222
Jennings, Robert, 45
Jesus Christ, 123, 174, 175
Johnson, Mary C., 58
Julius Kubasek Colony, 242

Kehot, 167
Kimball, Heber C., 176

Kingdom, The, 17–18, 26–29, 32
Kinkade, Kat, 257, 258, 264, 265
Kinsley, Jessie Catherine, 196–97
Kirby, Georgiana Bruce, 75, 77, 78 (illus.),
    79–81
Kirtland, Ohio (Mormon settlement), 165
Knight, Jane, 125, 126

Labkowsky, Sara, 229
Labor: in Catholic sisterhoods, 154–58,
    159; communal organization of, 60–
    61; denigration and trivialization of
    women's, 86, 95, 97–98, 128–29; and
    domestic duties, 27–28, 31, 38–44,
    76, 79, 100–101, 195, 197, 199; at The
    Farm, 211–12; Fourierist organization
    of, 82; and Mormon women, 176; in
    Oneida Community, 190, 196; and
    pioneer women, 55; Shaker division of
    by gender, 120, 125, 126–28, 135; and
    task rotation, 63; at Twin Oaks, 258–
    60; and women's roles, 22–23, 40–41,
    59
Lane, Charles, 80
LDS. See Church of Jesus Christ of Latter-
    day Saints
Lee, Mother Ann, 7, 72, 133–34, 142;
    and the dual nature of God, 119, 123–
    24, 137; gospel affection and symbolic
    presence of, 104, 106, 108, 109, 110,
    111–12; on her role as leader, 120, 123
Lesbianism, 10, 11, 240, 258
Letters from Brook Farm, 1844–47 (Dwight),
    81
Letters of Shaker sisters, 106, 108–9, 112
"Letters to My Gospel Companions in
    Zion's Domain" (Bathrick), 108
Lincoln, Abraham, 33
Lubavitcher Community, 5, 167, 221; and
    the Beth Rivkah school system, 222–
    27, 234; and the education of baalot
    teshuveh, 227–32, 234–35
Lucy Maria (Díaz), 84–85
Lyman, Maria (Sister), 110, 111

Machon Chana Women's Institute for the
    Study of Judaism, 227, 230–32, 234

Mack, David, 18
M'Knight, Eliza, 42–43, 44, 45
M'Knight, James, 45
McQuaid, Bishop Bernard, 155
McWhirter, George, 53
McWhirter, Martha, 19, 55, 56, 57, 59,
    60, 63, 65; and celibacy, 19, 56; re-
    ligious experiences of, 52, 53, 54,
    62
Male continence (coitus reservatus), 166,
    197. See also Contraceptive practices
Manifesto, or a Declaration of the Doctrine
    and Practice of the Church of Christ, The
    (Dunlavy), 123–24
Manifesto, The (Shaker periodical), 125–
    26, 127, 129, 131n. 1
Manufacturing: and financial manage-
    ment, 128–29, 130; and product mar-
    keting, 91–92, 128; women's role in
    communal, 83, 91–92. See also Fancy
    goods; Fancywork
Marijuana, 166
Markham, Esther (Sister), 111
Marriage, 4, 6, 71; and community, 39;
    complex, 166, 183–84, 196–97, 219n. 5;
    synergistic, 206, 207, 217. See also
    Celibacy, Celestial marriage, Monog-
    amy, Plural marriage, Polygamy
Marshall, Paule, 12
Material culture analysis, 89, 102n. 1. See
    also Fancy goods
Matthews, Robert. See Matthias
Matthewson, Angell, 135
Matthias (Robert Matthews), 17–18, 26–
    28, 32
Meacham, Joseph (Elder), 120, 123, 126,
    134, 135
Merkos L'Inyone Chinuch, 167
Messiah, dual, 123, 124, 134
Methodism, 22, 25, 53
Midwives, 6, 167, 208–9, 210, 211, 213–
    14, 215–16
Miller, Charlotte Noyes, 184–85
Monogamy, 166, 201, 203–4, 205, 217,
    258; at Brook Farm, 71; dissatisfaction
    with, 56–57; at The Farm, 205; and
    women's status at New Harmony, 39–
    44. See also Marriage; Plural marriage;
    Polygamy

Mormons. *See* Church of Jesus Christ of Latter-day Saints
Mormon War of 1857, 170
Mormon women silk workers, 177 (illus.)
Morrison, Toni, 12
Mount Lebanon, N.Y. (Shaker community), 126, 130. *See also* New Lebanon, N.Y.
MOVE (of Philadelphia), 12
Mutual criticism, 166
"My First Visit to Brook Farm" (Kirby), 79
Mysticism, eastern, 202

Nashoba, 46, 48
National Freedmen's Relief Association, 35
Nauvoo, Ill. (Mormon city), 165, 172, 173, 174
Neale, Emma and Sadie, 144 (illus.)
"Negro State," 35–36
Neshei Chabad, 226, 230
Neshei Chabad (newsletter), 225
New Harmony, 19, 39, 49; gender inequality of work in, 40–42, 43; women's powerlessness in, 44–45
New Harmony: An Adventure in Happiness (Pears), 40
New Harmony Gazette, 45
New Lebanon (later Mount Lebanon), N.Y. (Shaker community), 100, 125, 128–29, 136, 139, 141, 142
New Rosedale Colony, 243, 245
No Man Knows My History (Brodie), 173
Northampton Association of Education and Industry, 18, 29–31, 32
North Union, Ohio (Shaker community), 129, 141
Noyes, Corinna Ackley, 188, 189
Noyes, Harriet Holton, 185
Noyes, John Humphrey, 10, 166, 185, 194 (illus.); and children's education and socialization, 191, 192, 197, 198; and Oneida family hierarchy, 182–83, 184
Noyes, Pierrepont B., 188, 189, 193
Noyes, Polly Hayes, 198

O'Connell, Cardinal William, 154
Oneida Circular, 185, 186, 187; on children's education and socialization, 190, 191, 192, 196, 197
Oneida Community, 5, 166; birth statistics of, 190; and complex marriage, 183–84, 196–97; early childhood education and socialization in, 191–95; education after primary school in, 198–99; hierarchy of, 182–83; ideal woman in, 184–85; and prohibition of philoprogenitiveness, 185–90, 191, 192
Oneida Company, Ltd., 166
Only a Flock of Women (Díaz), 85, 86
Orphan's Home (Georgetown), 33
Owen, Robert, 18–19, 29, 48–49
Owenite communities, 6, 12, 18–19, 38–39, 49–50n. 1; Franklin Community, 42, 43–44, 45; Nashoba, 46, 48; New Harmony, 19, 39–42, 43, 44–45, 49

Pantagamy. *See* Plural marriage
Parochial schools, 156, 157, 159
Patriarchy, 65–66, 165, 239, 242; and female intimidation at The Farm, 207–8; feminist critique of, 85–86; and midwifery at The Farm, 216; in Oneida Community, 182–83, 184; role in Catholic sisterhoods, 153–54, 158
Pears, Sarah, 39–40, 41, 43, 44–45
Philoprogenitiveness, 185–90, 191, 192
Pierson, Elijah, 17–18, 25, 26, 27–28
Pierson, Sarah, 25, 27
Pillsbury, Parker, 31
Pioneer women, 54–55, 176
Pious societies, 152
Plenty (social service organization), 166, 212
Plural marriage: as complex marriage in the Oneida Community, 166, 183, 219n. 5; criminalization of in Utah, 177; at The Farm, 166, 203, 205
Poems, 6, 109–12
Polyandry, 174
Polygamy (Polygyny), 165, 169, 170, 171, 172–74, 175, 179
Polygyny. *See* Polygamy

Pontifical communities, 152, 154, 155, 157, 159
Poplar ware, 92–93, 97
Pote, James (Elder), 139
Pratt, Agatha, 57
Price, Hannah Fisher, 42, 44, 49
Price, William, 42
Prindle, Mary, 192
Procter-Smith, Marjorie, 12, 117
Pronatalism, 166, 201, 211, 212, 215, 216; among Hutterites, 242; and the sex/gender system, 217, 218
Prostitution, 23, 24, 25
Putney Community, 166

Quakers, 22, 31, 134

Rancier, Josephine, 56, 57
Rathbun, Reuben, 134–35
Reform: and anti-slavery, 32–33, 36, 46; at Brook Farm, 80; and labor, 39; and religion, 27; and Shaker communities, 125–26, 142; and women's sexuality, 24–25
"Reminiscences of Brook Farm" (Kirby), 79, 80
Retrenchment Society, 25, 27
Revival meetings, 53, 54
Rich, Adrienne, 6, 7
Ripley, George, 71, 75, 76
Ripley, Marianne, 79
Ripley, Sophia Dana, 75, 77
Rohrlich, Ruby, 13
Rosengarten, Sudy, 223
Rubin, Gayle, 217
Russell, Amelia, 77

Sabbathday Lake, Maine (Shaker community), 73, 92
Saint Elizabeth's Hospital for Women (Boston), 157, 158
Saint John's Hospital (Lowell, Mass.), 157
Salt Lake City, Utah, 172, 173, 178
Sanctified Sisters. See Woman's Commonwealth
Scheble, Martha McWhirter, 63, 65

Schenierer, Sara, 222
Schneersohn, Rebbe Joseph Yitzchak, 167, 222, 223
Schneersohn, Rebbe Menachem, 234
Schoolmaster's Trunk, Containing Papers on Home-Life in Tweenit, The (Díaz), 85
Sears, Chauncy (Brother), 141
Sedgwick, Ora Gannett, 77
Sellick, Harriet (Sister), 137
Separatism, feminist, 263–64
Sex/Gender system, 217
Sexuality, 4, 10, 17–18, 24, 25, 56–57, 134, 196–97, 205; and bisexuality, 258; and communal affection, 185, 204; diversity of at Twin Oaks, 240, 258; at The Farm, 205–6; and premarital relations, 239; and romance among the Hutterites, 253; and sexual initiation of children in the Oneida Community, 197. See also Celestial marriage; Celibacy; Marriage; Monogamy; Polygamy; Plural marriage
Shaker, The, 117, 141
Shaker and Shakeress, 142
Shakers. See United Society of Believers in Christ's Second Appearing
Shepard, Lucy Ann (Sister), 100
Sister Formation Movement, 156
Sisterhood of Single Mothers of Brooklyn, N.Y., 12
Sisters of Charity, 157, 158
Sisters of Mercy, 153
Sisters of Notre Dame de Namur, 118, 155 (illus.)
Sisters of Saint Joseph, 118, 154, 156
Skinner, B. F., 240, 257
Skinner, Harriet Noyes, 186
Slavery, 22–23, 47, 177
Smith, Alice, 105 (illus.)
Smith, Hyrum, 165, 172
Smith, Joseph, 165, 173, 174, 175; and the rise of Mormonism, 170, 171, 172
Smith-Rosenberg, Carroll, 6, 40, 62–63, 104, 106, 113n. 1
Spiritualism, 31, 32; among the Shakers, 124, 137–39
"Spiritual midwifery," 166. See also Childbirth, natural
"Spiritual wifism," 172

Sprigg, June, 73
Stenhouse, Fanny, 170–71
Stenhouse, T. B. H., 170
Stirpiculture experiment, 166, 186, 189, 190
Stowe, Harriet Beecher, 33, 177
Sturgis, Caroline, 77
Summary View of the Millennial Church or United Society of Believers, Commonly Called Shakers, A (Green and Wells), 124
Synergistic marriage. *See* Marriage, synergistic

Taylor, John (President, LDS), 179
Testimonies Concerning the Character and Ministry of Mother Ann Lee and the First Witnesses of the Gospel of Christ's Second Appearing . . . (Green and Wells), 120
Testimonies of the Life, Character, Revelations and Doctrines of Mother Ann Lee and the Elders with Her (Bishop and Wells), 120
Testimony of Christ's Second Appearing Containing a General Statement of All Things Pertaining to the Faith and Practice of the Church of God in This Latter-Day (Young), 123, 124
Transcendental Club, 75, 76
Transcendentalism, 29, 71, 75–76
Transmission: or, Variation of Character through the Mother (Kirby), 80–81
Truth, Sojourner (Isabella Van Wagenen), 4–5, 9, 21, 34 (illus.); and attempts to establish a "Negro State," 35–36; and the Freedmen's Village, 33, 35; and Harmonia, 31–32; and The Kingdom, 17, 18, 26–29, 32; as lecturer on abolitionist and woman's rights movements, 32–33; moves to New York City, 22–24; and the Northampton Association of Education and Industry, 29–31, 32; and religious reform movement, 24–25
Twin Oaks Community, 8, 240; ideals and values of, 257–58; men's-only activities in, 263; and non-sexist language, 265; planner-manager system of government in, 258–59; and separate women's activities, 256, 262–64; value of work in, 259–60, 262

Udall, David King, 175
Unitarianism, 71
United Society of Believers in Christ's Second Appearing (Shakers), 6, 7, 71–73, 104, 106; demographics of, 141, 146n. 2, 146n. 5; disagreement on gender equality within, 130, 133, 142–43, 145; and dual godhead, 119–20, 123–24; and dual system of government, 120, 123, 128, 134–35; and financial records of women's work, 128–30; gender equality and early communities of, 119–20, 123–24, 133–35; influence of utopian-socialist movement on, regarding women's rights, 124–26, 130; male apostasy in, 136–37; and Mother's Work revival, 137–39; and office of Trustee, 129, 135; and sexual division of labor, 126–28, 135, 136; and Sisters' epistolary tradition, 108–9; and Sisters' poetry, 109–12. *See also* Fancy goods

Van Houten, Catherine and Phebe, 107 (illus.)
Van Wagenen, Isabella. *See* Truth, Sojourner
Vegetarianism, 72, 166, 202

Wagner, Jon, 258
Walden Two (Skinner), 240, 257
Walker, J. W., 31
Watervliet, N.Y. (Shaker community), 140
Webster, Ruth (Sister), 127
Wells, Freegift (Elder), 139
Wells, Luther (Brother), 128, 130
Wells, Seth (Brother), 128, 130
Welter, Barbara, 4, 169
White, Anna (Eldress), 141–42, 143
White Rose Mission of New York City, 12
Whittaker, James (Elder), 134
Wife abuse, 6, 57, 207

William Henry Letters, The (Díaz), 84

Willis, Susan, 11–12

"Wolfing" (Twin Oaks), 264–65

"Woman" (Ripley), 77

Woman's Commonwealth, 6, 9, 19, 58, 64 (illus.), 66; and background of members, 54–55; constitution of, 64–65; creation of, 52–53; financial success of, 59–60; importance of kin and friendships in, 62–63; and marriage and sexuality, 56–57; moves to Washington, D.C., 63–65; work patterns and leisure in, 60–61

Woman's rights movement, 5, 30–31, 32–33, 53, 79; and Shakers, 124–25, 126

Woman's suffrage, 36, 142, 177–78

Women's artistry and crafts, 7

Women's Educational and Industrial Union, 86

Women-identified women (Rich), 7

Women's spirituality, 9

Women's studies, 3–4

Woodruff Manifesto, 165, 177

Worden, Harriet M., 187–88, 192, 198

World War I, 90

Wright, Camilla, 48

Wright, Frances, 46, 47 (illus.), 48

Wright, Lucy (Eldress), 110, 123, 124, 136, 137, 138; and Joseph Meacham, 134, 135

Wright, Sue, 9

Years of Experience (Kirby), 77, 80

Yeshiva Hadar Hatorah, 227

Yeshiva Tiferes Bachurium, 228

Young, Brigham, 165, 172, 175, 176, 178 (illus.)

Zalman, Shne'ur, 167

Zen, 166

Women in Spiritual and Communitarian Societies in the United States

was composed in 10 on 12 Galliard on Digital Compugraphic equipment
by Metricomp;
printed by sheet-fed offset on 50-pound, acid-free Antique Cream,
Smyth-sewn and bound over binder's boards in ICG Arrestox B,
and notch bound with paper covers
by Maple-Vail Book Manufacturing Group, Inc.;
with paper covers printed in 2 colors by Johnson City Publishing Co., Inc.;
designed by Victoria Lane;
and published by
Syracuse University Press
Syracuse, New York 13244-5160

Utopianism and Communitarianism
Lyman Tower Sargent and Gregory Claeys, Series Editors

This new series offers historical and contemporary analyses of utopian literature, communal studies, utopian social theory, broad themes such as the treatment of women in these traditions, and new editions of fictional works of lasting value for both a general and scholarly audience.

Other titles in the series include:

The Concept of Utopia. Ruth Levitas
Low Living and High Thinking at Modern Times, New York, Roger Wunderlich
The Southern Land, Known. Gabriel de Foigny; David John Fausett, trans. and ed.
The Unpredictable Adventure: A Comedy of Woman's Independence. Claire Myers Spotswood Owens; Miriam Kalman Harris, ed.
Unveiling a Parallel. Alice Ilgenfritz Jones and Ella Merchant; Carol Kolmerten, ed.
Utopian Episodes: Daily Life in Experimental Colonies Dedicated to Changing the World. Seymour R. Kesten
Women, Family, and Utopia: Communal Experiments of the Shakers, the Oneida Community, and the Mormons. Lawrence Foster
Writing the New World: Imaginary Voyages and Utopias of the Great Southern Land. David John Fausett